HARLAN
HINEY

THE MISSABE ROAD

...The Duluth, Missabe and Iron Range Railway

FRANK A. KING

Golden West Books

San Marino, California

THE MISSABE ROAD
... The Duluth, Missabe & Iron Range Railway
Copyright © 1972 by The Duluth, Missabe & Iron Range Ry.
All Rights Reserved
Published by Golden West Books
A Division of Pacific Railroad Publications, Inc.
San Marino, California 91108 U.S.A.
Library of Congress Catalog Card No. 74-190177
ISBN No. 87095-040-1

ACKNOWLEDGMENTS

It would be difficult to single out all of those who have assisted in the preparation of this book, since so many have been involved.

Special appreciation is expressed to Donald B. Shank, vice president and general manager of the Missabe Road, whose valuable suggestions and enduring enthusiasm have made the project possible.

Recognition is due Harold H. McLean and Robert R. Firestone, both of Pittsburgh, for research and editing.

Appreciation is also expressed to the St. Louis County and Lake County Historical Societies and to the railroad enthusiasts who made photographic material available. Also to Gerald M. Best for his assistance with the locomotive roster.

To be a book, any story requires a publisher. Donald Duke, publisher of Golden West Books, has done a great deal more than set type, form layouts and bind paper. He has provided publishing talents, encouragement and his own knowledge of the railroad.

Last, and certainly not least, appreciation is extended to all those officers, supervisors, and employees of the Missabe Road, both active and retired, who supplied valuable information and continuous encouragement.

TITLE PAGE ILLUSTRATION

Duluth, Missabe and Iron Range Mallet type No. 200 hauling a train of ore empties up Proctor Hill in 1945. Acquired from the Baldwin Locomotive Works in 1910, she served the Missabe Road for 43 years. The oil painting, in the collection of the DM&IR, was painted by railroad artist Harlan Hiney.

Golden West Books

A Division of Pacific Railroad Publications, Inc.

P.O. BOX 8136 • SAN MARINO, CALIFORNIA • 91108

Yellowstone No. 230 hurls exhaust skyward lugging close to an 18,000 ton train over the Missabe Division's southbound ruling grade through Saginaw. — FRANK A. KING

PREFACE

RAILROAD mileage grew very rapidly in the United States in the several decades following the Civil War. Hundreds of railroad companies were chartered, many of which never laid any track, but so many others were actually built that by 1900 there were 258,784 miles of railroad, providing a network throughout the country. The railroad whose history is here recorded represents only a small part of the rail mileage. But for three-quarters of a century it has carried much of the raw material that, in finished form, has helped equip and supply all of the nation's railroads; has assisted the United States in fighting two world wars and other smaller conflicts; and has been used to construct many of the buildings, bridges, automobiles and countless consumer products that are so vital to our American way of life.

Many of the early railroads were speculative ventures, built into virgin territory with the expectation that once the railroad was there the traffic necessary to sustain it would soon be developed. Sometimes it did, and sometimes it did not, and often the initial builders did not have the financial resources required to hold out until the traffic materialized.

The development of the Duluth, Missabe and Iron Range Railway is not altogether typical of railroads generally, and in many respects it is unique. Most railroads have had to struggle to develop their traffic, but the Missabe's traffic base, one of the largest and most accessible iron ore deposits ever discovered, was assured from the beginning. Demand for transportation services was strong, for the iron ore was worthless where it lay. Shipment by rail to Lake Superior was a necessary first step in moving the ore to ports on Lake Erie and Lake Michigan where it would have value. The Missabe story therefore focuses initially on the problems involved in getting the component railroads organized, obtaining adequate financing for them, and finally making them efficient instrumentalities of transportation.

The present Duluth, Missabe and Iron Range Railway had two principal predecessors: the Duluth and Iron Range (D&IR), which is now the Iron Range Division, and the Duluth, Missabe and Northern (DM&N), which is now its Missabe Division. Both railroads were conceived as integral parts of mining endeavors and their destinies were linked with those of the larger mining enterprises. The iron ore deposits were off in the Minnesota wilderness, and railroads had to be constructed through swamp land, virgin forest and rocky ridges. The entrepreneurs who tried to develop mining properties, build railroads and enter the competitive iron ore market found that their resources were not equal to the task. Eventually they were assisted by others who were financially able.

The problems were many, but the rails of the D&IR were finally pushed through to the ore deposits of the Vermilion Range, and, on July 31, 1884, the first train of Minnesota iron ore moved over the new road to a just-constructed ore dock on Agate Bay at Two Harbors. Less than a decade later, the DM&N moved its first train of ore from the Mesabi Range to the head of the lakes.

From these dual beginnings evolved the Duluth, Missabe and Iron Range Railway Company. It has experienced successes and failures, changes of ownership and merger, prosperity and depression. It has seen the depletion of high-grade natural ores and excessive taxation threaten its very existence. Finally, and this constitutes the last chapter, is a new development: man-made pellets of high iron content produced from Minnesota's vast reserves of low-grade taconite, an encouraging development for the future of the Missabe Road.

FRANK A. KING.

April 1, 1972
Duluth, Minnesota

TABLE OF CONTENTS

The Duluth of 1870 resembles a western frontier town, or perhaps a motion picture set for a cowboy movie. False fronts exaggerate the size of buildings in its Superior Street business district. — HARVEY MILLER

1

THE VERMILION ENCOUNTER

GOLD! Nothing is so likely to attract people to a remote area as a rumor that gold has been discovered there, unless, of course, the rumor proves to be true. Vermilion Lake gold fever, based on a rumor that gold had been discovered near a lake by that name located in the wilderness about 100 miles north of Duluth, swept through that city from 1865 to 1868. Prospectors and adventurers, many of them just out of the Civil War, came from all parts of the country to Duluth, a fledgling city of about 3,000 population, located on Lake Superior at the head of the lakes. Reinforced by nearly all the able-bodied male population of the city, they spent most of a winter clearing a crude route through the wilderness near an old Indian trail to the "gold fields" on Lake Vermilion. The trail was passable for teams during the winter only, and most supplies and mining equipment were brought by sled from St. Paul, almost 300 miles away. A rail connection between Duluth and St. Paul (the Lake Superior and Mississippi Railroad) was not completed until 1870.

Whether any gold whatever was found is conjectural, but clearly it did not exist in sufficient quantities to warrant sustained interest in prospecting for it. The rumor was probably started by the finding of iron pyrites, a yellow sulphide of iron superficially resembling gold, which even now is discarded in preparing iron ore pellets. However, the flurry helped open up the country, and a few men remained to look for iron ore instead of gold. Unmistakable evidence of iron ore had attracted their attention while en route to the Vermilion.

George R. Stuntz, who was one of these men, attached great importance to the iron ore discovery and never relaxed his faith that iron ore would ultimately prove more valuable than all the gold in the world. His knowledge of the Vermilion area was extensive. He first learned of the presence of iron ore from N. A. Posely, a blacksmith who was the son of a fur trader in the area. Posely had been sent by the federal government to teach the Indians blacksmithing. The Indians showed him iron ore specimens they had picked up, which he took in 1863 to the Indian post at Fond du Lac, now part of Duluth, and gave to Stuntz. At first Stuntz was not impressed, entertaining the generally held belief that the worthwhile iron ore in the Lake Superior district was located in the Marquette Range of Michigan's Upper Peninsula, on the opposite side of the big lake.

Stuntz soon had second thoughts about the value of the new ore and personally explored outcroppings on the Vermilion, bringing back samples of high-grade ore he found there. Now convinced

Duluth's rail connection with the outside world was completed by the Lake Superior and Mississippi during 1870. The first locomotive used at the Head of the Lakes, a six-wheel switcher, reposes in front of the railroad's freight depot. (BELOW) Sailing vessels and steamboats vied for docking space on the Duluth waterfront around 1870. Grain elevator on the right was Duluth's first. — BOTH HARVEY MILLER

that he had discovered a veritable mountain of iron, he tried to interest monied men to join him in prospecting the area, but for a long time no one took a serious interest.

Among the men Stuntz contacted was George C. Stone, formerly of Duluth, then living in Philadelphia. Through him Stuntz learned that Professor A. H. Chester, a mining engineer and geologist of Hamilton College, Clinton, New York, was investigating an iron formation some 20 miles south of the Vermilion outcropping. The professor was working for a group of eastern investors, including Charlemagne Tower of Philadelphia. The area under study was actually the eastern end of the Mesabi Range, but Chester did not encounter there the rich dirt-like ore that was later to become so characteristic of the Mesabi. He saw just the taconite, a hard, low-grade ore that only now is coming into its own. Stuntz was thus more attracted to the lure of the high-grade ore that he had seen on the Vermilion.

Before dealing further with developments on the Vermilion, mention should be made, on account of the railroad they organized, of a syndicate from Ontonagan, Michigan, that was also exploring the eastern end of the Mesabi at this time. The syndicate was headed by Peter Mitchell, a well-known mining man, after whom Reserve Mining Company was to name its taconite mine some 80 years later. Mitchell's group, like Tower's, found only the taconite manifestations of the Mesabi Range at its eastern end, but they did organize a railroad company, the original Duluth and Iron Range Rail Road Company, and secured a land grant for it from the Minnesota legislature. The charter granted on December 21, 1874, called for construction of a line from a point near Babbitt to Duluth. W. W. Spalding was the first president of the company.

Professor Chester was so disappointed with the ore he had seen on the Mesabi that he would not accompany Stuntz on a trip from Duluth to the Vermilion, but staked him with black powder, provided two Indian guides and requested that ore samples be returned to him. Not long afterward one of the Indians came back bearing a note from Stuntz requesting Chester to come north immediately. He did so and found about 60 tons of ore that Stuntz and John Mallman had blasted loose from an outcrop. It was obviously heavy and when analyzed later revealed 63 to 67 percent iron. Upon seeing the chunks of almost pure hematite ore at the base of a cliff, Chester wrote Charlemagne Tower proclaiming it "a magnificent sight," and said that "nature had done the mining and that it was only necessary to break up these large blocks to have many tons of the finest iron ore ready for shipment when the railroad should come in."

Pleased with this Vermilion encounter, Chester returned to Duluth and shipped samples to Hamilton College, where detailed examination confirmed the field appraisal. In his report Chester condemned the low-grade Mesabi ore and recommended to Tower that the Vermilion "well deserved further most careful and exhaustive examination." Tower agreed, but he needed to acquire title to more of the land and a railroad to haul the ore after it was mined.

The bypassed Mesabi was to break all records in ore production within Chester's lifetime, but Tower never lived to see what might have been his. Had the early explorations been more complete, and had more accurate information been available, he undoubtedly would have acquired a substantial interest in what was to become the world's greatest iron producing range — the Mesabi!

George R. Stuntz, surveyor and prospector, went looking for gold, but found iron. Though his discovery made fortunes for many, he died penniless in 1902. — JOHN H. HEARDING JR.

W. W. Spalding, incorporator and first president of the Duluth and Iron Range Rail Road. — LAKE COUNTY HISTORICAL SOCIETY

Hard rock miners pause briefly in 1884 to have their picture taken for posterity. Air hammers greatly facilitated drilling into the rich and extremely hard ore. — TOWER-SOUDAN HISTORICAL SOCIETY

2

A RAILROAD THROUGH THE WILDERNESS

THE times were opportune for promoting new sources of iron ore. The Marquette or "Old Range," as it was beginning to be known, had been America's chief source of iron ore following its initial development in 1854, but by 1880 gloomy predictions were in circulation concerning its early exhaustion. Opening of the nearby Menominee Range brought in an additional half million tons per year by 1880, but the supply was thought to be insufficient to meet the anticipated demands, and the possibility of an iron ore shortage became a matter of national concern.

Charlemagne Tower had followed this development with interest and was therefore open to George Stone's persuasion to participate in the Vermilion adventure. But to mine on the Vermilion required a railroad through the wilderness and an ore dock on Lake Superior, difficult and expensive undertakings. Tower turned for advice to E. N. Breitung of Marquette, Michigan, an iron mining and furnace operator of considerable prominence, and Breitung's enthusiasm helped get the project in motion.

Meanwhile, Stone had been procuring title to iron ore lands on the Vermilion. The lands were in the public domain and were subject to federal homesteading laws. Although not suitable for farming, as were the prairie lands for which home-

stead laws were designed, such laws were applicable to these lands, and title to both the surface and the underlying minerals could be acquired under them. Stone handpicked his homesteaders and arranged to have them convey title to Tower in due time. Thus, by early 1881 most of the desired ore properties were assembled into Tower's Minnesota Iron Company.

Construction of a railroad by the most direct route, which would be from the small settlement of Agate Bay on Lake Superior, soon to be called Two Harbors, would cost about two million dollars. Tower formed the Duluth and Iron Mountain Railroad Company for this purpose on January 29, 1881, and to help finance construction sought a swamp land grant from the Minnesota legislature. The legislature controlled the disposition of swamp lands by virtue of an Act of Congress that passed swamp land fee titles to certain states on the premise that they were better able to construct the necessary levee or drainage systems, and the lands as improved could be sold to defray the cost of the improvements. The legislature, however, was unwilling to make the grant to Tower's new railroad.

Stone then reminded Tower of the grant in the possession of the Duluth and Iron Range Rail Road Company, which, as previously noted, was formed in 1874 to build a railroad from Duluth to

Charlemagne Tower, Sr., Philadelphia lawyer and capitalist, despite seemingly insurmountable legislative, financial and engineering problems, succeeded in constructing the Duluth and Iron Range Rail Road through the 68-mile wilderness separating his mining venture from Lake Superior. —LAKE COUNTY HISTORICAL SOCIETY

George C. Stone played a key role in the formation and development of Charlemagne Tower's Minnesota mining and railroad venture. He was president of the D&IR during 1882-1883. — LAKE COUNTY HISTORICAL SOCIETY

near Babbitt. Stone was a member of the Peter Mitchell syndicate involved in that venture. Under its land grant of 1875, the Duluth and Iron Range had until February 17, 1879, to complete its line. No track had been constructed, however, when Spalding, president of the company, organized another railroad company, the Duluth and Winnipeg, in 1877, to take over the land grant. The D&W was authorized to construct a railroad from Duluth to the international boundary somewhere between the Red River and Lake of the Woods, presumably to connect with the Canadian Pacific, then being built. An act approved by the Minnesota legislature on March 9, 1878, provided:

> That the lands granted to the Duluth & Iron Range Railroad Company, by (here describing the 1875 act), in case of forfeiture by the said Duluth & Iron Range Railroad Company, be and the same are hereby transferred and vested in the Duluth & Winnipeg Railroad Company . . .

and gave the D&W additional time, ten years from the passage of the act, to construct and complete the line. As president of both companies, Spalding doubtless felt that his position was secure; if his D&IR defaulted, which was largely within his control, then the land grant would pass over to his D&W, with ample time to complete the line.

In need of both a railroad charter and a land grant, Tower decided to obtain stock control of the D&IR and keep the land grant from going over to the D&W. Stone enlisted the support of seven of his fellow incorporators, and at a meeting held on March 1, 1882, moved for authority to issue and sell not less than 5,000 additional shares. Despite Spalding's protests, the resolution passed by a vote of eight to two. The meeting proceeded. The new stock was sold to Tower, and he thereby obtained voting control of the railroad. He was elected a director, along with his son, Charlemagne, Jr., his son-in-law, Richard H. Lee, and George Stone. Stone was elected president, Lee, chief engineer, and Henry F. Thompson, secretary and treasurer.

Since additional time was required to complete the railroad and permission was needed to change its terminal point from Duluth to Agate Bay, and as clarification of the swamp land grant was also necessary, Tower was obliged to seek legislative aid. The importance of the land grant to Tower may be gathered from its size; it eventually became 606,720 acres of land. George Stone was

Charlemagne Tower, Jr., headed his father's D&IR from 1883 to 1887. Years later, he had a distinguished career in the United States diplomatic service. — LAKE COUNTY HISTORICAL SOCIETY

morning, and there was four feet of snow on the ground, McGonagle's crew started working from Agate Bay toward the iron country. He described it as:

. . . a desperate winter for outdoor work, living as we did in tents, with temperatures running 40 degrees below zero and lower; but we plodded along, moving our camp every few days, until we connected our line with what was known as Case's Line near the Whiteface River, thereby giving us a connected line all the way to Tower.

Several changes in the alignment were made to reduce costs, and McGonagle and crew were sent back to Stone Lake where, some months later amid the torments of mosquito-infested swamps, they completed the final survey.

Construction came next. On June 20, 1883, John S. Wolf and Company of Ottumwa, Iowa, a railroad contractor well known in the west, was awarded the construction contract on the basis of

given the task of securing legislative relief for the D&IR, and William Spalding was his adversary in endeavoring to retain the land grant for his D&W.

The Minnesota House of Representatives had already approved a bill favoring the D&IR, but the evening of March 1, 1883, found the legislature ready to adjourn and the Senate deadlocked on the bill. Senator Charles Gilfillan of St. Paul, spokesman for the D&IR, was so ill that he had to be carried into the Senate chamber. He spoke nevertheless, stressing that the D&IR, unlike the paper D&W, was a going concern and that its construction would facilitate development of iron mines, create new jobs and benefit the state. The bill was approved, 25 to 15, with the Senate adjourning at 3:30 A.M.

Surveys for the D&IR had been started during 1880-1881, following as direct a route as possible from the iron ore deposits near Tower to Agate Bay on Lake Superior, a distance of 68 miles. W. A. McGonagle, who almost 50 years later headed both the D&IR and DM&N, left a vivid account of laying out the route of the line. On December 6, 1881, an engineering corps in his charge assembled in Duluth near Fifth Avenue East and traveled by sled on the ice to Agate Bay, arriving there late on the second day. Though it was snowing the next

Appropriately garbed for Minnesota's winter cold, D&IR President Charlemagne Tower, Jr., (extreme right) posed for this photograph in the comfort of a Duluth photographer's studio. Group included Isaac P. Beck, secretary of the D&IR, on extreme left; Mrs. R. H. Lee, sister of Tower, and her husband R. H. Lee, chief engineer of the D&IR. Tower no doubt sent this picture to his family and friends back in Philadelphia to illustrate the hardships endured "out west." — DM&IR COLLECTION

a low bid of $12,519 per mile. He agreed to complete the 68-mile railroad to Agate Bay on or before August 1, 1884, or pay a $50,000 forfeiture bond. He was to clear and grade the roadbed, supply and lay the ties, with the company furnishing rails and fastenings. It was standard gauge (4' 8-½"), of course, and 60-pound rail.

Typhoid fever, the scourge of construction camps, and probably due to bad water, struck in the fall and winter of 1883 and claimed many victims. Lack of nourishing food was not one of the hardships. McGonagle, years later, affectionately recalled hotel keeper Ma Blake, "...who served us, literally, with the fat of the land and with dishes that were at times fearfully and wonderfully made."

Construction money was a constant problem. Under terms of the land grant Tower would not receive the title to the swamp lands until the line was completed all the way to Duluth, so the lands were not yet very good security for raising money. The D&IR issued $2,500,000 worth of bonds, giving a first mortgage on all its property, including lands to be obtained under the swamp land grant, and the Minnesota Iron Company mortgaged its lands and other property as security for the bonds. To tie the mining and railroading enterprises together, Tower vested full ownership of the railroad's stock in the Minnesota Iron Company.

Stone was at his best in the role of promoter, financier, and organizer, but he disliked the daily detail of the presidential job and urged Tower to place his son in the position. Tower was reluctant

to do so, but finally gave in and at a board meeting held on April 26, 1883, young Tower was elected president and George Stone vice president and treasurer. Thus, at age 35, Charlemagne Tower, Jr. was given an opportunity to show his ability. In his new office in Duluth, he was the epitome of eastern reserve and refinement, in contrast to the more western type of informality then prevailing in Duluth. Though separated by over a thousand miles from his father in Philadelphia, he

The original D&IR merchandise dock at Two Harbors, on the right, received materials for construction of the railroad. — LAKE COUNTY HISTORICAL SOCIETY

18

MINNESOTA'S FIRST ORE TRAIN

Glistening under the bright summer sun, Duluth and Iron Range Rail Road Consolidation locomotive No. 8 heads for Two Harbors on July 31, 1884, with the first train of iron ore in the State of Minnesota.

maintained almost daily correspondence with him, reporting on the construction of the railroad. Strangely enough, the father never personally visited his mining and railroad empire.

The first 450 feet of track, laid with 60-pound rail rolled by the Pennsylvania Steel Company, was put in place at Agate Bay on August 29, 1883. Assistant Superintendent George H. White telegraphed the Duluth office, "First wheel rolls on the steel of the D&IRR Company at about 4 o'clock this p.m." Construction of the remainder of the 68 miles proved to be more difficult, but it was soon progressing on many fronts. A merchandise dock extending into Agate Bay, complete with railroad tracks, was used to receive rails and other material arriving by lake steamer. During 1884, 46 pockets of an ore dock, which later became Dock No. 2, were made ready to receive ore from cars and transfer it to boats. Piling had been driven for Dock No. 1 immediately east of Dock No. 2, but problems encountered during construction led to the decision to complete Dock No. 2 first. The dock stood 40 feet above water and extended 644 feet into the harbor. Approximately a million board feet of lumber went into the making of the first half of the dock.

At the direction of Charlemagne Tower, Sr., Stone attempted to control the sale of lots in the town of Two Harbors, formerly the settlement of Agate Bay, to insure their acquisition only by men who intended to build on them and live in the town. This was only partly successful, for speculators came in and an enterprising individual set up a shanty-town haven nearby and for a time did a thriving business in nefarious activities designed to separate workmen from their pay. Organized local government came on January 7, 1885, with the setting up of the Township of Two Harbors by officials of the iron company. A church was established by Presbyterians in 1887, and the Town of Two Harbors was incorporated a year later. Two Harbors was made the county seat of Lake County in lieu of Beaver Bay in 1889. These developments reflected the good progress made by the railroad and the mining company in their joint enterprise.

With August 1, 1884 as Wolf's completion date for the railroad, Tower had to start mining well in advance to have plenty of ore ready to ship. He had earlier selected Captain Elisha Morcom of Quinnesec, Michigan, as mining superintendent, and after a year of successful test-pitting, Morcom

The first ore dock at Two Harbors as it appeared during the summer of 1884. The young lady at the oars was the daughter of D&IR Assistant Superintendent G. H. White. —LAKE COUNTY HISTORICAL SOCIETY

returned home in the fall of 1883 to organize a party of miners to come to northern Minnesota. About 350 people, mainly Cornish, including men with families, signed up to migrate to the Vermilion Range, cost of transportation to be borne by Tower's mining company. The travel time via the slow and roundabout railroads, and finally by horse-drawn sleighs over the Vermilion Trail, was about seven days. But, waiting for them at Soudan,

Captain Elisha Morcom headed Charlemagne Tower's mining operations on the Vermilion Range. — TOWER-SOUDAN HISTORICAL SOCIETY

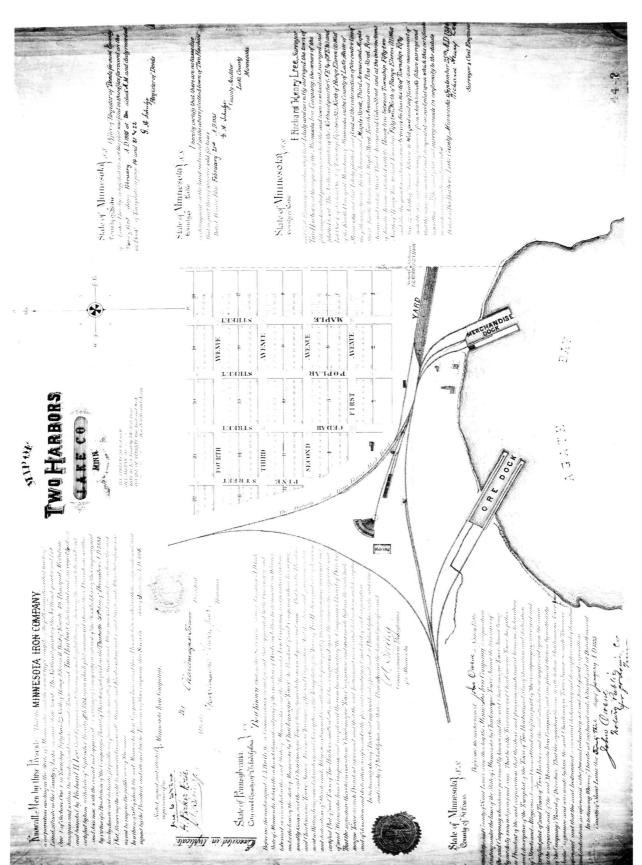

An 1884 map of Two Harbors, prepared by Minnesota Iron Company, showing the townsite and initial yard layout of the D&IR. — DM&IR COLLECTION

ready for occupancy, the Michigan miners and their families found sturdy two-story houses which had already been constructed by company carpenters. Some of these houses are still standing. So mid-1884 found several hundred miners at work, assuring that ore would be ready to ship by the time railroad construction was completed.

The initial mining was in the outcrops, which soon turned into open pits or cuts, principally seven, known as Breitung, Tower, Stone, Ely, Stuntz, Lee and Montana, all near a place called Soudan, about two miles east of the town of Tower. Most of these outcrops united with the main ore body at deeper levels. Being extremely hard, the ore had to be blasted loose, and horse-drawn carts were used to haul it out of the pits. As operations drove the pits deeper, skip hoists were installed to lift out the ore, and it was not long before all mining was being conducted underground.

Skip hoists were used to lift the ore out of the original open pits. This view shows the skip at the Minnesota Mine at Soudan about 1885. The open pits gave way to underground mining within a short time. — TOWER-SOUDAN HISTORICAL SOCIETY

The perilous voyage of the *Three Spot* between Duluth and Two Harbors is depicted in this painting by Albert Headley, a pioneer resident of Two Harbors, who later became general car foreman of the D&IR. — LAKE COUNTY HISTORICAL SOCIETY

Moving the D&IR's first locomotive, assigned No. 3, and later known as the *Three Spot*, from Duluth to Two Harbors seemed like a routine job. The lake was calm when the *Ella G. Stone*, the company tug named after George Stone's wife, started out with the scow carrying its precious locomotive cargo. Upon reaching Knife River, about 20 miles up the lake, a moderate northeaster began to blow. It soon increased to such gale proportions as to endanger the lives of the men. Tug Captain C. O. Flynn gave orders to the crew to stand by and be ready at his command to use an axe to cut the lines securing the tug to the scow, but fortunately this did not become necessary. In the words of William McGonagle, who was one of the men aboard, "A kind providence and the excellent seamanship of

The *Three Spot* was the first locomotive to see service on the D&IR. She was originally built for a railroad in Brazil, the San Juan and Vera Cruz, who refused her for some obscure technical reason. The pioneer locomotive was restored to its original appearance in 1923, at which time this photograph was taken. — AUTHOR'S COLLECTION

Captain Flynn saved us from the necessity of sending the *Three Spot* to Davy Jones' locker, and instead we sailed into the peaceful waters of Agate Bay and delivered our cargo safely on the rails that projected from the timbers at the shore line." Perhaps, like sailors as far back as Ulysses, he exaggerated the danger to improve the tale.

In any event, the little wood-burning Mogul, built by the Baldwin Locomotive Works, was immediately put into service hauling rails and other supplies to the advancing railroad as contractor Wolf pushed the 60-pound steel northward. He was determined to get back his $50,000 penalty bond, and the Towers, who were as anxious as he was to see the line completed by August 1, gave him complete support.

By early July 1884, the track was about 12 miles from Tower, and Franklin Prince, the mining engineer, was emboldened to proclaim, "We hold with pleasure the coming of the road, and to my ears no music can sound as sweet as the rumbling of an ore train as it threads its way through this wilderness." The margin for completion of the road on time was getting short.

As the date approached, contractor Wolf was at the end of the line driving his men, and finally there was but one day to spare to meet the August 1 deadline, but it would come on a Friday! By superstition, Friday was an unfavorable day, so plans were made for the first shipment to move on Thursday, July 31, 1884. Early Thursday morning found the contractor's forces working on the rock cut at mile post No. 64 near Tower. The rock was hard to drill and blast, so the alternative of laying a temporary track over the granite outcrop was

chosen, and the line was completed substantially, though probably not precisely, according to contract.

President Tower had been at the end of the line since the previous Tuesday overseeing the construction activities. The siding under the loading chutes was completed early Thursday morning (the 31st) and ten ore cars that had been brought up to within a short distance of the mine on Tuesday were spotted for loading. Contractor Wolf, whose special day it was, since he completed the road on time, was given the honor, at Tower's request, of dumping the first wheelbarrow load of ore into car No. 406, and Captain Morcom was given the honor of raising the American flag because he too had kept to the schedule and was ready with ore to be loaded. His men then eagerly went to work loading the cars.

Meanwhile, a train consisting of ten empty ore cars and trailing caboose No. 21, which served as the president's private car, steamed out of Two Harbors at 7 A.M. The special guests were in the caboose. Blasting up the three percent grade leading from the lake, the train climbed some 1,100 feet in the first 12 miles. It was headed for Soudan, where the loaded cars were to be picked up and local Chippewa Indians were to entertain the guests with a powwow. The locomotive pulling the train was No. 8, a resplendently new Consolidation type (2-8-0) Baldwin locomotive weighing about 115,000 pounds exclusive of tender. It was the road's first coal burner. The engineer in charge was Thomas Owens, later to become superintendent and vice president of the railroad. The ore cars in the train, as well as those being loaded at the mine, were of 20-ton capacity, reputedly the first of this size in the Lake Superior region. All previous ore cars had been four-wheeled *jennies* of seven to ten-ton capacity.

As the little train proceeded northward it passed through points given the names of Wabegan, Sibiwissa, Gakadina, Matawan, Cloquet River, Wissakode, Bassett Lake, White Face River, St. Louis River, Binisibi, Okwanim, Mesaba Heights, Embarrass River, and finally Tower. Charlemagne Tower, Jr. was interested in Indian lore and had given Indian names to most of these projected stations. Some of the names were either too long or too colorful and were changed about ten years later to avoid confusion in train orders.

The people of Tower and Soudan turned out in force that morning to cheer the arrival of the first train to be loaded with ore, and all that it symbolized. To further emphasize the importance of the occasion, there was no work at the mine that day, the company having declared it to be a holiday. But where was the train? Time seemed to drag. Finally, No. 8 steamed out of the forest and rolled to a stop near the ore-loading dock at Soudan at about 11 A.M. The guests upon alighting from the train were greeted by President Tower, Chief Engineer Richard Lee, Contractor John Wolf, Sr., and Mine Superintendent Elisha Morcom. The day was beautiful. There was handshaking all around, and the guests spent the next hour looking at the mine and the surrounding area.

The Chippewa Indians, who had been invited by President Tower to participate in the festivities, arrived at the site about noon. In Tower's own words, contained in a letter describing the events of the day to his father:

They came flocking in accordingly, men and women, painted and decked with beads and feathers, making altogether a very remarkable appearance and adding to the celebration of the opening of the road in such a way as to make an impression upon us which we should never

forget. They formed a large circle, all sitting on the ground with their drum in the center, and I went close to them in order to distribute the presents which, as I knew they were coming, I had provided beforehand. I had taken so many pipes and a large quantity of tobacco and pocket knives, also trinkets for the women, earrings, breast pins, and bright colored handkerchiefs, that every one of them received a gift of some kind, and before long their faces were beaming with satisfaction; they began to dance and sing with expression of evident joy. We gave them pork enough and flour to content them and left them cooking and eating, promising to come to see us again whenever we should send them word. I think there were rather more than a hundred of them.

While this was taking place, many of the miners and townspeople from Tower, caught up in the carnival atmosphere of the day, climbed onto the loaded cars to which the engine had been coupled. Efforts to discourage them from riding failed, and, as the cars were moved onto the main line, "They were," in Tower's words, "overflowing with people who resembled ants as they clustered upon them." The train stopped a little way down the line to let them off.

The plans had called for departure of the train from Tower at about 2 P.M. in order to arrive at Two Harbors before dark. However, due to a number of delaying incidents, this schedule could not be met. Finally, at 4 P.M. the 10-car train pulled out for Two Harbors, trailing caboose No. 21 with President Tower and his dozen guests.

The train moved more slowly on the southbound trip because engineer Owens was not sure of the new roadbed and was concerned that his cars would get away from him on the downgrades because they were overloaded. As he recalled later, "Morcom was to measure each carload by the number of wheelbarrow loads per car. He did not make a very good guess as each was overloaded by an average of ten tons. Captain Morcom was noted for his generosity." The ten cars actually contained 220 long tons of ore and were not seriously overloaded. Before the year was out, the loads were averaging 22.87 long tons of ore per car with 20 cars per train.

Part of the slow movement was attributed to the stops required en route to siphon water from streams, since water tanks had not yet been erected. Nor did having some of the top officials of the railroad and their wives riding behind in the caboose help any. Upon reaching the station of St. Louis River, now Skibo, President Tower sent a telegram to his father in Philadelphia announcing that the first ore train was en route to the docks and that, according to contract, the $50,000 performance bond would be returned to contractor Wolf. The party reached Two Harbors without incident at about 11 P.M., and as Tower said, "All well contented with our day."

The ten carloads from the first train were dumped on the dock on August 1 and more cars arrived daily. The steamer, *Hecla,* and her towed consort, the schooner *Ironton,* shortly took on about 1,400 tons each of the ore consigned to G. H. and S. P. Ely of Cleveland. Before the shipping season was over, 62,122 tons of Vermilion lump passed through Two Harbors. This was a good start, even though the Elys were having, as could be expected, some difficulty in selling the new ore.

Eleven new Baldwin locomotives and 350 ore cars were on hand as the railroad started operation. Passenger service between Two Harbors and Tower commenced on August 11. D&IR timetable No. 1 showed Trains 1 and 2 running daily except Sunday, with 5 hours and 10 minutes required for the 68-mile run in either direction.

Two Harbors Dock No. 2, with steamer *Hecla* and schooner *Ironton,* taking on the first ore cargoes from Minnesota. Piling was being driven on the left for Dock No. 1. — DM&IR COLLECTION (BELOW) Wood chips and scraps of lumber scattered on the ground attest to the newness of the D&IR's roundhouse at Two Harbors. The four engines in the house were among eleven in service during 1884. — AUTHOR'S COLLECTION

D&IR engine No. 1 on a mixed train at Tower Junction in 1884. Man with oil can is Thomas Owens, who was the engineer on the first ore train. He later became superintendent and vice president of the D&IR. — LAKE COUNTY HISTORICAL SOCIETY

There was, however, little time for elation because the iron ore market rapidly went into a tailspin. Even ore from the proven ranges went begging, which made it difficult to dispose of ore from the unknown Vermilion Range, regardless of its quality. Then, too, the enterprise needed much more money, and Tower's personal resources were about exhausted. He called upon George Stone for help and, capitalizing on Tower's reputation, Stone successfully negotiated loans from St. Paul banks secured by notes of the Minnesota Iron Company. Other efforts to obtain more capital support had little success. Men of means regarded the operation as speculative, and neither the stock of the iron company nor the bonds of the railroad were attractive to outside investors. Moreover, times were so hard in early 1885 that receivership appeared to be the only way out. Stone even formulated plans to have himself appointed receiver, and Tower Sr. observed dejectedly in one of his letters to Stone that "it will be a pity to let this thing stick in the mud."

But enough money was raised in time to keep the enterprise from going under. The remarkably high iron content of the Vermilion ore — it was averaging 68 percent iron — at last began to appeal to furnace operators, and sales began to climb. The Elys made their first major sale, 45,000 tons, to Carnegie Bros. & Company, Limited, of Pittsburgh. By September 1885 Tower did not have to worry about covering next month's expenses. The year 1885 ended with 227,075 tons of ore having moved through Two Harbors. Construction of a second dock (Dock No. 1) was well underway, since it would be needed to handle the increased tonnage anticipated during the coming year.

In view of the brightening outlook, a contract was let to John S. Wolf to construct a 26-mile extension of line, then known as the Lake Division, from Two Harbors to Duluth. This was completed during December of 1886, thus fulfilling the requirement of the swamp land grant. Ore sales continued to climb, with the Carnegies now buying 100,000 tons of the Vermilion ore at a clip. By 1886 the top grade of Vermilion ore, "Minnesota Bessemer," was selling at $6.50 per ton, and "Red Lake," the lower grade, at $5.65 per ton. Company

27

Brand new Baldwin-built No. 4 spots the Soudan Mine loading pocket during 1884. The little four-wheeled, diamond-stacked switchers were the smallest locomotives ever owned by the company. — TOWER-SOUDAN HISTORICAL SOCIETY

auditor A. H. Viele estimated overall mining and railroad profits at $2.50 and $1.65 per ton, respectively.

The mines produced 318,324 tons of ore in 1886, of which 307,949 were shipped to lower lake ports, the balance being stockpiled at the mine. About 100,000 tons were divided between Joliet Steel and Union Steel companies at Chicago, and another 100,000 tons went to Carnegie Bros. & Company. The remainder was sold in smaller quantities, largely throughout the iron-making districts of Ohio and Pennsylvania. Profits were now sufficiently high to permit the Minnesota Iron Company to pay off its loans, and the future seemed to be secure. The annual report showed that the year 1886 ended with a surplus of nearly $300,000, and Charlemagne Tower, Sr., congratulated all those responsible for the "promising condition of the business of the Minnesota Iron Company."

However, the activities of H. H. Porter, head of the newly formed Illinois Steel Company, soon presented a very serious problem. Porter was a nationally known financial figure who had allied himself with some of the great capitalists of the time. His group had already acquired a rich deposit of Vermilion ore at Ely 20 miles east of the Tower property, later called the Chandler Mine, through a mining syndicate that included such

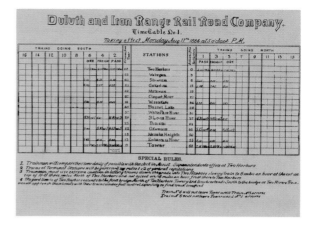

D&IR Timetable No. 1, effective August 11, 1884, was hand-lettered. It shows one ore, one freight, and one passenger train daily in each direction. — DM&IR COLLECTION

American type engines Nos. 1 and 2 were the first passenger locomotives on the D&IR. By the late 1880's, engine No. 2 had already lost her original diamond stack. — STATE HISTORICAL SOCIETY OF WISCONSIN

The D&IR's first office building was constructed at Two Harbors during 1883. — DM&IR COLLECTION (BELOW) The D&IR's first general offices in Duluth were located on the southeast corner of Lake Avenue and Superior Street, just a block away from the original depot. On the sidewalk can be seen provisions waiting to be carted to the depot for placement on the train bound for Two Harbors and the iron mines. — HARVEY MILLER

prominent capitalists as Marshall Field, Cyrus Mc Cormick and John D. Rockefeller. The group was determined to acquire the D&IR and made clear to the Towers that they were prepared, if necessary, to bring a competing trunk line to the Vermilion and would also contest the legality of his Vermilion ore land acquisitions.

Tower was first inclined to fight it out, but on Stone's advice concluded not to do so. In April of 1887, Stone, Tower, Jr. and Richard Lee met with Porter in Chicago. He offered $51.50 a share for all of the Minnesota Iron Company stock. Tower wired his father that this was a final offer and urged him to take it, which he did. Porter agreed to pay approximately $6,400,000.

The Tower group resigned their offices on October 18, 1887, with Jay Morse becoming president of the Minnesota Iron Company, and H. R. Bishop, president of the D&IR. Although Tower, Jr. was given a place on the board of each company, it was soon evident that his services were not wanted in any official capacity, and he left for Philadelphia to become vice president of the Finance Company of Pennsylvania. He later had a distinguished diplomatic career, first being appointed

Station at Tower, constructed during 1885, was the first on the D&IR. — DM&IR COLLECTION (LEFT) By the mid-1880's, Duluth had taken on a very cosmopolitan look. After all, how many cities could boast at the time of a street railway system featuring mule cars! — HARVEY MILLER

Minister to Austria-Hungary by President McKinley in 1897 and Ambassador to Russia in 1899. Three years later he became Ambassador to Germany. He retired from the diplomatic service in 1908.

Charlemagne Tower, Sr., though unhappy about losing control of the Minnesota mining and railroad enterprise he had so carefully nurtured to success, was doubtlessly solaced by almost doubling his money in five years. He died in 1889 at the age of 80.

George Stone did not participate in the affairs of the Minnesota Iron Company after 1887, but retained an interest in the Porter syndicate. He continued to live in St. Paul, his original home, where he was active in promotional and political affairs until his death in 1900.

31

D&IR No. 24, resplendently new, posed at some long-for-gotten location. She, along with two other engines of the same type, was received from Baldwin Locomotive Works during 1888. The train on the right carried D&IR President Bishop's original private car *Vermilion* on the rear. — AUTHOR'S COLLECTION

3

THE DULUTH
AND IRON RANGE
COMES OF AGE

THE passing of control of the D&IR to the Porter interests was a major change in the fortunes of the company and ultimately led to its becoming a part of the United States Steel Corporation in 1901. From its inception the railroad had been regarded primarily as a means of getting iron ore, mined and controlled by its owners, into the stream of commerce. Once the ore reached the docks at Two Harbors it could go to any customer that purchased it. Acquisition by the Porter interests tended to integrate the railroad into the steel industry, insuring both a market for the ore it transported and access to funds for capital improvements.

The first executive committee meeting following takeover of the railroad was promptly held at 15 Broad Street, New York City. The committee consisted, in addition to Bishop, of Porter, who had engineered the takeover, R. P. Flower, an eastern financier and ex-governor of New York, and Charlemagne Tower, Jr. President Bishop reported exchange of the $2,500,000 of six percent registered bonds for $3,000,000 of D&IR five percent coupon bonds, and gave bond Number 1 of the canceled series to Charlemagne Tower, Jr., for presentation to his father. President Bishop reported having authorized the immediate purchase of 200 flat cars of 30-ton capacity and 200 ore cars for delivery in

May of 1888. The executive committee also confirmed Bishop's action in contracting for a 21-mile extension from a point near Tower to Ely, to serve the Chandler Mine, thus accomplishing one of the primary purposes of the takeover.

The Chandler extension to Ely was completed the next year with expectation that mining would start the following season and provide additional ore traffic for the railroad of approximately 300,000 tons per year. Other improvements during 1888 included the purchase of five Consolidation-type locomotives, one switch engine, three American-type passenger locomotives, and 426 freight cars. Included in the latter were 200 ore cars of the new 24-foot standard length to be constructed in the company shops at Two Harbors. Ore cars previously used on the D&IR were 28 feet in length. Expenditures were also made on the ore docks and other facilities at Two Harbors, bringing the total for improvements and developments in this one year to a figure in excess of $950,000. Traffic was slightly over one-half a million tons in the year 1888, the first full year under the new management.

A sure indication that the railroad was prospering was the purchase of a business car, given simply the letter "A," from the Pullman Palace Car Company. It replaced the original homemade *Ver-*

milion, constructed in the company shops at Two Harbors. Trips to the north woods could now be made in the style that city folks were accustomed to enjoying. That year also saw Westinghouse air brakes applied to 20 locomotives and 839 cars. The D&IR is reputed to have been the first railroad in the country to fully equip its locomotives and cars with the new type brake, which contributed enormously to the safety and efficiency of train operations.

M. J. Carpenter succeeded Bishop as president in November 1891. Carpenter was also president of the Chicago and Eastern Illinois Railroad, a line extending south from Chicago to the Ohio River. Like the D&IR, it was also controlled by Illinois Steel Company, and for a time the president, treasurer and purchasing agent were the same for both roads.

The discovery of soft, high-grade iron ore on the Mesabi Range in 1890, first at Mountain Iron and then at Biwabik, presented both a threat and a challenge to the management of the Duluth and Iron Range. The new ore lay to the west, and if served by other railroads, the D&IR's opportunities to expand would be threatened; by the same token, the development presented a challenge to expand by projecting new lines to serve the area.

Porter's first reaction to the opening up of the Mesabi field was to project a new line of railroad from a point on the Lake Division of the D&IR directly into the heart of the Mesabi mining district. Surveys were made for a line extending from

a point only two miles west of Two Harbors to Fayal, near Eveleth, on the Mesabi Range. The line, which was to have maximum grades against the southbound ore movement of 0.3 of one percent, was never built because the estimates revealed that the costs would be excessive. Instead, the decision was made to construct a branch line extending from Allen Junction, on the D&IR, to McKinley, in the vicinity of Biwabik, 18 miles to the west, thus setting up a rivalry with the Duluth, Missabe and Northern, whose line was soon to reach the same area.

Other events of importance to the D&IR in the 1890's may seem less interesting, especially in contrast to the more exciting events occurring on its western counterpart, the Duluth, Missabe and Northern. But the steady physical improvement and the traffic growth of the D&IR during the 1890's bear on the desirability of bringing both lines under common control soon after 1900.

For almost a decade, commencing March 8, 1892, J. L. Greatsinger was in charge of the D&IR, first with the title of general manager. Prior to this he had been superintendent of motive power and

M. J. Carpenter (left), who was president of the D&IR between 1888 and 1892, concurrently headed the Chicago and Eastern Illinois Railroad. Both railroads were controlled by Illinois Steel Company. — LAKE COUNTY HISTORICAL SOCIETY (RIGHT) J. L. Greatsinger headed the D&IR between 1892 and 1901, during which years the line attained its ultimate form. He subsequently became president of the Brooklyn Rapid Transit Company in New York City. — DM&IR COLLECTION

cars. Before 1892 was over he was promoted to president, succeeding M. J. Carpenter. He was an able manager and deserves much of the credit for making the D&IR into a first-class railroad. A remnant of his name lingers on in the *Edna G* steam tug of the Missabe Road, which is still in use. Edna was his daughter.

Extension of the line of the Duluth Street Railway to Lester Park during the year 1892 brought about the discontinuance of the D&IR's suburban passenger service to that point. People preferred to use the more convenient trolley line. Begun in 1887 and operated jointly with the St. Paul and Duluth Railroad, the rail service had provided 15 round trips daily. Motive power, provided by the D&IR, was engine No. 99, an old shotgun-stacked 4-4-0 purchased from the Chicago and Eastern Illinois Railroad.

Iron ore tonnage first exceeded the million mark in 1892, with the D&IR loading 1,166,016 tons into vessels at Two Harbors. Dock No. 4, on which work had begun in 1892, was extended the following year from 84 to 168 pockets. Ninety pockets of Dock No. 3 were completed during 1893, with the dock being rebuilt and extended to its ultimate length in 1904 and 1905. Work was completed on Dock No. 5, the last and largest of the D&IR's wooden docks at Two Harbors, in 1895. It contained 168 pockets and was 54 feet 6 inches in height. In 1899 Dock No. 1, which had become badly deteriorated and grossly inadequate for

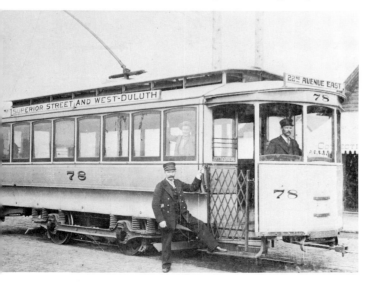

Duluth Street Railway trolleys, as represented by car No. 78, were responsible for discontinuance of D&IR's commuter train service in 1892. — WAYNE C. OLSEN

loading the larger lake vessels, was rebuilt out of wood.

When additional motive power was required to handle increased tonnages, consisting largely of iron ore coming from the Mesabi Range, the D&IR turned away from the well-known Consolidation type and in 1893 began ordering Mastadon type (4-8-0) locomotives. These new engines, manufactured by the Schenectady Locomotive Works and Baldwin Locomotive Works, were among the largest in the world at the time and could handle much greater tonnages than the Consolidations. By the turn of the century, 30 Mastadons were on the motive power roster.

The principal extensions built during this period were (1) Western Mesaba Branch from McKinley to Virginia Station, 6.3 miles (1893); (2) Main line from Ely to Winton, 4 miles (1894); (3) Auburn Branch, from Winston on the Western Mesaba Branch to the rapidly growing mining community of Eveleth, 4.94 miles (1894); and (4) Western Mesaba Branch from McKinley to Fayal, to reach newly opened mines near Eveleth, 8.53 miles (1895). The entire main line from Allen Junction to Two Harbors, a distance of 45 miles, was double tracked with 80-pound rail starting in 1895, with completion in 1899.

A major project of the 1890's was the relocation of the main line between Rollins and Waldo, completed in 1898. The severe 2.8 percent northbound grade and 1.5 percent southbound grade between these points were such operating handicaps that the entire 18 miles was relocated. Initially referred to as the Stewart River Branch, the line relocation project required the removal of three million cubic yards of earth and was an expensive undertaking.

D&IR Timetable No. 24, effective November 24, 1889, listed 15 commuter trains daily between downtown Duluth and suburban Lester Park. — DM&IR COLLECTION

Ore Dock No. 5 at Two Harbors, completed during 1895, was the last wooden dock built by the D&IR. Tow barge *Sagamare* in the foreground was of "whaleback" construction. — DM&IR COLLECTION

Frozen iron ore in cars has always plagued the Lake Superior district ore-carrying roads during the early spring and late fall shipping periods. This early scene shows how ore steaming was carried on by the D&IR in the days of wooden ore cars and 12-Wheelers. Steam generated by locomotives was fed to lances inserted into the tops of the cars, thereby thawing the frozen ore. (BELOW) The big Class J 12-Wheelers were in full command of all D&IR main line ore service at the time this photo was taken, around the turn of the century. Trim-lined, Schenectady-built No. 66 is shown at the head end of an empty train of 25-ton capacity ore cars. — BOTH AUTHOR'S COLLECTION

Busy turn-of-the-century scene at Two Harbors roundhouse. It required the efforts of three men to turn the big-boilered Mastadon type No. 71. Note its unusual headlight. — AUTHOR'S COLLECTION

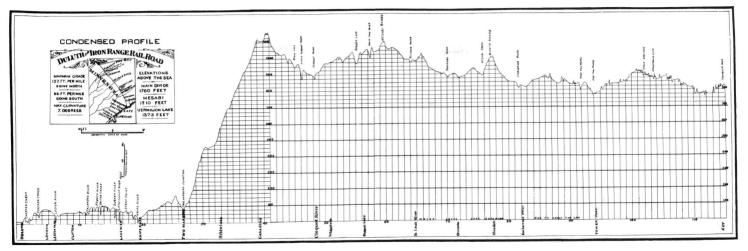

CONDENSED PROFILE

DULUTH AND IRON RANGE RAILROAD

MAXIMUM GRADE
132 FT. PER MILE
GOING NORTH

66 FT. PER MILE
GOING SOUTH

MAX. CURVATURE
7 DEGREES

ELEVATIONS
ABOVE THE SEA

MAIN DIVIDE
1760 FEET

MESABI
1710 FEET

VERMILION LAKE
1375 FEET

Profile of the D&IR which shows the grade from Two Harbors into the Vermilion.—DM&IR COLLECTION

Because of limited financial resources Charlemagne Tower, Sr. had rejected this more desirable alignment when constructing the original road, but traffic density now made it well worth the cost.

The final project of the decade was the completion of the Loop Line out of Two Harbors during 1899. This reduced the northbound grade from 3.0 to 1.5 percent and completed the double tracking into Two Harbors.

With a new tonnage record being set almost every year, it is understandable why the D&IR management felt justified in expending large sums to improve the property during the waning years of the 19th century. By 1899 annual iron ore shipments reached almost 4,000,000 tons, with about 55 percent of the tonnage coming from the Mesabi Range. During that year, orders were placed for 340 all-steel 50-ton capacity ore cars, the first all-steel cars on the railroad. Such cars now become the standard.

The year 1901 proved to be a good one for the D&IR, with more than five million tons of ore moving between the mines and the docks. The railroad had indeed come a long way since that momentous day in July of 1884 when Charlemagne Tower, Jr. rode triumphantly in the caboose behind the first cars of iron ore moving from the Soudan Mine to Two Harbors on Agate Bay.

Rebuilding old Dock No. 1 at Two Harbors was the big construction project for 1899. The upper photo shows the old dock almost dismantled to the water line as of February 4. On June 16, only four and one-half months later, the rebuilt dock was about ready for loading vessels, a remarkable construction feat. — BOTH DM&IR COLLECTION

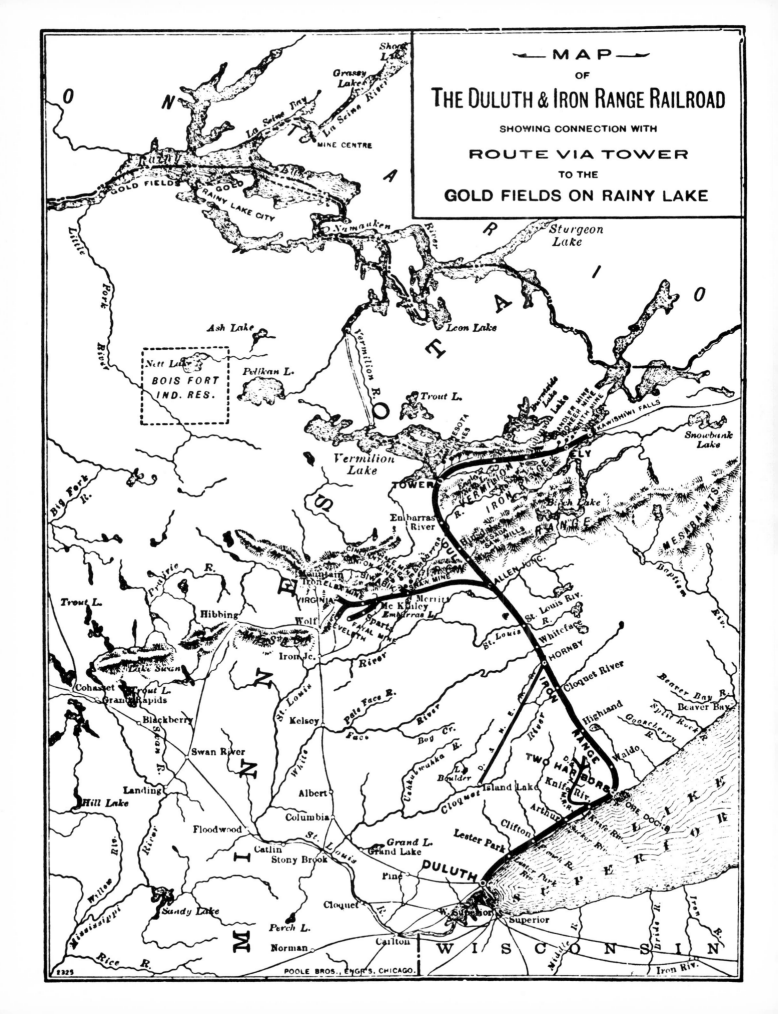

When the map at left was included in an 1897 time-table, the D&IR had almost reached its ultimate mileage. The last major line construction, involving relocation of 18 miles of main line north of Waldo, was completed the following year. Interestingly, the timetable still advertised the road as a means of travel to the gold fields on Rainy Lake. — DM&IR COLLECTION (ABOVE) On June 7, 1895, the Minnesota Iron Company ran a complimentary trip over the D&IR, covering the Vermilion and Mesabi Ranges. The party, which traveled by lake steamer from Buffalo to Duluth, included many of the most influential financiers and capitalists of the time. Among the 160 guests were such personalities as P. D. Armour of Chicago meat-packing fame; merchandiser Marshall Field of Chicago; R. P. Flower, industrialist and former governor of New York State; Pittsburgh coal and coke producer, H. C. Frick; Robert Todd Lincoln, son of the late President and president of the Pullman Company; D. O. Mills, a leading West Coast banker; Pittsburgh industrialist, Henry W. Oliver; Illinois Steel Company's H. H. Porter; George M. Pullman, board chairman of the Pullman Company; and Charlemagne Tower, Jr. Shown is the 16-car special headed by Consolidation No. 51. Another Consolidation at the rear assisted the train out of town.

The year was 1893. Engine No. 2 had only recently arrived from the Pittsburgh Locomotive Works and was the
pride of the Missabe Road. Optimism concerning the
newly-discovered Mesabi ran high, yet none could then
visualize the hundreds of millions of tons of "red rust"
that would pass by the Iron Junction depot during the
next eight decades. Iron Junction served as the first operating headquarters of the DM&N during the 1892-93
period of Merritt control. An engine house and rip track
situated there enabled most locomotive and car repairs
to be made at that location during the early years. —
DM&IR COLLECTION

4

THE MERRITTS' GREAT ADVENTURE

THE Mesabi Range lies along the south side of a 100-mile ridge of granite extending diagonally across the state of Minnesota. At its closest point the Range is about 60 miles north of Duluth. Mesabi, sometimes spelled Mesaba, Missabe, or Missabay, means giant in the Chippewa language, and the Range is sometimes referred to as the Giant's Ridge. The name is appropriate, considering the 2.9 billion tons of iron ore hauled from it during the first 80 years of its productive life.

The earliest direct references to Mesabi iron ore are those of Henry H. Eames, Minnesota's first state geologist. He recorded making field trips in 1866 in the upper reaches of the St. Louis River as far east as Embarrass Lake on the eastern end of the Range, right on top of the ore formation. He wrote of seeing immense bodies of iron ore, both magnetic and hematite, and that, "... In some of these formations, iron enters so largely into its composition as to affect the magnetic needle." He traveled up the Prairie River, a short stream northwest of Grand Rapids, and reported seeing iron ore at Prairie Falls. As early as 1866 the geologists had thus established, in an academic way, almost the full extent of the Mesabi Range.

The eastern end of the Mesabi Range had become accessible with the building of the main line of the Duluth and Iron Range to the Vermilion.

For 20 years after its initial exploration by Peter Mitchell, most of the prospecting of the Mesabi was confined to its eastern end. Consequently, reports concerning the commercial value of its ore were unfavorable. But not everyone was satisfied with these reports. Lewis H. Merritt of Duluth, a man with seven stalwart sons, was one who was not satisfied. In the mid-1860's, after a lonely journey through the high country the Chippewa Indians called Mesabi, he returned with a promising iron ore sample; "I tell you, there's iron up there worth more than all the gold in California," he often told his boys. Many years later, fired by their father's zeal, three of his sons, Leonidas, Alfred, and Cassius, set out in 1885 to prove him right and make themselves a fortune. Five years of hard work proved him right, but the fortune they sought to make escaped their grasp.

The brothers' earliest explorations for iron ore were on the Vermilion Range, but they soon became discouraged there because most of the good properties were already in the hands of the Minnesota Iron Company. They did, however, find a sizable ore deposit, later to be known as the "Section 30" mine, near Winton.

A real break came in 1888 when Cassius Merritt was employed by the Duluth and Winnipeg Railroad as head surveyor in laying out a line from

Duluth's famous Merritt family in 1871. Top row, from left: Leonidas, Lewis, Andrus, Alfred, and Lucien; bottom row: Cassius, Mother Hephzibah and Father Lewis; Jerome and Napoleon. — ST. LOUIS COUNTY HISTORICAL SOCIETY

Duluth northwesterly toward Winnipeg. After two earlier efforts, one that never passed the planning stage and one that died in a rock cut on the hill above Duluth, the D&W was finally ready to build a railroad. While not employed to look for iron ore, Cassius always had an eye out for it. He picked up a piece of high-grade ore in the very area where the first mine on the Mesabi would be located. Spurred by this discovery, the three brothers, assisted by three nephews, began searching in earnest. Equipped with only a surveyor's compass and dip needle, they set out to track down a big ore body, drawing rough maps as they went.

The spring of 1890 found the three Merritt brothers and their men test-pitting an area around what is now called Mountain Iron. Where their dip needle showed maximum deviation they found only low-grade taconite, to them a worthless, jaspery rock. However, on November 15 as they moved a little farther south below the crest, their wagon wheels sank through a carpet of pine needles and disclosed reddish, powdery soil in the ruts. Alfred picked up several handfuls, and sensing at once its unusual heft, knew that at last their long search had been successful. Captain J. A. Nicols, the head of the test-pit crew, was given orders to start digging at the foot of the crest. Nicols hesitated. He had spent many years exploring the Michigan ranges and knew that ore would be found only at the crest of a range. After all, wasn't he the most experienced miner of the lot? Only after Alfred turned up several shovelfuls of soft, heavy soil did Nicols undertake to dig where Leonidas indicated.

The next day made history. H. V. Winchell, a leading authority on Minnesota geological affairs, recorded it as follows:

On the sixteenth day of November, 1890, workmen, under the direction of Captain J. A. Nicols, of Duluth, Minnesota, encountered soft hematite in a test-pit on the Northwest Quarter of Section Three, Township Fifty-eight, Range Eighteen, West of the Fourth Principal Meridian. This mine, now called the Mountain Iron, was the first body of soft ore discovered on the Mesabi Iron Range.

After digging down 14 feet Captain Nicols was elated. He returned to Duluth the next day with 50 pounds of what proved to be ore of 64 percent iron content in his packsack. Lewis H. Merritt's prophecy and George Stuntz's prediction about iron on the Mesabi had been verified. Since winter would soon be closing in, Nicols wanted to stop digging until spring, but Alfred and Leonidas would not permit it and ordered him to go back and uncover all the ore he could. They were determined to convince the learned geologists and mining experts that here on the Mesabi, where they had scoffed at finding high-grade ore, was the real thing, a veritable mountain of ore. They named the place Mountain Iron.

The next year two woodsmen, John McCaskill and John McKinley, told the Merritts about seeing iron ore in the base of an uprooted tree located on their land 20 miles east of Mountain Iron. The Merritts acquired this parcel from them, and in August of 1891 their test-pit crew found good ore there. This property became the famed Biwabik Mine. All doubts about Mesabi iron ore soon vanished, and the Mesabi iron ore rush was on.

Transportation by railroad was essential to get the iron ore to Lake Superior. The railroads then nearest this area were the Duluth and Iron Range, running between Ely and Two Harbors, considerably to the east of Mountain Iron, and the Duluth and Winnipeg, a Canadian-backed railroad, later part of the Great Northern, the closest point on which was at Stony Brook Junction, 48 miles southwest. The Merritts were primarily interested in mining the iron ore and did not want to get themselves involved in constructing and operating a railroad. They first tried to interest the Duluth and Iron Range in constructing a branch from a point on their main line, westward to Mountain Iron, but the D&IR was not receptive. Approaches were then made to the Northern Pacific and the

The Merritt brothers first discovered high-grade Mesabi ore in a test pit near Mountain Iron, marked with an "X" in the scene below. Stripping operations were already well underway when this photograph was made, using small, narrow-gauge locomotives and three-yard capacity cars. — ST. LOUIS COUNTY HISTORICAL SOCIETY

At the left, Leonidas Merritt led the brothers in their long search for iron. (RIGHT) Alfred Merritt, who became president of the Missabe Road on February 7, 1893, held down the top position for only one year. — ST. LOUIS COUNTY HISTORICAL SOCIETY

St. Paul and Duluth railroads, but connections to them would be long and expensive, and neither road was interested. It was soon obvious to the Merritts that they would have to build a railroad of their own. Leonidas Merritt wrote a fanciful prospectus, hoping to woo investors:

> We are going to build a railway, with easy grades for transportation, from the mines of the Mesabi to the smokestacks of the Zenith, to the furnaces for smelting, to the mills where cunning fingers fashion articles for commerce, structural steel, and heavy castings, tools, and rails and nails and whatnot.

He begged bankers, merchants, and small businessmen of Duluth to:

> . . . put some cash in the Missabe, lend a helping hand to others who are working for you. Let us bind with bands of iron the Mesabi to the Zenith.

The *Zenith* referred to by Leonidas was the City of Duluth, sometimes called the *Zenith City of the Unsalted Seas.*

Obtaining authority to use the 1882 charter of the Lake Superior and Northwestern Railway, which had not done any building, the Merritt group incorporated the Duluth, Missabe and Northern Railway Company on June 23, 1891. The capital stock was stated to be $5,000,000, but raising that much money from sale of stock was an-

other matter. The board of directors elected K. D. Chase, president, Leonidas Merritt, vice president, S. R. Payne, secretary, Cassius Merritt, treasurer, and Moses E. Clapp, counsel.

On August 6 the directors authorized a survey for the location of the railroad from Stony Brook Junction, on the Duluth and Winnipeg, north to the Mountain Iron mine on the Mesabi Range. Between that date and the end of the year the survey crew, which included Cassius and Wilbur Merritt, both of whom were experienced railroad surveyors, operating under the direction of C. H. Martz, chief engineer of the DM&N, laid out the preliminary line for the new railroad. Twenty-five of its 48 miles headed north across the muskeg straight as an arrow. Running the survey was a formidable task because the country was uninhabited and all supplies for the survey crew had to be packed in by Indians. At times the crew would run out of provisions for two or three days. For miles the survey line ran through a great swamp, necessitating knee-deep wading. The line was to slope down gently from the Mesabi Range to Lake Superior, so gently, said the Merritts, that ore-laden cars, if given a good shove at the mines, would almost roll by themselves the entire 48 miles to the St. Louis River. This was not entirely a dream, for the route had, and still has, excellent grades.

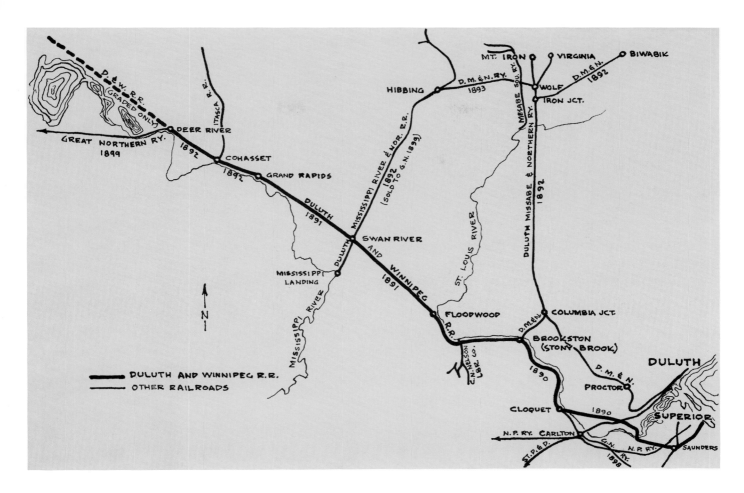

Map showing the Duluth and Winnipeg Railroad and the years of line extension. — DRAWN BY AUTHOR (BELOW) Newly constructed DM &N depot at Mountain Iron as it appeared in late 1892. Architecture was very similar to the nearby depot at Iron Junction. Recently laid main line track in the foreground is badly in need of ballast and lining. — MT. IRON PUBLIC LIBRARY

A construction contract was let on January 28, 1892 to Donald Grant, a well-known railroad contractor of Faribault, Minnesota. He subcontracted the work to Foley Brothers and Guthrie of St. Paul, Minnesota. The sum of $1,300,000 was raised through sale of bonds, three-fifths of which were purchased by Grant, the contractor, and Chase, the president.

Since the Merritts also controlled most of the high-grade ore deposits at Biwabik, construction of a branch from Iron Junction to Biwabik, a distance of 16.5 miles, was undertaken before the original line was completed. That contract was signed with Grant on March 2, 1892, the work to be completed late in the fall. A five-mile branch from Wolf to Virginia was also completed that year.

The operating headquarters was placed at Iron Junction, where both an engine house and rip track for handling locomotive and car repairs were located. A two-stall engine house, a 60-foot turntable, and fuel and water facilities were constructed at Stony Brook Junction, the southern terminus. The facilities were minimal, but adequate for the early operations.

47

The arrival of the first carload of Mesabi Range ore in Duluth on October 18, 1892, was cause for much excitement among Duluthians, who began gathering at the Union Depot hours before its appearance. Note the pine tree on top of the load, which has ever since been a tradition for the first car loaded from any new mine. — ST. LOUIS COUNTY HISTORICAL SOCIETY (BELOW) In November 1892, the historic first cargo of Mesabi Range ore from the Mountain Iron Mine was loaded into whaleback barge No. 102 at the dock of the Duluth and Winnipeg (now Burlington Northern) at Allouez, Wisconsin. — BURLINGTON NORTHERN

The Merritts wanted to have their road terminate at Duluth, but due to initial inability to procure rights-of-way within the city, they made a connection with the Duluth and Winnipeg at Stony Brook and entered into a contract, dated April 14, 1892, which permitted the DM&N to operate over D&W tracks and use the D&W dock and terminal facilities at Allouez (Superior), Wisconsin. In actual practice, the DM&N elected to terminate its operation at Stony Brook and have the D&W handle its trains into Allouez.

The need to complete the Duluth, Missabe and Northern as soon as possible was quickly apparent. Leonidas received an order from Henry W. Oliver of Pittsburgh, on August 4, 1892, for 200,000 tons of "your best quality blue ore" for delivery during the 1893 shipping season. This was the first sizable order for Mesabi ore.

Throughout the summer and early fall of 1892 construction of the railroad moved ahead at a rapid pace, with the 60-pound rail being laid at rates as high as two miles per day. The line was completed into Mountain Iron by mid-October, and to properly celebrate the occasion, and their mother's eightieth birthday as well, the Merritts ran a special train to the mine on October 15, 1892. The train was routed over the Northern Pacific from Duluth to Cloquet, over the Duluth and Winnipeg from Cloquet to Stony Brook and over the DM&N's own line to Mountain Iron. Two days later the *Duluth News Tribune* reported that:

> . . . A jolly party of excursionists took a trip to Mountain Iron Saturday on the Duluth, Missabe and Northern Railway, given by the Merritt brothers in honor of their mother, Mrs. Hepzibeth Merritt, of Oneota, it being her eightieth birthday (Saturday, October 15, 1892). In the party were her seven sons: Leonidas, Alfred, Lucien, Lewis, Napoleon, Cassius and Andrus, together

with their families, including grandchildren and great-grandchildren, numbering 55 of the Merritt family — several being absent. The party left the Union Depot at 8:15 a.m., in a special train of four coaches in charge of G. H. White, General Superintendent of the DM&N Railway, who gave his personal attention to all the details and did much to add to the pleasure of the trip. Prominent among the invited guests were some 200 ladies and gentlemen.

The run to the mine was made without incident, and refreshments were served on the train at noon. Since the Merritts were teetotalers, there was no champagne, but 25 gallons of milk were provided. Upon arriving at the mine the party walked immediately to the edge of the pit, observed the loading of ore cars, viewed the stockpile, reassembled, and were photographed. While standing on the waste dump, the Reverend Doctor Forbes, a Methodist minister, made a speech. After looking over the grounds for a short time, the party returned by train to Duluth.

Thus was the Merritts' great day celebrated. Two days later the first train of ore from the Mesabi Range, containing ten cars of rich hematite from Mountain Iron, was dispatched to the Duluth and Winnipeg ore dock at Allouez. The cars were set out at Stony Brook Junction, where they were picked up by the D&W local and hauled the remainder of the way to Allouez. One car of ore was taken from the train at Superior and moved to Duluth, where it was spotted at the Union Depot in order to give Duluthians, some of whom were still a bit skeptical about Mesabi ore, an opportunity to examine it. The 20 tons of dark, soft ore, assaying better than 63 percent iron, got considerable attention and remained on a track under the train shed for several days.

Ore started moving in 40-car solid trains between Mountain Iron and Allouez during November. It was necessary to double-head these trains over the Duluth and Winnipeg because the only locomotives available were small standard 4-4-0's. All DM&N trains were handled by leased power in 1892 because the three Ten-Wheeler type (4-6-0) locomotives ordered from the Pittsburgh Locomotive Works did not arrive until 1893. A total of 394 cars were on order or in service of which 200 were 25-ton capacity ore cars.

The first cargo of Mesabi Range ore was loaded into whaleback barge No. 102 at the new Allouez dock of the Duluth and Winnipeg on November 11, 1892. This dock was constructed by the D&W under terms of its contract with the DM&N covering handling of the Merritts' ore. The shipment, consisting of 2,078 gross tons, was consigned to the Oglebay-Norton Company, of Cleveland, Ohio.

It is of interest that difficulty was experienced that fall with frozen ore, both in cars and in dock pockets. This was always a problem with the soft, wet Mesabi ore and was never fully overcome. As a result, only one other vessel was loaded at Allouez before the season closed. First year shipments had totalled 4,245 tons.

Ore shipments were resumed through Allouez in the 1893 navigation season. However, the Merritts were becoming increasingly dissatisfied with the Duluth and Winnipeg operation, and commenced talking about building into Duluth. They contended that the D&W had failed to provide the number of ore cars required under the contract and that the D&W's share of the line haul rate was excessive. St. Louis County, where Duluth was located, offered the DM&N $250,000 worth of county bonds as an inducement to build into Du-

luth. Perhaps the basic motivation for taking what proved to be a disasterous step was the intense rivalry between the cities of Duluth and Superior, evidenced by the Merritts insisting that theirs should be a Minnesota road throughout. Many years later Leonidas Merritt acknowledged that ". . . This was a fatal mistake and, seemingly the only one we made in the whole enterprise, as it involved us in debt, whereas, while at Allouez Bay we were facing a safe business and practically uninvolved in any way."

Chase, the DM&N president, and Grant, the contractor, who were both heavily involved in the road, did not share the Merritts' enthusiasm and determination for building into Duluth at that time. Since the necessary funds were not available locally, they felt that the company would be placing itself in a precarious financial position should it move ahead with the Duluth extension. They had no doubts about the ultimate desirability of building into Duluth, but were of the opinion this should wait until the business of the railway justified it, and they were right.

Not only was more capital required to build the Duluth extension, but the Merritts also felt obliged to buy out their dissenting partners Grant and Chase, and they could not get the necessary money from local bankers. The timing could not have been worse for outside financing, for the year 1893 turned out to be a panic year. What a time for the Merritts to be launching new capital-demanding ventures.

The corporate vessel in which the Merritts floated downstream into the hands of John D. Rockefeller was the American Steam Barge Company, with C. W. Wetmore as the unwilling pilot. In addition to Rockefeller, the principal stockholders of the company were Captain Alexander McDougal, of Duluth, inventor of the whaleback steam barge, then highly regarded as an ore carrying vessel, A. D. Thomson, a grain exporter, also from Duluth, and Cleveland vesselmen represented by Colgate Hoyt. Wetmore, the secretary of the company, was considered by his contemporaries to be a shrewd lawyer of excellent connections.

Negotiations for the movement of Mesabi ores via their vessels had already brought American Steam Barge Company officials into contact with the Merritts. A pooling of mine, railroad and ship properties was proposed as the additional basis for

The first train of ore from the Mesabi Range to the newly built DM&N dock at Duluth arrived on July 22, 1893. Many members of the Merritt family can be seen to the left of the train, proudly observing the events of their great day. — AUTHOR'S COLLECTION

financing required for the railroad. Wetmore was to raise two million dollars, to be used to complete the Duluth extension, an ore dock at Duluth, and the Superior Branch to extend from Wolf to Hibbing. There would normally have been nothing wrong with this proposal, but under the circumstances prevailing in the panic year of 1893 it was ill advised. Messrs. Chase and Grant stood against the American Steam Barge contract, but with Wetmore's help the Merritts prevailed. On January 30, 1893, a Merritt representative told the local press:

> The Merritt syndicate has complete control of the DM&N. They propose to take the road into their own hands and make it the best iron road in the world, as fast as money and men can do it. They own and control it for all time, and the Rockefellers and the Barge Company behind them will furnish all the money that may be needed.

Perhaps Wetmore allowed the Merritts to believe that he carried Rockefeller's checkbook in his pocket, but those who had dealt with that gentleman knew that he carried his own checkbook and required very good security for his loans. Frederick T. Gates, one of Rockefeller's trusted lieutenants in this and other ventures, later wrote:

> Mr. Wetmore . . . undertook the serious task of raising among capitalists by the sale of bonds, the $1,600,000 then supposed to be enough for the railroad. In January, 1893, Mr. Rockefeller took a quarter of the whole lot, but scarcely anyone else wanted any. Mr. Wetmore tried in vain to sell them to banks . . . No one would take bonds on a small, distant ore road, to undeveloped mines of doubtful ore values. Wetmore was reduced to borrowing from banks in driblets on short time, with the bonds as collateral widely margined. As to investments in the Missabe, Mr. Rockefeller declined to join the syndicate and formally sent him (Wetmore) word that he would neither invest in, nor loan money on, Missabe mines.

Chase soon agreed to sell the Chase-Grant block of stock for $250,000 to the Merritt-Wetmore syndicate, thereby giving them control of the DM&N. Alfred Merritt succeeded Chase as president on February 7, 1893, and Leonidas Merritt continued as vice president. Wetmore was appointed second vice president and D. M. Philbin, general manager. At a director's meeting held the same day, Leonidas Merritt stated:

> The Company expects to cover the entire Mesabi Range with branches and spurs. Extensions to some of the new mines are already underway. The important timber interests will not be neglected. The company has $400,000 in its treasury, and not a cent of debt. The Chases and Grant received $250,000 for their 5,000 shares; the Merritts took half and the Rockefeller interests one-half. Of the $400,000 sold at par, the Merritts bought $300,000, and the Rockefellers $100,000. The Merritts and their associates have therefore a greater proportionate interest than ever.

While this statement appears optimistic, it must be remembered that the Merritts had not yet been confronted with paying the full expenses associated with the Duluth extension and ore dock, both of which were in the early stages of construction.

The New York and Missabe Company was formed by Wetmore and the Merritts to carry out the financial and consolidation plans. Wetmore had numerous meetings with Rockefeller interests without obtaining the help needed. Conditions were becoming precarious, and it was especially difficult to attract new investors following the failure of the Philadelphia and Reading Railroad Co. in the spring of 1893. By midsummer the panic

Looking north at Columbia Junction, where the new Duluth Extension (track on the right) connected with the main line. Track on the left, which went southwest to a connection with the Duluth and Winnipeg at Stony Brook Junction, was the original route for Mesabi Range ore. — DM&IR COLLECTION

was in full swing, with failure of the Erie, and shortly thereafter, the Northern Pacific, Union Pacific, and Santa Fe railroads going into the hands of receivers. Rockefeller would take no more than the first block of bonds. The Merritts had men working on the railroad and the dock who had to be paid. Contractors Wolf and King completed work on the Duluth extension in July, the 36-track receiving yard at Proctor was well along, and the big dock at Duluth was almost completed. On the surface everything looked right, but actually the end was near for the Merritts.

By July, some $3,200,000 in bonds and a mountain of floating debt were owed, equipment note obligations of $50,000 to $60,000 were falling due each month, and contractors were demanding payment for work done. The Duluth offices of the railway company were several times at the point of being mobbed, and the company's notes were being offered at 60 percent discount. Most of the time Leonidas Merritt was in New York with Charles Wetmore attempting to raise the money required to keep from going under. But before recording the downfall of the Merritts, note should be made of what they had accomplished.

The great ore dock jutting some 2,300 feet into St. Louis Bay in the City of Duluth was ready in the midsummer of 1893 to receive and dispatch iron ore shipments. The largest of its kind on the Great Lakes, the dock and its half-mile approach were comprised of 12.5 million board feet of timber. The dock boasted of 384 pockets, each with a capacity of 150 long tons of ore, and it stood 52 feet 8 inches above the water. The Merritts had reason to be proud of everything about it, except its cost. Brother Lucian, a Methodist minister, proudly wrote to Leonidas in New York on July 20, 1893 that "... Work on the railroad and the dock have been and are now pushed and this day will find track laid on the dock;" further describing it as a great big institution. Writing on he consoled, "... While you have sweat blood in New York, Alf and the boys have done likewise here and it has been pushed right along — you all deserve great credit."

Lucian's letter also expressed strong resentment against the Minnesota Iron Company and the Duluth and Iron Range Rail Road, presumably because of their refusal to handle the Merritts' ore. He confidently told Leonidas that they would regret their action "... when ore comes in on that dock."

The first commercial shipment of Mesabi ore to come to Duluth, ten carloads from the Mountain Iron Mine, arrived on July 22, pulled by engine No. 15, a gleaming Ten-Wheeler, newly arrived from the Pittsburgh Locomotive Works. A description of this event was penned on that date to Leonidas Merritt by his wife. She wrote:

You ought to have been here this afternoon to help us celebrate the coming of the first ore onto the new dock ... The largest part of the Merritt family were there, children and all ... We had to wait a couple of hours before we saw the train, then away up the hill through the smoke and haze we could see a black line that looked like a black caterpillar creeping slowly along . . . Soon it came onto the trestle and then over the dock where we all stood waiting for it . . . It moved out until the ore cars were over the pockets and then stopped to unload. Nobody made a sound, not a hurrah or anything, while they came on the dock, but we were so glad to see it there that we didn't feel like making a noise . . . After they had unloaded three or four cars, we came home, with Alf's folks. He is home now . . . I will send you a little of the ore from the cars that came down today so that you will realize that they have really begun to ship ore . . .

The Superior Branch, extending for 16 miles between Wolf and Hibbing, the last major construction by the DM&N while under Merritt control, was completed during October. Hibbing, then only a logging camp sitting on top of hundreds of millions of tons of iron ore, was destined to become the iron ore capital of the world. By the end of 1893 the DM&N had 116.83 miles of main line and branches, and 7.20 additional miles of second track on Proctor Hill. Slightly more than half a million tons of iron ore moved over the road that year, of which approximately 20 percent was handled through the Duluth and Winnipeg's dock at Allouez and the balance through the DM&N's new dock at Duluth.

Eighteen locomotives were received during 1893, including two of the 4-4-0 type for passenger service, ten 4-6-0's for ore and freight, and six 0-6-0 switchers. All were built by the Pittsburgh Locomotives Works, a Carnegie enterprise. Rolling stock consisted of 1,001 ore, 35 box, 210 flat, 50 logging bunks, 13 cabooses, eight miscellaneous passenger and head-end cars, and the business car *Missabe*. The logging bunks were received with-

FIRST ORE DOCK AT DULUTH

Whalebacks loading ore at the Duluth, Missabe and Northern's first ore dock at Duluth. The original of this painting, by marine artist Howard Sprague, has been a treasured possession of the Missabe Road ever since 1893 when the dock was completed.

out trucks, inasmuch as they were in service only during the winter, or non-ore season, and could use the trucks taken from idle ore cars.

This was the railroad the Merritts had succeeded in putting together hardly two years after its date of incorporation — June 21, 1891. That they built well is not to be disputed; that they built too well may be argued; that they built too much too quickly soon became apparent.

By mid-1893 Rockefeller became aware of the true status of his DM&N bonds and realized that claims of the contractors who built the road and not his bonds were the first lien on the property. He was advised that a million dollars or more owing to the contractors came ahead of the bonds. There was no question that he had to step in and save the Merritts in order to protect his own investment.

Frederick T. Gates and G. Welwood Murray were sent by Rockefeller to arrange matters with the Merritts and Wetmore. Gates has summarized the agreement, dated August 28, 1893, as follows:

Mr. Rockefeller was to finance the railroad with $500,000. (He actually put in over $2,000,-000). Mr. Rockefeller was to take over without recourse the Adams and Lone Jack mining properties, which the partners, Wetmore and Merritt, had recently bought for $428,000 short paper. Mr. Rockefeller was to advance Merritt and Wetmore, as partners, considerable sums of needed cash, and to the Merritts, personally, $150,000 that they might retain control of their stocks. Mr. Rockefeller was to buy all the ore the Mountain Iron Mine could produce and ship over the railroad that fall, so as to put the mine in operation. The Merritts on their part, were to put their railroad stock and all their best mining stocks, the 'Mountain Iron,' 'Biwabik,' 'Missabe Mountain,' 'Rathbun,' and 'Shaw,' into one basket, or company, to be called the Lake Superior Consolidated Iron Mines, issuing the Consolidated stock to themselves on valuations to be fixed by themselves. Leonidas Merritt to be president, and the Merritts to control. The company was to buy from Mr. Rockefeller all his mining stock, including the Adams and Lone Jack, now his, paying for their stock in debenture bonds of the Consolidated Company, so many bonds for so much stock.

The arrangement appeared fair and satisfactory to all concerned, Rockefeller putting in the money and retaining solid security in the form of bonds,

the Merritts putting in equities of great potential value, and, in turn, receiving stock of great potential value. Although Lake Superior Consolidated became worth many millions of dollars within eight years, it was, as one unidentified writer aptly described, ". . . at the time only a golden hope, led along an improvised railroad, to a group of explorations and expectations in which few mining men, and fewer furnace men, had any confidence."

To outward appearances the Merritts were now on sound financial footing. They were, however, still under tremendous pressure. They had a failing bank, the Southern National, to stave off from collapse, and had many other pressing financial commitments. The pressure against them mounted to the point where, in January 1894, the Merritts offered Rockefeller 90,000 shares of their Lake Superior Consolidated stock at $10.00 per share. Rockefeller took up the offer, giving them the option to redeem 55,000 of the shares within one year at the same price, plus interest. They shortly sold additional shares to Rockefeller and soon the Merritts had sold so much of their Consolidated stock that they no longer held control. This became evident at the annual meetings of the DM&N and the principal mining companies, held on February 6, 1894. Shorn of their voting power, Leonidas and Alfred refused to continue in office, though both were offered the reins under Rockefeller's guiding hand. Headlines in the February 7, 1894 issue of the *Duluth News Tribune* told the story:

Merritts step out — John D. Rockefeller in full control of Consolidated mines — elections held yesterday . . . Alfred Merritt declines Missabe's Presidency . . . will devote full time to straightening his private affairs . . . the Presidency of the Missabe Road was not filled yesterday and will not be for some time . . . D. M. Philbin re-elected General Manager . . . Control and management of the mines in hand of W. J. Olcott of Ironwood, Michigan.

The Merritts made another attempt to become involved in the Mesabi when, on September 11, 1895, they incorporated a new ore railroad, the Duluth and Northwestern. The five incorporators and directors were all Merritts, with Alfred as president. Active operations were to begin the following year, with Duluth as the southern terminus and headquarters, and ore docks located on the St. Louis River. "It will be a Merritt road, run in

the interest of Duluth, built to give an outlet for the independent mines," said the Merritts, but it died for lack of the required capital.

Disappointed over the loss of their Mesabi holdings, the Merritts continued to explore for ore. This time, their attentions were focused on such diverse areas as Canada, New Mexico, Idaho, Oregon, and even south of the border in Mexico. Silver and copper replaced iron in the latter explorations, which were spearheaded by Leonidas and Alfred. Through it all the brothers stuck steadfastly together. Only one was to leave the family and Duluth, Lewis, who went to California where he later became a wealthy man.

The bodies of Alfred, Cassius and Leonidas Merritt are buried together high atop the hill overlooking West Duluth. The earth of their graves may tremble a bit from the passage of heavy trains of iron ore rolling day and night over the tracks of the railroad they conceived and built almost 80 years ago. It is easy to feel sympathy for the Merritt brothers and try to lay their downfall to others. The Merritts did bring suit against Rockefeller charging fraud, and won in the trial court. However, the judgment was reversed on appeal, and the case was then settled out of court, reputedly for half a million dollars, which went to the Merritt creditors.

The real villain in the piece was the Panic of 1893. The commitments of the Merritts would not

Duluth, looking east in 1893. The Union Depot on the right (with spires) was the scene of much activity, with seven railroads serving the city at that time. — ST. LOUIS COUNTY HISTORICAL SOCIETY

have been too difficult to handle a year earlier, when credit was easier, and, had the crunch come a year later their enterprises might well have been on such secure footing as to weather it. But, as Chase and Grant had warned, they need not have built the Duluth extension when they did, and so the argument goes.

A fine tribute to the Merritts was given on the floor of the House in 1911 by Congressman Augustus O. Stanley of Kentucky. Speaking of them he said: "The people of Minnesota regard these men, in a way, as we regard Boone in Kentucky, and as they regard Houston in Texas, with gratitude and reverence; and while they are ruined in fortune, and broken in spirit, they will find their reward some day, I hope, in monuments commemorating their genius and their courage." One monument to their genius and courage is the railroad line they built, still running where they laid it out. It has already carried iron ore tonnages beyond their wildest dreams, and there is more to come.

5

THE DM&N
UNDER ROCKEFELLER
CONTROL

THE history of the DM&N now begins to parallel that of the D&IR. By 1894 control of both roads had passed from the entrepreneurs who had endured the hardships and taken the risks, over to the financially strong.

The D&IR became associated with the steel making industry when it was acquired from the Towers by Illinois Steel Company interests in 1887. While the DM&N appeared to be allied only with the mining end of the industry as a segment of Rockefeller's Lake Superior Consolidated Iron Mines Company, it became a part of Andrew Carnegie's integrated empire in 1896 when Rockefeller leased all the iron ore properties to Carnegie Steel Company, which guaranteed to take at least 600,000 tons of ore a year out of the mines and ship it over the railroad.

Although Rockefeller now had a going railroad, much remained to be done to make it the railroad it needed to be. Main line tracks had settled so badly in swamp areas, under the weight of heavy ore trains, that considerable upgrading was necessary. Derailments were occurring with such alarming frequency that General Manager Philbin issued this bulletin on August 13, 1894:

I find some trains are running entirely too fast, and slow orders and yard limit boards are not

honored as they should be and while I am anxious to get trains over the road without unnecessary delay, our roadbed is new and in many places still soft and track rough and we must hold ourselves down to *safe rate of speed* which should not exceed 18 miles per hour at any point and not over 12 miles per hour over bad track and around sharp curves.

He urged that special care be taken in bringing the trains from Mountain Iron, down Pine Hill, and approaching all yards and junctions, and warned that any carelessness would be "severely dealt with," probably meaning that those responsible would be fired.

After Alfred Merritt's departure, General Manager Philbin acted for a time as the chief operating officer. Serving with him were A. D. Allibone, first vice president and treasurer, and Alexander McDougal, the Duluth whaleback shipbuilder, as second vice president. Important changes in top management came in 1895 when Rockefeller's emissary, Frederick T. Gates, was made president and J. T. McBride first vice president, succeeding Allibone. McBride had been general superintendent of The Everett and Monte Cristo Railroad in the State of Washington and had been with the Great Northern as an operating officer when that road was being extended to the Pacific Northwest.

DM&N 10-Wheeler No. 9, shown with a loaded ore train of 25-ton capacity ore cars near Wolf, was representative of main line power during the Rockefeller period.—DM &IR COLLECTION

Frederick T. Gates, one-time Baptist minister and church fund raiser, was president of the DM&N from 1895 to 1901. His fund-raising ability brought him to the attention of John D. Rockefeller, who placed him in charge of many of his business activities. Gates had an exceptional talent for big business and saw to it that Rockefeller's investments produced the greatest possible returns. — DM&IR COLLECTION (RIGHT) Ore train pile-up on the DM&N during the 1890's. With the 35-man wrecking crew taking time out to have their photographs taken, it took a little longer to clean up the derailment. — ST. LOUIS COUNTY HISTORICAL SOCIETY

Wooden headframe for shaft No. 1 at the Adams Mine at Eveleth. Note the small H. K. Porter-built narrow-gauge wood-burning locomotive which was typical of those used at the time on the Mesabi Range for handling trains of overburden. — ST. LOUIS COUNTY HISTORICAL SOCIETY

The Adams Branch, constructed during 1895, terminated at the DM&N's Eveleth depot, which is seen in this view framed between the No. 1 Spruce Mine headframe on the left and the water tank on the right. — JOHN H. HEARDING JR. (BELOW) DM&N officials proudly inspect the newly completed locomotive coaling station at Proctorknott during 1896. The man third from left is J. T. McBride, who had become first vice president of the road the previous year. Next to him, toward the track, is Edward Harriman, famous railroad financier. Locomotive taking on coal is 10-Wheeler No. 16. — MARGARET MC BRIDE

The extent of the rehabilitation work necessary after the takeover may be inferred from the fact that the only extension made in 1895 was the short (3.71-mile) Adams Branch from Spruce, on the Biwabik Branch, to Eveleth. Work was completed that year on the big sorting yard near Duluth, at which time the name of the nearby community was changed from "Yards" to "Proctorknott." The name of the community was later shortened to "Proctor" and the railroad facility is now known as "Proctor Yard."

A second dock was placed in service at Duluth in 1896, Dock No. 1 being no longer adequate to handle the tonnage. DM&N ore volume for the year 1896 was just under two million tons exceeding by about 180,000 tons that handled through Two Harbors by its older rival the D&IR. The up-start DM&N was on its way to becoming the major iron ore carrier in the area, though its tonnage did not again exceed that of the D&IR until 1902, when they were under common control.

The DM&N's second ore dock at Duluth was constructed during 1895 and 1896. In the upper view, timber-framing of the dock pockets is in progress. The 60-foot piling on the flatcars in the foreground came from the West Coast. (BELOW) The lower view, taken from near the outer end of Dock No. 1, shows the timber-framing for Dock No. 2 nearing completion. — BOTH MARGARET MC BRIDE

DM&N Consolidation No. 300 heads up the two percent grade to Proctor with a long string of wooden empties. This photograph shows the train operating in the normal right-hand fashion. In the early 1900's, the DM&N became a "southpaw" road, and to this day operates left-handed in double-track territory. The D&IR also operated in a left-hand manner. — WAYNE C. OLSEN COLLECTION

First shaft house at the Hull-Rust Mine near Hibbing in 1897. The Hull-Rust, later an open pit, was for many years the most productive iron mine in the world. — AUTHOR'S COLLECTION

J. W. Kreitter, who had previously been with the Fremont, Elkhorn, and Missouri Valley Railroad, which was shortly absorbed into The Chicago and North Western system, was appointed superintendent in 1896, taking over some of the duties of General Manager D. M. Philbin, who resigned to become superintendent of the Duluth, Mississippi River and Northern and lead that former logging road into the Great Northern system. Kreitter held the post of superintendent for 32 years, retiring in 1928. Within a short time Philbin became superintendent of the Mesabi Division of the Great Northern, the DM&N's newest and from then on its greatest rival in the movement of iron ore.

J. W. Kreitter was superintendent of the Missabe Road for a third of a century, retiring in 1928. — DM&IR COLLECTION

By 1899 the DM&N again found itself short of dock capacity and let a contract for construction of a third dock at Duluth. The specifications initially called for the construction of only 192 pockets, instead of the final configuration of 384 pockets. When completed to ultimate length it would have greater storage capacity than either of the two previous docks, and its greater height permitted the expeditious loading of the largest vessels on the Lakes.

During 1899 the DM&N took delivery of its first Consolidation type (2-8-0) locomotive, No. 302, designed specifically for road service. The DM&N ultimately had 51 locomotives of this type moving ore between Mesabi mines and the Duluth docks. Worthy of note during that year was the completion of the program to install automatic couplers and air brakes on all motive power and rolling stock.

In the opening year of the new century (1900) the DM&N undertook an extensive program of additions and improvements to its property. *First,* surveys were continued for an eastward extension from a point on the Biwabik Branch to Henry Oliver's Stevens Mine, a distance of 11 miles, thus invading deeply into D&IR territory; *second,* double-tracking of the main line all the way from the ore docks at Duluth to Wolf on the Mesabi Range was commenced with the laying of a second track between Shaw (St. Louis River) and Wolf, a distance of 6.20 miles, and north from the Proctor ore scales for a distance of 4.60 miles; *third,* 15 miles

A busy 1899 late-season scene at DM&N's Duluth docks showing six vessels waiting for ore to be thawed so they could be loaded. Locomotive on the left, Consolidation No. 300, was built for service on Proctor Hill. Construction of a third ore dock (No. 3) was under way at the time. — DM&IR COLLECTION

Forest products have always constituted an important source of revenue for the Missabe Road. This late 1890's scene shows Mitchell & McClure logging Shay No. 4 headed for the DM&N's Adolph interchange with a capacity train of white pine logs. Note the auxiliary water tank behind the locomotive. — ST. LOUIS COUNTY HISTORICAL SOCIETY

John D. Rockefeller, at the left, controlled the Missabe Road's affairs from 1894 through 1901. — DM&IR COLLECTION (ABOVE) During the late 1890's, many DM&N employees working in and out of Proctor found it necessary to live in boarding cars such as these. To alleviate this undesirable situation, the company constructed a number of homes shortly after the turn of the century. These were later sold to employees. — AUTHOR'S COLLECTION

The steamer *Emory Owen* taking on an ore cargo at newly completed DM&N Dock No. 2 at Duluth in 1900. With a cargo capacity of 1,739 gross tons, she was a typical lake vessel of the period. — JOHN H. HEARDING JR.

By the turn of the century, the famed Mountain Iron Mine was one of the leading producers on the Mesabi Range. This scene shows a Lake Superior Consolidated Iron Mines 0-4-0 type Pittsburgh-built switcher with a train of seven cubic yard capacity stripping cars in the foreground. Farther down in the pit, two trains are being loaded with high-grade ore. — AUTHOR'S COLLECTION

of 60-pound rail in the main line were replaced with 80-pound rail; *fourth,* a major line change, including 3.17 miles of relocation, was completed on the Biwabik Branch in order to avoid rebuilding two bridges situated on unstable ground near Crooked Lake; and *fifth,* work was completed on the initial 192 pockets of new ore dock No. 3, the major project of the year, and the first vessel was loaded from it on September 22. In addition to these improvements in fixed facilities, the DM&N acquired ten new locomotives from the Pittsburgh Locomotive Works (eight for road and two for switching service), and 800 ore cars of 35-ton capacity from Pullman during 1900, in time to assist in handling just under four million tons of ore. These 800 ore cars were the last of wooden con-

struction to be acquired. Five experimental all-steel ore cars also arrived that year, forecasting the pattern of things to come. By now, the average tons of ore per train had risen to 1,401, with 51 cars per train. These improvements are noted in order to indicate the health and vigor of the line and its prospects as it was about to enter into a new phase of its history.

It is clear that Rockefeller played an extremely important role in the development of both the Mesabi Range and the DM&N. His financial resources permitted an orderly expansion of the various mining properties, and, in addition, his influence with eastern industrialists led to the acceptance of Mesabi ores, thus hastening development of the Mesabi Range by perhaps a decade.

Passenger service to the iron ranges flourished in the early 1900's before buses and automobiles took over. In the photo an almost-new Schenectady-built 10-Wheeler (No. 102) is about to depart Endion station at Duluth for the north country with D&IR train No. 1. — AUTHOR's COLLECTION

6

THE VIEW
FROM THE YEAR 1901

THE year 1901 represents a turning point in the history of the two railroads that were ultimately to form the present Duluth, Missabe and Iron Range Railway Company, for that is the year which saw them acquired by the United States Steel Corporation. The year is also a good vantage point from which to take an overall look, not only at the stage of development reached by the two railroads as of that date, but also at the Mesabi Range as a whole and at the other railroads then serving it. By 1901 the lines of development were fairly well established that would hold until about the mid-1950's, when the high-grade soft ore began to run out and the taconite development began.

The Vermilion Range that was discovered first, and to which Charlemagne Tower, Sr., directed his D&IR railroad in 1884, continued to produce iron ore for many years, but was eclipsed by the more productive Mesabi. The high quality hard-rock iron ore found in the Vermilion Range kept the railroad to Soudan and Ely in operation, but there was little new development. The Mesabi, however, developed rapidly after the early discoveries by the Merritt brothers at Mountain Iron and by John McCaskill at Biwabik. The whole Range soon swarmed with prospectors trying to penetrate the glacial drift that covered the erratic

streak of high-grade soft ore so typical of the Mesabi. The area, which was intensely cold in the winter, was covered with heavy pine timber and bush, and for a time there was an intermingling of bustling lumber camps, temporary test-pits and actual mining operations.

The first new strikes were in the Mountain Iron-Biwabik region where the Merritts began their mining operations. Captain J. G. Cohoe, working for the Merritts, discovered the enormous Mesabi Mountain (Virginia) deposit in March 1892, and shortly thereafter it was leased to Henry W. Oliver of Pittsburgh. Other deposits were found somewhat further west in the same township, and Virginia soon became the center of a vast complex of mines, all initially served by the DM&N. Nor were these riches all. Frank Hibbing, a young immigrant from Germany working in the Virginia area, had a hunch that the series of ore bodies continued much further to the west. So west he went. At a booming lumber camp about 25 miles from Virginia he came upon a likely area, took out leases, and then located the largest body of high-grade iron ore ever found in the Lake Superior region. The pit from which ore has been taken at this location is now so vast that it looks, on account of both color and depth, like a miniature Grand Canyon. The original town of Hibbing,

which rested on top of a segment of the ore body, was moved about a mile south shortly after World War I to permit recovery of the ore lying beneath it.

The deposits of the Mesabi's high-grade soft ore were gradually explored and identified during the 1890's. Never more than two miles wide, and thinning to nothing in places, the body of soft ore turned out to be about 100 miles long, extending all the way from Babbitt on the east to beyond Grand Rapids on the west. In addition to the soft ore, which yielded from 60 to 65 percent iron, there was the taconite having 25 to 30 percent iron. This, then, was the great incentive to building railroads into the territory—an enormous supply of a valuable, heavy-loading commodity in continuous demand.

By chance the Merritts had come upon the Mesabi at about the center of one of its most productive areas, and their DM&N found itself even more strategically placed than the Merritt brothers had any reason to believe at the time they surveyed the route. The D&IR, operating some 30 miles to the east, was able to serve only the eastern end of the highly productive Mesabi, by means of extensions, and using Two Harbors as its port.

About 1900 there was a threat that another railroad would be built directly into the eastern part of the Mesabi where the D&IR and DM&N were established. Henry W. Oliver, the Pittsburgh industrialist who had placed the first large order for Mesabi ore with Leonidas Merritt in 1892, became one of the early mine operators, leasing, among others, many Rockefeller properties. For a time things ran smoothly, but late in the 1890's Oliver charged that Rockefeller was selling ore to his competitors at 20 cents a ton less than to him, and he claimed that the freight rates over Rockefeller's DM&N railroad and Illinois Steel's D&IR railroad were excessive. Unable to obtain satisfaction of his grievances, Oliver incorporated the Virginia and Ely Railroad Company. As reported in the September 7, 1899 issue of *Iron Age*:

> The Oliver Mine is not turning out as well as Lessee would like and he may abandon this leasehold. . . . The Oliver people have on the Mesabi a number of mines and prospects whose ore is tied to no traffic contract. These include the Stevens, Shaw, Sheridan and the Security Land and Exploration Company properties. There will be ample business for a fourth ore road.

The next development was an announcement from Oliver that he intended to free himself from dependence upon Rockefeller's fleet of ore carriers. He ordered five large ore boats which, through Carnegie Steel Company's ability to supply the necessary steel, were rushed to completion. However, the war so bravely begun soon ended in a negotiated peace, and Oliver's proposed railroad was never built. Additional railroads were, however, built by various interests into other parts of the Range.

One line-haul railroad to build into the Mesabi was the Great Northern. It was natural that the promoters of this railroad, in projecting their line to the head of Lake Superior in 1898 as an outlet for grain shipments from the west through acquisition of the old Duluth and Winnipeg, by then reorganized as the Duluth, Superior and Western, would also be interested in tapping the newly discovered Mesabi as a source of additional traffic. The vehicle for the Great Northern's penetration of the Range was the Duluth, Mississippi River and Northern (DMR&N) railroad, a rickety logging line extending south from Hibbing to Swan River on the Duluth and Winnipeg. This line was

Spotting cars at the Pioneer stockpile at Ely during 1901. Twenty-five ton capacity wooden ore cars were still standard equipment on the D&IR, although the all-steel 50-ton ore car was beginning to make its appearance. The Pioneer was the last mine to operate on the Vermilion Range. Before closing in 1963, it had produced over 41,000,000 tons of high-grade ore. — AUTHOR'S COLLECTION

The great Mahoning pit was one of the first mining properties to be developed in the Hibbing area. In this turn-of-the-century scene, high-grade ore is being loaded directly into cars by steam shovels. The mine was originally served by the Duluth, Mississippi River and Northern Railway (later absorbed by the Great Northern Railway), which owned no ore cars. The cars shown were leased from the Duluth, South Shore and Atlantic Railway, an ore carrier that serviced the mines on Michigan's Marquette Range. — MINNESOTA HISTORICAL SOCIETY

Henry W. Oliver, Pittsburgh industrialist, played an important role in the development of the Mesabi Range. — DM& IR COLLECTION

avoid burdening the railroad with too speculative an investment. Exploration revealed considerable ore and the mining properties were later organized into the Great Northern Iron Ore Properties. The line between Hibbing and Swan River was integrated into the Great Northern system and was later extended both east and west of Hibbing so as to make the Great Northern a substantial Mesabi iron ore carrier as early as 1901.

By 1901 both the D&IR and DM&N had assumed the basic forms they would ultimately take. The D&IR's main line extended from Two Harbors 68 miles directly north to Tower Junction, with a 21.5-mile branch going east to Ely and another extending west for 30 miles along the Mesabi to the city of Virginia. Although the D&IR had a 26-mile line extending along the shore of Lake Superior to Duluth, the company did not have iron ore docks of its own at Duluth or access to the docks of other railroads. Its port was Two Harbors, at which it then had five wooden ore docks

controlled by the Wright and Davis logging interests, who also owned about 25,000 acres of lands denuded of virgin timber at the western end of the Mesabi. The mineral resources of the property were uncertain. The potential of this combination of lands and railroad appealed to D. M. Philbin, general manager of the DM&N. He became superintendent of the DMR&N in 1895 and set about making arrangements with the Duluth and Winnipeg to accept at Swan River iron ore originating on his line and transport it to Allouez, much as the D&W had moved Merritt ore received at the Stony Brook connection to Allouez before construction of their own ill-fated line to Duluth.

An opportunity to buy the Wright and Davis property, with the line between Hibbing and Swan River thrown in for good measure, was presented to James J. Hill, the famous *Empire Builder*. Philbin helped sell the idea to Hill and his two sons, who were in official capacities on the Great Northern. The upshot was the acquisition of the whole package in 1899, the railroad line going to the Great Northern and the acreage to Hill personally for the sum of $4,050,000, apparently to

James J. Hill, the famed "Empire Builder," whose acquisitions of Mesabi Range ore properties was responsible for his Great Northern Railway becoming a major ore carrier, second only to the Missabe Road. — BURLINGTON NORTHERN

with a total storage capacity of 162,000 tons. Up to 1901 the D&IR had handled 24,915,417 tons of ore through Two Harbors, and during the year 1901 handled 5,008,518 tons. Starting earlier, it then had a good lead over its DM&N rival.

The main line of the D&IR, which was completely double tracked by 1901, was originally laid with 60-pound rail. By 1901 its southbound track was being replaced by 80-pound rail. Its main line between Tower Junction and Two Harbors ran through much rougher country than the line of the DM&N, and in consequence it had, and still has, a less favorable grade. Even after construction of the 18-mile Stewart River Branch in 1895-1898, which became a part of the main line, the southbound ruling grade was 0.62 of one percent. The northbound ruling grade up the hill and out of Two Harbors became 1.5 percent after construction of the Loop Line in 1899.

Branches of the D&IR had penetrated into the Mesabi by 1901 and in the area between Biwabik and Virginia were offering competition with the DM&N. It was seldom the practice of both roads to serve the same operation. Extensions, mine tracks and sidings were put down and taken up with great frequency as mining operations changed from place to place.

By 1901 the D&IR had 70 locomotives. Its rolling stock consisted of 3,635 cars, as follows: 2,634 wooden ore cars, 340 steel ore cars, 647 freight and miscellaneous cars, and 14 passenger cars of various types. The 1901 D&IR was a tidy little railroad, well conceived and well managed and with a good future, even though not as well placed with respect to the Mesabi iron ore deposits as the DM&N.

The 1901 situation of the DM&N was even more promising than that of the D&IR. Its 72 miles of main line from Duluth to Mountain Iron, as laid out by the Merritt brothers in 1891, had the advantage of the easier terrain of the western part of St. Louis County; the ruling southbound grade was only 0.30 of one percent. By 1901 the main line was double tracked with 80-pound rail in the

Gigantic, spectacular, and impressive, are words which describe this 1902 view of the Duluth and Iron Range ore docks at Two Harbors. Considering their size and the millions of board feet of lumber used in their construction, they were at the time, truly "wonders of the engineering world."

Construction of the first ore dock commenced during the winter of 1883-1884 and the dock itself was 552 feet long, excluding the approach. It stood 36 feet high and contained two tracks; each pocket held about four wooden cars of ore. The original dock was enlarged and four additional docks built, the highest of which was No. 5, being 66 feet 9 inches from surface of the water to the top of the deck. These huge wooden structures were short in length compared with some other ore docks on the Great Lakes owing primarily to the harbor limitations. The five wooden docks were in time torn down and replaced by the three existing docks of concrete and steel.

Two Harbors was a beehive of activity in 1902. In this scene one can count at least 10 steam locomotives working around the yard or on the docks which had a total storage capacity of 162,000 tons. The first Two Harbors depot is visible in the center background to the left of the large brick building. In the immediate foreground the *Horace S. Wilkinson* waits for her cargo, part of which is about to be unloaded from a string of cars. — DM&IR COLLECTION

DM&N train No. 2 heading south out of Iron Junction, pulled by 10-Wheeler No. 30. The baggage car on the head end had been borrowed from the Chicago and North Western. The booming passenger business at the turn of the century created occasional passenger equipment shortages. — AUTHOR'S COLLECTION

southbound track. The decision of the Merritts to extend their line directly to Duluth, instead of using the D&W to Allouez, proved to be right in the long run and by 1901 there was a fine operation all the way to the docks. Proctor Yard was then well established and main line drags were broken up there, not only to allow change in motive power for the sharp descent to the ore docks but also to permit cars to be held and reclassified so that dock trains could carry the mixture of ore required for individual boats. The 600-foot descent from Proctor Yard to the docks was, and still is, accomplished on an S-shaped line almost seven miles long having a ruling 2.2 percent grade favoring the loaded movement. The valley of the St. Louis River created the break in the ridge that rims Lake Superior and makes access to the lake at Duluth much easier for railroads than at other points.

Including branches constructed prior to 1901, the DM&N network consisted principally of the following lines:

	Miles
Main line from Duluth to Mountain Iron	72.24
Biwabik Branch from Iron Junction to Biwabik	16.50
Virginia Branch from Wolf to Virginia	6.40
Superior Branch from Wolf to Hibbing	17.00
Adams Junction to Spruce to Eveleth	3.71
Stony Brook Junction to Stony Brook to Columbia Junction	5.20

The docks of the DM&N at Duluth, while not as conveniently situated for the boats as those of the D&IR at Two Harbors, were adequate for the DM&N's 1901 tonnage. They consisted of three wooden docks with total storage capacity of 167,040 tons, including the completed part of Dock No. 3, then in the course of construction. Starting eight years later than the D&IR, the DM&N by 1901 had already handled 17,904,024 tons of ore through either Duluth or Allouez, and in 1901 handled 3,437,158 tons. Its tonnage was soon to surpass and then remain continuously ahead of that of the D&IR. By 1901 the DM&N had 37 locomotives. Its rolling stock consisted of 3,877 units, as follows: 3,475 wooden ore cars, 5 steel ore cars, 383 freight and miscellaneous cars, and 14 passenger cars of various types. Thus, by 1901 the DM&N was already a thriving property, very well located, both physically and in respect to Mesabi ore deposits, but not yet fully come into its own.

These, then, were the two ore-carrying railroads in remote Minnesota that were caught up in the series of events that culminated in the formation of the United States Steel Corporation in 1901. Their inclusion in the new corporation resulted in a stronger, more efficient steel industry, one better able to respond to the requirements for steel in the ensuing decades, including two world wars.

The D&IR, which was part of Federal Steel Company, successor to Illinois Steel Company, came into the Corporation as part of the steel-making complex assembled by Judge Elbert H. Gary. Rockefeller sold his Minnesota iron ore properties and the DM&N to United States Steel shortly after the original members had entered into basic arrangements to form the Corporation.

DM&N Class C-1 Consolidation No. 305 blasts up Proctor Hill in 1904 with a train of 28 ore empties. The Duluth docks can be seen in the distance. The engine was almost new, having arrived from the Dickson Works of the American Locomotive Company only two years before. — AUTHOR'S COLLECTION

7

PEACE AND PROGRESS
1901 - 1914

WORLD War I brought on such great changes in everything as to make 1914, the year of its beginning, a suitable breaking point in relating the history of the Missabe Road. The interlude between 1901, when the D&IR and DM&N were acquired by the United States Steel Corporation, and August of 1914, when the war began, probably did not seem as untroubled to those experiencing it as it now does to those looking back on it. But in comparison to what followed these were halcyon days, an age of innocence, when things were more simple and progress could be related solely in terms of industrial development, without giving much thought to what was happening elsewhere in the world. The railroads were supreme in the movement of freight and passengers. The automobile was a novelty; paved roads were a rarity; trucks had hardly been invented; airplane riding was considered a risky adventure; and the only form of land transportation offering any competition to the railroads was the interurban electric railway. World War I changed all of this and ushered in the modern era with its new devices, complications and insecurities.

From 1901 to 1914 the D&IR and DM&N were free of traffic and financial concerns and were able to concentrate on the job of providing service equal to the demands of a rapidly growing volume of traffic. Compared with the earlier days of exploration and development, this will be a more prosaic story, but it will illustrate how a great industry in a time of freedom from governmental restraints could, under capable management, produce the technology and machinery required to solve the problem of efficiently transporting an ever increasing volume of iron ore.

Although the DM&N and D&IR were now under common control, they were not merged, either corporately or in terms of operations. They were to continue side by side as separate entities until 1938.

William J. Olcott, who first appeared in this narrative as the man from Ironwood, Michigan, whom Rockefeller put in charge of the mining properties taken over from the Merritts in 1894, was made president of the DM&N in 1901, succeeding Rockefeller's trusted lieutenant Frederick T. Gates. He soon found his responsibilities too burdensome for one man and secured the help of William A. McGonagle in running the railroad. McGonagle was assistant chief engineer of the D&IR. He was mentioned earlier as the young engineer who laid out the original line of the D&IR in 1881. He came to the DM&N in 1902 as assistant to the president, became vice president the following year, president in 1909 and ultimately

During 1901 Duluth area mining man William J. Olcott, shown at the left, became head of the Duluth, Missabe and Northern. Veteran railroader Francis E. House, shown at the right, presided over the Duluth and Iron Range Road. — BOTH DM&IR COLLECTION

assumed, in 1930, the additional responsibilities of the presidency of the D&IR.

Francis E. House, who had been general manager of the Bessemer and Lake Erie Railroad, became president of the D&IR on June 7, 1901, succeeding J. L. Greatsinger, who left to become president of the Brooklyn Rapid Transit Company. House held the presidency of the D&IR for the next quarter century.

The record of iron ore tonnages handled by the two railroads in the 1901-1915 period, which is shown along with other years in Appendix A, tells to a considerable extent its own story. The leap to 11,233,170 tons for the two roads from 1901 to 1902, most of it coming on the DM&N, shows that the new U. S. Steel Corporation was getting off to a good start, and the new high of 21,654,197 tons in 1907 for the two roads shows that it was indeed a success. The sharp drop to 14,529,031 tons in 1908 reflects the short industrial depression following the Panic of 1907, but the climb was resumed again in 1909 and 1910. The drop from 22,448,692 tons in 1913 to barely half that total in 1914 reflects the economic lull that preceded the opening of the war and continued for a time until that shock had been absorbed. Most of the significant physical developments on the two railroads in the 1901-1914 period, the new locomotives and cars,

Caricature of W. A. McGonagle which appeared in a book showing prominent Duluthians. McGonagle came to the DM&N from the D&IR in 1902 as assistant to the president. He later became president and headed the DM&N for 21 years. — WILLIAM A. MC GONAGLE, JOSLYN ART MUSEUM, OMAHA

The DM&N ore sorting yard at Proctor, by the early years of the new century, was the scene of considerable activity, with thousands of cars handled daily. Building to the left of the caboose track was the first car shop. Some years later it was replaced by a much larger facility located in the wooded area on the far left side of the yard. (LEFT) The train in the foreground is moving loads from Proctor Yard to the Duluth docks. In the early 1900's, hardy brakemen were required to ride on top of the car, ready to set hand brakes in case the train speed became too great on the 2.2 percent grade to the docks. — BOTH MINNESOTA HISTORICAL SOCIETY

DM&N Consolidation engine No. 306 blew itself asunder near Birch while northbound with a train of ore empties. This tragic accident, which occurred during 1902, claimed the life of the head brakeman and seriously injured the engineer and fireman. The engine received a new boiler and remained in service for another 46 years, being finally retired in 1948. — BOTH AUTHOR'S COLLECTION

line extensions, rebuilding of docks, yards and facilities, were required to accommodate the expanding traffic.

There were, however, some other concerns. President Olcott wanted Y.M.C.A. quarters built for the men at Proctor. He said in the DM&N annual report for 1900 "... It is for the best interest of the company to have sober, efficient, and industrious men. Conditions at Proctor are not attractive, to say the least. The men do not feel that the place is permanent, and therefore hesitate to invest any money in the place." He pointed out that employees had nowhere to go for amusement or relaxation other than several saloons and urged that something be done to counteract the influence of such "degrading resorts." He proposed that the company establish a Railroad Y.M.C.A. at Proctor. The facility was provided in 1903.

Olcott also expressed concern over the lack of suitable facilities for locomotive storage and heavy

This D&IR ore train came to an abrupt halt at the foot of the 3.0 percent grade into Two Harbors yard during the summer of 1905. The new steel ore cars fared much better than the old wooden cars at the end of the train, many of which were reduced to kindling. — DM&IR COLLECTION

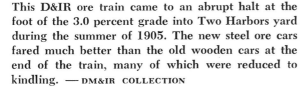

repairs, lamenting "... It certainly is a poor practice, and almost inexcusable, to have 20 expensive engines, costing over $200,000, standing out of doors, exposed to the rain and snow." He recommended that a building be erected at Proctor, which was done in 1905.

One DM&N project conceived under the old regime that was not completed under the new one was the proposed East Missabe Branch, to serve the Stephens Mine. Considerable grading had been done and the stone abutments for a bridge over the Embarrass River, which still stand, had been constructed, but, with the D&IR now under common ownership and having a track right by it, the work was discontinued in April of 1901. Bridge material intended for use on the line was refabricated and used to replace timber structures on Proctor Hill and on the Superior Branch.

DM&N passenger service between Duluth and Hibbing had consisted of only one train daily in each direction during the first decade of the road's existence. Commencing in 1902 a second daily train was added. The Company annual report for the year reported that "... This train was successful from the beginning and has accommodated our patrons in Duluth and the various mining towns, as well as giving us very satisfactory increased business."

The growing ore traffic volume shown in Appendix A is reflected in the types of motive power acquired and disposed of during the 1901-1914 period. As early as 1901 the standard train load on the DM&N was established at 55 all-steel cars carrying

The locomotive back shop at Proctor completed during 1905 and used continuously until the end of the steam era. The old roundhouse to the left had already been superseded by a new engine facility at the north end of the yard, when this photograph was taken in the 1920's. — DM&IR COLLECTION

The Proctor roundhouse force took time out to pose on the turntable at the old south end engine terminal during 1907. The man standing eighth from the left was George W. Martin, general roundhouse foreman. — AUTHOR'S COLLECTION

2,750 long tons of iron ore. The DM&N's Ten-Wheelers were inadequate for handling trains of this tonnage and, in 1901, six of them were sold to the Indiana, Illinois and Iowa Railroad. The DM&N began to rely more heavily on the Consolidation (2-8-0) type. The D&IR followed suit in 1905 with the purchase of nine Consolidations from the Baldwin Locomotive Works to be followed by 25 more in the next few years.

The superiority of the D&IR Consolidations over the Mastodons (4-8-0) they replaced was that, in addition to being heavier locomotives, they carried a higher percentage of their total weight on the driving wheels, thereby creating greater tractive effort and making them more suitable for handling heavier trains. They could haul an additional 400 tons per train over the rugged D&IR main line to Two Harbors. The Mastodon was never a very popular locomotive, and only about 600 were ever built for service in the United States, most of them in the 1890 to 1900 decade. Conversely, the Consolidation type, for many years the workhorse on practically all the railroads in the country, was built in greater numbers than any other wheel arrangement. About 21,000 of them saw service in the United States.

A D&IR Class K Consolidation rounds "Pork City Hill" at Two Harbors with an empty ore train, bound for Biwabik on the Mesabi Range. The year was 1910, by which time the new "K's" had just about taken over all main line ore hauling. (BELOW) With steam up, DM&N Consolidation No. 315 prepares to pick up its train of 55 ore empties at Proctor Yard and head for the North End. With their long, narrow fireboxes, the C-2's were tough to fire. — BOTH AUTHOR'S COLLECTION

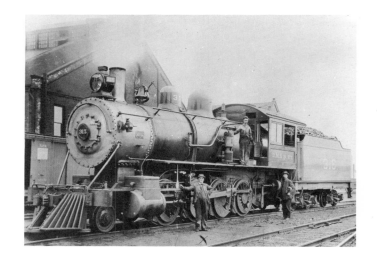

D&IR No. 74, a Mastadon type, was one of six locomotives received from the Baldwin Locomotive Works during 1896. The 4-8-0 type, first developed experimentally about 1855, was reintroduced by Baldwin in 1882. It offered more boiler capacity and a better distribution of weight on drivers than the Consolidation 2-8-0 type. During the period between 1893 and 1900, the D&IR purchased 30 Mastadons from Baldwin and the American Locomotive Company. — AUTHOR'S COLLECTION

The DM&N Biwabik local pauses for orders at Iron Junction depot around 1910. All of the slide-valved C-3 Consolidations were eventually superheated. The long ladder on the pilot deck facilitated servicing the headlight. — DM&IR COLLECTION

Mallets were synonymous with the Missabe Road for over 40 years. No. 205 is shown drifting into Proctor Yard with a train of empties from the Duluth docks. Note the locomotive coaling facility in the background. — AUTHOR'S COLLECTION

Gleaming new Lima-built D&IR Mikado No. 305 poses for the photographer on the go-out track at Two Harbors during 1913.—AUTHOR'S COLLECTION

Good as the DM&N's Class C-2 Consolidations were, they could only haul 28 empties up the two percent grade on Proctor Hill, often creating a situation requiring that trains be scheduled as frequently as 15 minutes apart. A locomotive capable of handling at least 55 empties per trip was required. Electrification was first studied, but dropped when it was found that Mallets could do the job and earn a better return on the investment.

A powerful locomotive like the Mallet was required to handle empties up the steep grade of Proctor Hill and prevent congestion and interference with the loaded movement downhill. The Baldwin Locomotive Works was asked to work up specifications for eight big 16-drivered Mallets, the like of which had never been seen in the North Country.

The big Mallets began to arrive at Proctor for service on the Hill in the spring of 1910. They caused considerable excitement and concern. Weighing some 320 tons with tender, and approaching 100 feet in length, they were awesome. Some of the "old head" engineers wanted no part of them, and bid into other assignments. Firemen were apprehensive about their huge appetites for coal. Even with the combined efforts of the two firemen initially assigned, difficulty was encountered in keeping up steam. However, reliable mechanical stokers were being perfected and were applied within a short time, thereby permitting one fireman to do the job. Baldwin had conservatively guaranteed that the Mallets could handle 55 steel empties, plus a 4-wheeled caboose, up the Hill at a speed of 12 miles per hour. Before long

the Mallets were handling as many as 85 empties per trip. Some of these locomotives continued to render excellent service on the Hill for more than 40 years.

The final locomotive development in this pre-World War I period was the introduction by the D&IR in 1913 of six large Mikados (2-8-2), four from the Baldwin Locomotive Works and two from the Lima Locomotive Works, for main line ore service, and four Pacifics (4-6-2) from Baldwin for passenger service. The DM&N also received three Pacifics for its passenger service. The Mikados, being approximately 50 percent heavier than the Consolidations, were rated to haul 3,250 tons of ore southbound over the D&IR's ruling grade of 0.6 of one percent. This was an increase of 1,000 tons over the Class K Consolidations, which engines had, only three years before, displaced the well-known Class J (4-8-0) in main line ore service. With the acquisition of all-steel passenger equipment on both roads, the Pacifics held down all main line passenger assignments, bumping the Schenectady and Baldwin-built Ten-Wheelers onto less demanding service.

The advantages of superheaters were now well known in motive power circles, so the D&IR decided, as an experiment, to so equip one of its Class K Consolidations. Use of superheated steam increased the horsepower output of a simple two-cylinder engine by 25 to 30 percent or more. The result on the D&IR was to increase tonnage ratings from 2,250 to 2,650, so all 25 Class K locomotives were equipped with superheaters within four years. The DM&N did the same with its 32 Class

C-3 Consolidations. As a sign of the times it might be noted in passing that the effectiveness of the electric headlight was being established, and they were applied to the ten new locomotives received by the D&IR in 1913 and to 90 other D&IR locomotives in 1914.

During 1902 the D&IR rebuilt Dock No. 4 at Two Harbors, extending it to 168 pockets in length. The cost of repairing and maintaining wooden ore docks became prohibitive by 1907. Construction of steel and concrete was the answer. During 1907 the D&IR began construction at Two Harbors of ore Dock No. 6, the first steel structure of its type on the Great Lakes. It was 888 feet long, stood 74 feet above the waterline, contained 148 pockets, and had a capacity of 44,000 tons. The project was completed in 1909.

By 1910 D&IR Dock No. 1 at Two Harbors, was in need of such extensive repairs that the decision was made to replace it with a new steel dock similar to Dock No. 6. The new steel dock, designated No. 1, contained 224 pockets, with a total storage capacity of 56,000 tons. It extended 1,344 feet into the harbor, stood 75 feet above the waterline and was placed in service in 1911.

The D&IR's third steel dock at Two Harbors (Dock No. 2) was completed in 1916, replacing old wooden ore Dock No. 2, last used in 1910. It was the largest ore dock at that location, standing 80 feet high and extending 1,368 feet into the harbor. The storage capacity of its 228 pockets was 68,400 tons. The three remaining wooden docks, Nos. 3, 4 and 5, were shortly dismantled because they were no longer needed.

Work was begun by Barnett and Record of Minneapolis in 1904 on an extension of DM&N Dock No. 3 at Duluth, the contract specifying that it was to be ready for 1905 operation. DM&N Dock No. 1, badly decayed and too low for loading the larger lake vessels, was taken out of service in 1905. The same year, wooden Dock No. 2, constructed in 1896, was given a general rebuilding. Construction of Dock No. 4, at Duluth, containing 384 pockets with a storage capacity of 76,800 tons was undertaken in 1906. It was the largest and last wooden dock constructed for either the DM&N or D&IR.

Contracts were let in 1907 for construction at Duluth of a coal unloading and storage dock 1,800 feet long and 604 feet wide, with a storage capacity of 650,000 tons. Coal from the lower lake ports was then an important inbound commodity. It was used by the railroads in their steam locomotives and was the principal fuel for domestic heating. The dock had three rigs to provide for fast unloading of vessels. The St. Louis Bay Dock Company was organized to finance construction of the dock, which was to be operated by the DM&N. It was to handle coal used by the DM&N, as well as tonnage expected to be shipped to the Oliver Iron Mining Company, and the steel plant of the Minnesota Steel Company, then being projected in the far western part of Duluth. The coal dock was completed and placed in service in 1909. It was finally dismantled in 1968 to make way for the new Lakehead Taconite Storage Facility at the same location.

Contracts were let by the DM&N in 1913 for

Panoramic view of the four DM&N wooden ore docks at Duluth around 1910. Recently completed Dock No. 4 is at the extreme right. Dismantling operations are under way on Dock No. 1 at the extreme left. — AUTHOR'S COLLECTION (RIGHT) An ore carrier takes on its cargo at DM&N Dock No. 3 in Duluth around 1910. The vessel's first mate directs loading operations. — DM&IR COLLECTION

construction of a new steel and concrete iron ore dock, known as No. 5. Standing over 80 feet above the waterline, and extending 2,304 feet into St. Louis Bay, with storage capacity of 115,200 long tons of ore, it easily eclipsed in size any ore dock constructed until that time. The three million dollar price tag was in keeping with the immensity of the project. The big dock was placed in service in 1914, ready to handle the war-generated traffic soon to follow. Construction began during 1917 on still another steel ore dock for the DM&N, No. 6, at Duluth. With a total storage capacity of 153,600 long tons, it still stands as the largest structure of its kind on the Great Lakes.

Line extensions during the 1901-1914 period were primarily on the DM&N, since it serviced the area experiencing the greater traffic growth. The D&IR constructed the four-mile Eastern Mesaba Branch from Mesaba to Spring Mine in 1908, and two years later extended it 12 miles further to Dunka River. In addition, an eight-mile extension off that branch at Ridge served a heavily timbered area. Years later the Eastern Mesaba Branch was

DM&N steel Dock No. 5 at Duluth was the largest on the Great Lakes when completed during 1914. — DM&IR COLLECTION (BELOW) A winter scene on the Eastern Mesaba Branch of the D&IR during 1910. The engine is D&IR No. 49, a Class G Consolidation built by Baldwin in 1888. — AUTHOR'S COLLECTION

to play a useful role in the taconite development.

In contrast to this meager development of branch lines on the D&IR, the DM&N developed several important new lines and improved others. The Superior Branch to Hibbing underwent considerable upgrading and some relocation in 1902, including replacement of wooden bridges with steel to accommodate the new and heavier Consolidation type locomotives and the more heavily loaded steel cars soon to be carrying iron ore from Hibbing. The Troy Branch was completed the same year from the Biwabik Branch to Troy Mine near Eveleth. The straight-as-an-arrow Shaw Cut-Off, which eliminated doubling over Macon Hill on the Superior Branch and trimmed three miles off the ore haul from the Hibbing district to Duluth, was a significant project of the 1905-1906 era.

And so it went from year to year and mine to mine as the Mesabi Range developed. The huge pits and the great piles of refuse rock, and lower grade ore carefully laid aside for possible future use, are all that are now left to indicate where many spur tracks and lines of railroad once existed.

The most important extension project of the entire period was the Alborn Branch, begun in 1905 and finished in 1906. It was occasioned by the opening up of the far western end of the Mesabi, first by the Great Northern in 1903 by extending its line westward from Kelly Lake (near Hibbing) to Nashwalk, a distance of 9.29 miles. There were other iron ore properties still further west in adjoining Itasca County that were also being opened up and could not be reached directly by any DM&N line. A new line was therefore projected extending northwest from Alborn for a distance of 55 miles.

During the 1890's, heavy ore traffic from the Hibbing district necessitated replacing timber trestles on the Superior Branch with more substantial steel structures. This photograph shows a DM&N Ten-Wheeler at the head end of an ore train moving over one of the new steel bridges. — AUTHOR'S COLLECTION

This photograph shows the rear end of the same train shown above. The steel structure was erected within the old timber trestle without interrupting train movements. — AUTHOR'S COLLECTION

A temporary falsework trestle over the St. Louis River had to be dynamited open to release a log jam during construction of the Alborn Branch in 1906. — AUTHOR'S COLLECTION

Coleraine, the newest and most westerly mining community on the Mesabi Range, takes shape during 1907. The locomotives and shop buildings were owned by Oliver Iron Mining Company. — DM&IR COLLECTION

Section crew in early-day pose at Coleraine Junction tower, where the Alborn branch parts company with the main line. — DM&IR COLLECTION

A portion of the Alborn Branch was utilized in 1910 to provide improved access to the Hibbing area. The Hull-Rust Short Line was built at that time from Hull Junction on the Alborn Branch to the Hull-Rust pit. It was 18 miles long and provided a very direct route to Duluth. It relieved the Superior Branch of considerable congestion and avoided the necessity of providing additional yard capacity at Mitchell. Traffic was so heavy that the Hull-Rust Short Line was double tracked at the outset and a second track was installed on the Alborn Branch southward from the point where the new line reached it. With the near depletion of the Hibbing deposits, the Hull-Rust line, having served its purpose, was taken up in 1962. The Alborn Branch itself is no longer the lifeline that it once was, because joint arrangements with the Burlington Northern, formerly the Great Northern, now permit Missabe traffic originating in the Coleraine area to move over its line in an easterly direction across the Range when operationally desirable.

Construction of the Minnesota Steel Company plant at the western end of Duluth between the years 1910 and 1915 had a direct effect on the DM&N. Two connecting terminal railroad companies were organized and operated under lease by the DM&N. The 11-mile line of Spirit Lake Transfer Railway was to extend from a point of connection with the DM&N at Adolph, just north

This 1910 view of the main street in Iron Junction features a DM&N water tank. Residents at that time did not object to their settlement being called a "tank town." — DM&IR COLLECTION (RIGHT) For many years, Alborn was a busy point for passengers changing trains. The main line train on the right is headed south while its counterpart on the adjacent track points north. The branch line train for Coleraine is at the extreme left. (BELOW) Ore in the Coleraine district, being high in silica, has required beneficiation throughout the years. This giant ore concentration plant at Trout Lake, constructed during 1910, is still in use. — BOTH AUTHOR'S COLLECTION

of Proctor, to the center line of the St. Louis River draw span (Oliver Bridge, named for Henry W. Oliver of Pittsburgh), where it connected with the line of the Interstate Transfer Railway. *Spirit Lake* came from the name of a nearby widened out part of the St. Louis River.

The Interstate Transfer Railway was projected to extend from Oliver Bridge to proposed docks on Wisconsin Point. Although grading was completed almost to the end of Wisconsin Point, rails were laid only as far as the connection with the Omaha Road (Chicago, St. Paul, Minneapolis & Omaha) at South Itasca, which is about eleven miles from the Oliver Bridge. The 2,189-foot bridge, including a 300-foot draw span, was authorized under an Act of Congress (February 20, 1908) requiring that it be constructed with two decks ". . . one of which shall provide for the passage of wagons and vehicles, for all kinds of street railway and motor cars, and road travel, and one of which shall also have two passageways, one on either side, for the exclusive use of pedestrians." Designed more than 60 years ago, the big structure with its 24-foot roadway is still in use.

The Spirit Lake provided a means of moving iron ore from the DM&N's sorting yard at Proctor to the Minnesota Steel Company's new mill, and Interstate Transfer provided connections with the line-haul railroads radiating out of Superior. Sections of both lines were laid on an abandoned portion of the old right-of-way of the Duluth and Winnipeg which had been taken over in 1899 by the Great Northern. The new lines were completed in 1915.

Looking north along the well-manicured track of the DM&N north of Alborn. The Carnegie steel ties, installed during 1910 as an experiment, lasted until World War II. — AUTHOR'S COLLECTION

The 2,189-foot-long double-deck Oliver Bridge as it appears today. Both decks are visible in this illustration. — DM&IR COLLECTION

This 1950 bird's-eye view of Steelton Yard, looking east, shows a portion of United States Steel's Duluth Works. A Class C-3 Consolidation is about to depart for Missabe Junction with a train of ore empties. On the adjacent track, a Class K Consolidation takes on water at the standpipe. — DM&IR COLLECTION

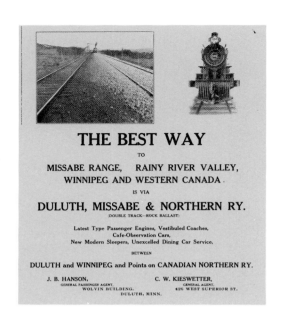

Before completion of the Duluth, Winnipeg and Pacific into Duluth, through-passenger service was provided between Duluth and Winnipeg utilizing the DM&N as far north as Virginia. This 1908 timetable extolled the virtues of the DM&N's new service, calling it "The Best Way" to reach Winnipeg and western Canada. — DM&IR COLLECTION

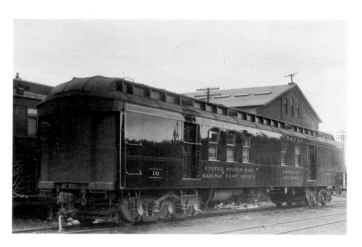

By 1913, DM&N and D&IR main line passenger trains were made up largely of new all-steel equipment. Shown at the left are representative all-steel cars of the period, DM&N coach No. 84 and D&IR mail and express car No. 10. (ABOVE) Elegant D&IR wood-sheathed parlor car No. 27 is shown at Ely in 1909 about to depart for Duluth on the end of train No. 2. — ALL AUTHOR'S COLLECTION

DM&N passenger train No. 4 drops down Proctor Hill into Duluth around 1910. The large white house above the locomotive belonged to the Merritt family, who were instrumental in building the DM&N. — DM&IR COL-LECTION

The Duluth Union Depot, left center in this 1910 scene, featured a huge train shed spanning the tracks. Passenger trains of both the DM&N and D&IR used this facility. — AU-THOR'S COLLECTION

All D&IR and DM&N passenger trains operating out of Duluth used the Duluth Union Depot owned and operated by the Northern Pacific Railway. During the last days of DM&IR passenger service trains terminated at the Endion station located on the lakefront, about two miles east of the Union Depot. No trains now use the Duluth Union Depot. However, plans are well along regarding its preservation as a cultural center housing the local historical society and other civic organizations.

There were parlor-cafe cars on the main line passenger trains of both the DM&N and D&IR. It was possible to make a 167-mile circle tour by leaving Duluth on the D&IR morning train, transferring to branch line trains across the Range, and finally back to Duluth via the DM&N in the late afternoon. D&IR parlor car No. 26 built by Barney & Smith, and No. 27 built by American Car and Foundry, were the most elegant in the area at the time of their receipt in 1908. What luxury to ride through the north woods in a parlor car, with your meal prepared in a kitchen and served to you in your seat. It might be hot in the summer, and you could get a cinder in your eye if you opened the window. There were few automobiles to look out for at the crossings, and the horses drawing wagons and buggies might shy a bit as the train went by. Though ominous clouds were gathering over Europe when the 1901-1914 era was drawing to a close, the possibility of war, and American involvement in it, seemed remote.

View of Proctor Yard, looking south from the overhead viaduct, showing some of the new trackage added during World War I. —AUTHOR'S COLLECTION

8

FROM WORLD WAR I THROUGH THE TWENTIES

THE onset of World War I in Europe in the summer of 1914, which was to change everything, had no immediate effect on the operations of the DM&N and the D&IR. It became apparent, however, that even if the United States did not become directly involved the demand for steel would greatly increase, so, without the necessity of official designation, both the production and transportation of iron ore became war industries.

Fortunately, the DM&N and the D&IR were ready. With the exception of wooden Dock No. 2 at Two Harbors, which was replaced in 1916, the docks were in good shape. The motive power was adequate for the existing traffic and could be and was supplemented as the demand increased. As of the end of 1914 the DM&N's locomotive roster stood at 51 Consolidations, 8 Mallets and 54 other locomotives of various types. Its car fleet aggregated 8,541 units, consisting of 8,504 ore, freight and miscellaneous cars, and 37 passenger cars. The D&IR owned at this time 55 Consolidations, 30 Mastodons, 6 Mikados, and 20 other locomotives of various types. Rolling stock consisted of 6,621 units, made up of 6,591 ore, freight and miscellaneous cars, and 30 passenger cars.

The impact of the war in Europe is reflected in the tonnages handled by the two railroads in 1915. As Appendix A shows, the combined tonnages for that year were double those of 1914, setting, at 24,212,801 tons, a new high. On a single day, 211,616 tons were loaded through the DM&N's docks, a new record. This tonnage represented 4,700 carloads of iron ore and required the running of an ore train down Proctor Hill as frequently as every 15 minutes. A vessel cargo record was set when the steamer *William P. Snyder,* of the Shenango Furnace Company, took on 12,749 tons. A record of 8,262 tons loaded into a vessel in one hour was also established that year.

Since indications were that the 1916 tonnages would be even higher, something had to be done to improve the performance of trains then powered by the Consolidations. Orders were placed by the DM&N for six Santa Fe type (2-10-2) locomotives having a rating of 135 carloads of ore between the Mesabi Range and Proctor, compared with 65 carloads for the Consolidations.

The combined 1916 tonnages reached a peak of 33,334,925, a figure not to be topped until 1941, a quarter century later during World War II. Most of the increase, as Appendix A indicates, came on the DM&N, but, even so, the D&IR tonnage reached 10 million for only the second time in its history. Six of the new Santa Fe type locomotives, and two additional Mallets for use on Proctor Hill, similar to but heavier than those acquired in 1910,

DULUTH, MISSABE A
DOCKS AT DU

The four DM&N docks at Duluth provided an impressive sight from the hillside above. The year was 1915, during which time the Duluth docks shattered all tonnage records up to that time. Newly completed steel Dock No. 5 is on the extreme right. To the far left can be seen the DM&N coal unloading rigs and a portion of the coal storage area. The small vessel taking on a cargo of lumber at the road's log dock near the center of the picture was called a "lumber hooker." — DM&IR COLLECTION

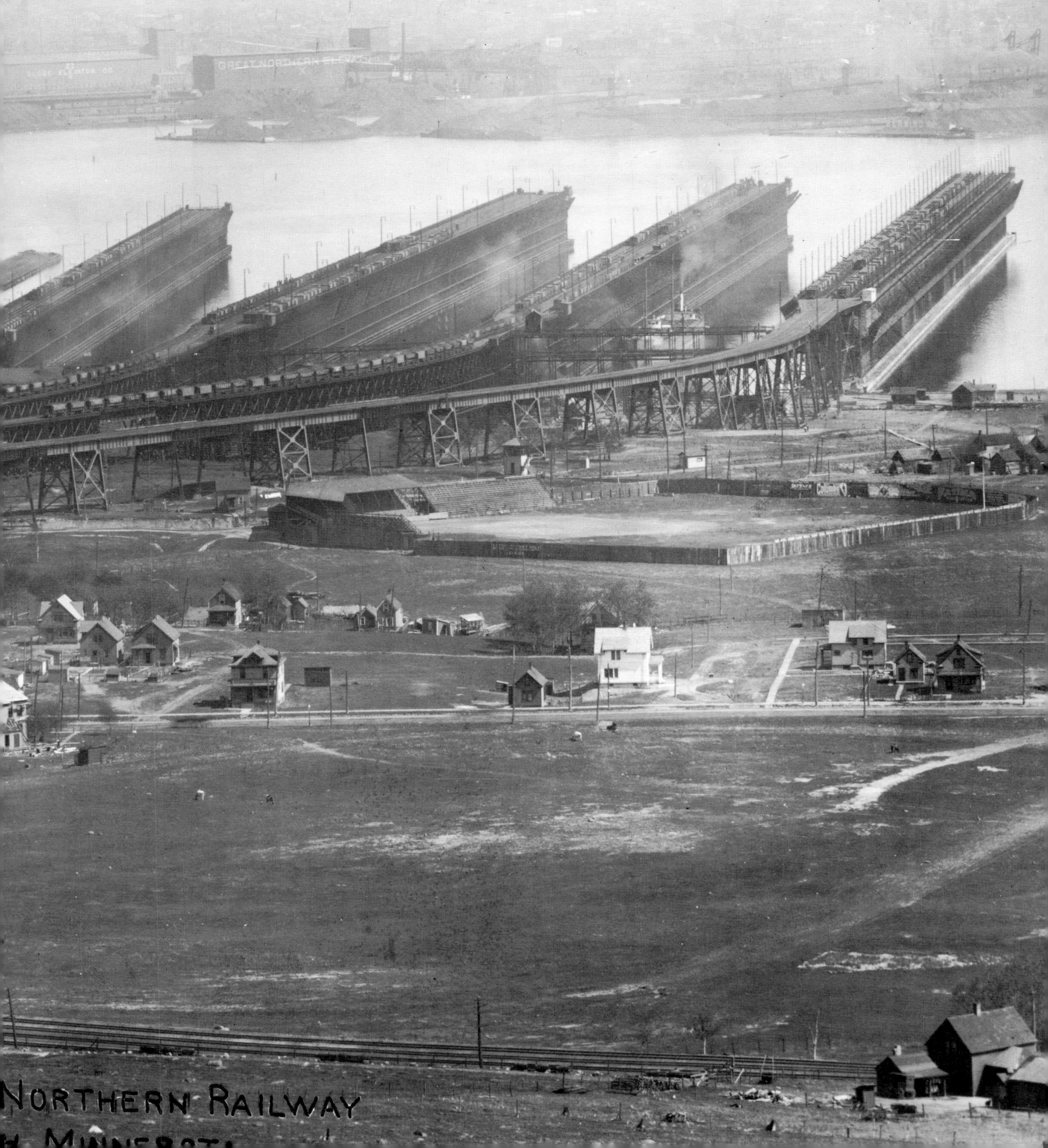

NORTHERN RAILWAY

MINNESOTA

During 1916, the DM&N placed six Santa Fe's in road ore service out of Proctor. One of them, No. 505, is shown weighing a 135-car train at the Proctor ore scales. — AUTHOR'S COLLECTION

DM&N ore train laboring upgrade through Saginaw holds the interest of a mother and her children. The track in the foreground belonged to the Duluth and Northeastern which until 1941 crossed the Missabe at this point. — E. KRUGER

were received by the DM&N in 1916, otherwise handling of this tonnage would never have been possible. Also contributing to this result were 1,000 new ore cars received by the DM&N.

Improved yard and engine facilities at Proctor were also of help. Fifteen miles of new track were added, bringing the total trackage at that location to almost 80 miles. The old South End engine terminal, long inadequate for servicing the larger power, was replaced with a new locomotive facility at the north end of the yard. The new terminal included a reinforced concrete engine house with 30 stalls, a 100-foot turntable and a coaling station of 1,000-ton capacity. New steel ore Dock No. 2 at Two Harbors, placed in service in 1916, and three additional Mikado type locomotives, together with 750 new ore cars that year, helped the D&IR achieve its record tonnage.

The year 1917, which in April witnessed the entry into the war of the United States, was not notably different on the DM&N and D&IR than 1916, except for the placing of both railroads under federal control on December 17. All railroads of the nation were placed under the direction of the United States Railroad Administration. The inclusion of the DM&N and D&IR was a matter of national policy and not on account of their own performances or inadequacies. President House of the D&IR was appointed federal man-

ager of both the DM&N and D&IR under the U. S. Railroad Administration, and President McGonagle of the DM&N took over as president of the D&IR.

Federal control lasted 28 months, or until March 1, 1920. It was not beneficial, nor, as in the case of some railroads, especially harmful to either the DM&N or D&IR. For instance, a new ore dock, No. 6 of the DM&N at Duluth, which was started in 1917, was completed under federal control in 1918. It increased the aggregate storage capacity of the DM&N's Duluth docks to 350,000 tons.

Total 1917 tonnages of the two railroads fell short by two million tons of equalling the record year 1916, and stood at 31,362,298 tons, still a fine performance. One significant 1917 development, though not related to the war effort, was completion of the 15-mile Wales Branch of the D&IR into the timber country north of Two Harbors. The new line paralleled to some extent that of the Duluth and Northern Minnesota Railway, a 99-mile common carrier logging road lying to the south which was abandoned in 1921.

Construction of the new 30-stall enginehouse at Proctor was well along by 1917. In addition, 15 miles of track were placed in service, giving a total of 80 miles of trackage at that location. — DM&IR COLLECTION

Elesco feed water heater-equipped D&IR Mikado No. 310 nears Fayal Yard with a train of ore empties. This engine, and two other Mikados received from Baldwin during 1923, were the last locomotives acquired by the D&IR. — AUTHOR'S COLLECTION

Operating efficiency declined during the period of federal control, not because of poor management of either the DM&N and D&IR but because of personnel and material disruptions caused by the war. One bright spot in the period of federal control was acquisition by the DM&N in 1919 of 10 United States Railroad Administration Santa Fe type locomotives. In keeping with other locomotives of U.S.R.A. design, they were good performers and lasted until the end of the steam era 40 or so years later. The return of the DM&N and D&IR to the control of their own managements, following the termination of federal control, was not marked by any fanfare, and time was needed to put back into the properties the extra wear taken out during the control period.

Aside from the abrupt drop in 1921 traffic, coincident with the recession commencing that year, the decade of the 1920's produced a generally high level of tonnage dropping only once below the 20 million ton mark. Since this was about 10 million tons less than the war-time peak, there was little need during the decade for expansion of facilities to handle the traffic. During 1923 the D&IR received its last locomotives, Mikados Nos. 309 to 311, from the Baldwin Locomotive Works.

DM&N No. 509, United States Railroad Administration design Santa Fe type locomotive, and crew pose at the Proctor coal dock during federal control. Note the "U.S." stenciled in large letters on the tender. (BELOW) D&IR log train from Knife River photographed at Milepost 1 in Duluth, in March 1913. — BOTH AUTHOR'S COLLECTION

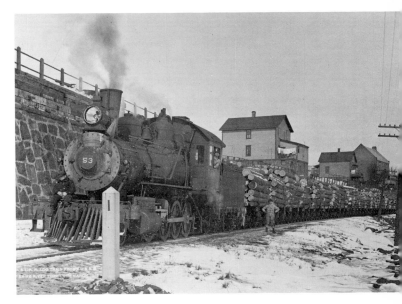

The gospel of safety was preached to DM&N and D&IR railroaders in this safety car. Instructor A. V. Rohweder is shown on the right. (ABOVE RIGHT) The receipt of a coveted safety award was always a proud occasion. Accepting a 1935 award for the Missabe Road are Safety Superintendent A. V. Rohweder, extreme left, and President C. E. Carlson, second from left. (RIGHT) Over the years the Missabe has won the Harriman Safety Award 13 times. The 1927 award is shown here. — ALL DM&IR COLLECTION

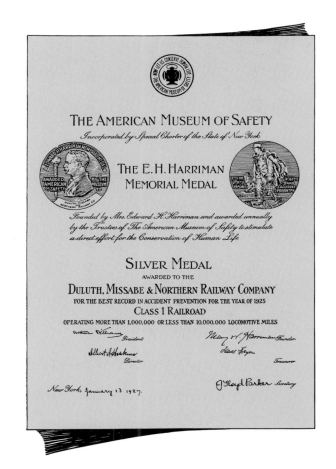

One development of which President McGonagle was particularly proud, and justly so, was the safety record following the employment of Arthur V. Rohweder as supervisor of safety for both the DM&N and the D&IR in 1917. Rohweder came from the Chicago and North Western on the recommendation of its Ralph Richards, a leading authority in the field of railroad safety, and did an outstanding job. Safety committees were organized under his direction, employee suggestions were solicited and the gospel of safety was preached in a stripped-down passenger coach provided with displays of safety equipment, posters, and visual aids. Every employee was expected to visit the safety car and learn how to protect himself from injury. From a combined DM&N-D&IR high of 643 lost-time accidents in 1917, including seven fatalities, the record steadily improved to an all-time record of only two reportable accidents in 1938. The Missabe has won Harriman Safety Awards 13 times during the last 30 years.

The timetables and travel literature published by the D&IR were colorful and attractive. Each edition extolled the accommodations afforded the out-of-door pleasure seeker and the bountiful hunting and fishing possibilities. Train service information described the modern first class passenger trains available and the fine parlor car and dining service on the main line. — AUTHOR'S COLLECTION

During the first few decades of the depot's development, so many ingenious experiments were being conducted that the evolving depot types elude classification. The D&IR's Biwabik depot was a study in Victorian elegance.—DM &IR COLLECTION

High tide of the passenger business was reached on the DM&N and D&IR, as on the railroads generally, in the early 1920's. The peak for these two railroads was in 1920 when passenger train revenues, including handling of mail and express, attained an all-time high of $1,067,373. During this period the DM&N provided two round trips daily between Duluth and Hibbing, and one round trip daily between Duluth and Virginia, all offering parlor-cafe service. Connections were made at Allen Junction with branch line trains for the various Range towns along the D&IR as far west as Virginia. The D&IR operated two trains daily in each direction between Duluth and the end of the line at Winton, both providing parlor-cafe accommodations.

However, for those able to read it, the handwriting was already on the wall. As early as 1913 two enterprising men at Hibbing bought a Hupmobile touring car and started a motorized livery service that is credited with being the beginning of the

The May 1922 passenger timetable of the DM&N listed three trains daily in each direction between Duluth and the Mesabi Range. A year later one train was gone, the beginning of the end. From here on, passenger revenues showed a steady decline. — AUTHOR'S COLLECTION

The spartan architecture of the DM&N's Biwabik depot contrasted sharply with that of the D&IR's on the preceding page. (BELOW) The design of the DM&N's Hibbing depot was undoubtedly influenced by the Mission style used by the San Pedro, Los Angeles & Salt Lake Railroad (now Union Pacific) in California. — BOTH DM&IR COLLECTION

Greyhound System. Their operations had no initial impact upon railway revenues because they were confined to local areas between North Hibbing and Alice, where Hibbing now stands. Nor were DM&N revenues affected when regularly scheduled intercity bus service, thought to be the first such service in the United States, was established between Hibbing and Nashwalk 15 miles to the west. After all, that was in Great Northern territory. Nor was there any concern when the new buses began competing with the interurban for passengers, since the DM&N was still doing a respectable amount of business between Range points and Duluth. Electric interurban service was offered by the Mesaba Railway between Hibbing and Gilbert, a distance of 34 miles, as early as 1913, and by the early 1920's hourly service, which the steam roads could not match, was being supplied between the communities across the Range.

Shortly after 1920 intercity bus service commenced between Hibbing and Duluth, using Fageol buses of the Blue Goose type. Not only was the railroad fare undercut, but the buses also

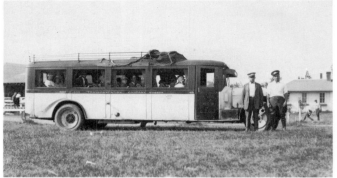

Famous *Blue Goose* intercity bus used between Hibbing and Duluth, during the 1920's. This service is reputed to be the forerunner of today's vast Greyhound bus system. — AUTHOR'S COLLECTION

Mesaba Electric Railway 2-car interurban train pauses at Thomas. These medium weight steel-sheathed cars were built by the Niles Car Company in Ohio. — WAYNE C. OLSEN COLLECTION (BELOW) Interurban No. 10 was one of 5 motorized combination cars. Niles also provided the line 5 motorized passenger cars, 2 express cars, and 4 trailers to begin service. — DONALD DUKE COLLECTION

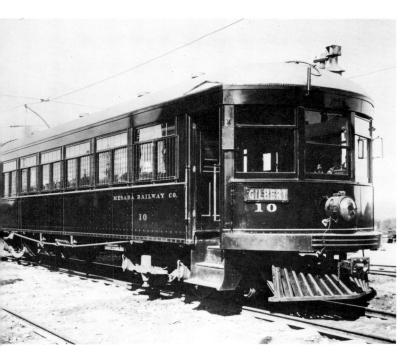

During the first quarter of this century, America witnessed a great transportation revolution, with the rapid development of the electric interurban railway. The interurban filled a travel void for rural America. Aside from what infrequent and slow local passenger service might be available from the steam railroads, travel in the countryside was still restricted to horse and buggy range. The interurbans were new, swift and clean, stopping anywhere, and running more frequently than the steam trains. A single car or three cars composed a complete train. In town, the interurban line ran down the main street.

One of the most isolated interurbans in the country was the Mesaba Electric Railway, whose 35 miles of line between Hibbing and Gilbert, via Virginia and Eveleth, began operation in March 1913. The line was built to high standards and its equipment was typical of the period. Owing to a good passenger traffic potential across the Range, the road prospered in its earlier years and lured passengers from the D&IR and DM&N local steam trains.

The road began to fail with the introduction of the automobile, and the motor coach. The Mesaba Electric Railway, which was abandoned in 1927, was one of Greyhound's earliest victims.

offered faster and more convenient schedules. So, between the buses and the increasing use by individuals of Henry Ford's Model T automobile, passenger train patronage declined, and during 1923 DM&N trains Nos. 5 and 6 between Duluth and Virginia were withdrawn from service and four years later parlor-cafe car accommodations disappeared. Highways along the D&IR were not as conducive to bus operation, and passenger train operations continued there without much change until 1926.

Rail-motor car service was tried out on the D&IR's Western Mesaba Branch in 1926 without much success. Car MC-1, was an open platform combine, powered by two below-floor Red Seal Continental engines, but, along with the transmissions, they malfunctioned with annoying regularity and called into service the Ten-Wheeler in the Biwabik enginehouse, which was always fired up ready to bring 'er in. The DM&N likewise tried out internal combustion transportation on the Alborn Branch using motorized wooden combine Car M-108 but, as on the D&IR, it was not satisfactory. Within a couple of years steam was back on the job.

The 1920's witnessed the moving of an entire town to get at the millions of tons of iron ore beneath it. The great Hull-Rust Mine complex had grown steadily in size until it enveloped North Hibbing on three sides. The immense project of

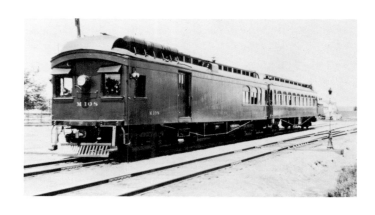

In an effort to reduce passenger train operating expenses, both the D&IR and the DM&N tried out internal combustion powered rail cars during the late 1920's. The DM&N's two self-propelled units, M-55 and M-108, are shown here. — BOTH AUTHOR'S COLLECTION

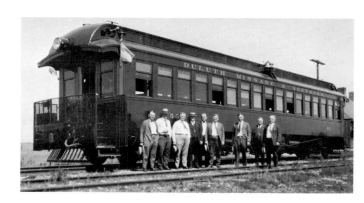

Starting in 1919, dwellings were moved from old North Hibbing to South Hibbing, to make way for an expansion of the Hull-Rust Mine. Steam log haulers, resembling a cross between a small Shay-geared locomotive and a caterpillar tractor, did much of the work. — AUTHOR'S COLLECTION

moving the town to a new site, previously referred to as Alice or South Hibbing, was well under way by 1921. Even the electric interurban line between North Hibbing and Chisholm had to be relocated, requiring several miles of new construction, for it ran right through the center of the famous "North Forty" which was about to become part of the big pit.

A shock ran through the railroad on April 3, 1926, when President Francis E. House of the D&IR, who had been in charge since 1901, died very suddenly of a heart attack. He had seen the railroad grow to maturity and had carried it through many trying times. He was succeeded as president on May 11, 1926, by Horace Johnson, vice president of the D&IR. A veteran whose career began before the turn of the century, he continued to head the D&IR until retirement on July 1, 1930.

As the mid-twenties were reached and passed, and the war period receded into memory, it seemed that an economic plateau had been attained. Employment was high, both in the iron ore pits and on the railroads. Automobiles became more plentiful; employee outings and picnics were held. Baseball teams were organized and there was keen rivalry between the DM&N and D&IR units. There appeared to be no reason why good times could not continue forever, but of course they could not.

Horace Johnson was the last president of the D&IR before the road was leased to the DM&N. — DM&IR COLLECTION

The Missabe band was always on hand to supply color and sound at both company and community gatherings. — AUTHOR'S COLLECTION

In 1927 the D&IR published a condensed history of the road featuring this map of the route and the mines served. — DM&IR COLLECTION

Two projects of the 1920's remain to be discussed before recounting the shattering of the dream of perpetual prosperity. One was the construction by the D&IR of the Embarrass Lake Cut-Off, a 1.5-mile relocation designed to eliminate the old Summit Line east of Biwabik with its 0.6 percent southbound grade that set the ruling grade on runs between Biwabik and Aurora. The job required over a million yards of fill which, fortunately, was available from stripping operations at the nearby Mary Ellen Mine.

The D&IR's Embarrass Lake cut-off near Biwabik under construction during 1927 is shown in the view at the upper right. — AUTHOR'S COLLECTION (RIGHT) Mining company train dumping overburden from Mary Ellen Mine into Embarrass Lake. Over a million yards of fill were required to span the lake. — DM&IR COLLECTION (BELOW) Snowbound D&IR Mikado No. 300 had to be dug out of deep drifts near Two Harbors on February 14, 1923. — MINNESOTA HISTORICAL SOCIETY

111

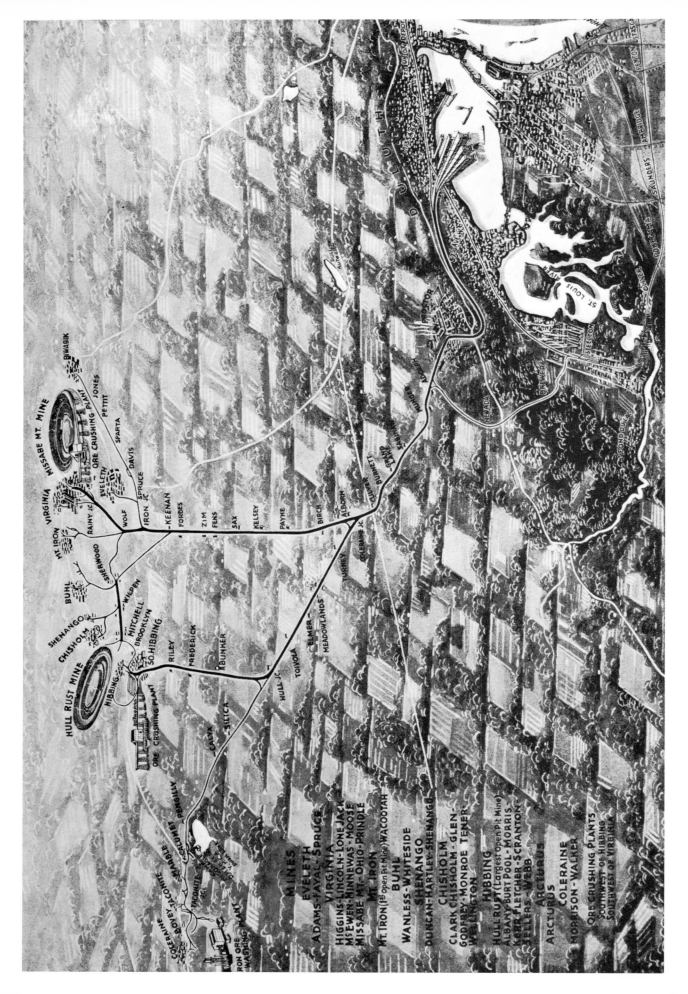

This map showing the DM&N route and mines served was published in a 1927 condensed history of the road. — DM&IR COLLECTION

The ore car repair shop at Proctor was a busy place during the 1920's. — DM&IR COLLECTION

In 1928, President Calvin Coolidge, accompanied by his wife and son, visited the Mesabi Range. They traveled by special train over the DM&N between Duluth and Hibbing as guests of W. A. Mc-Gonagle, the Missabe Road's president. — DM&IR COLLECTION (BELOW) DM&N engine No. 210, after her 1929 rebuilding, sported a double stack. — AUTHOR'S COLLECTION

The other project was the adaptation of Mallets, previously used only on Proctor Hill, to road service. President McGonagle had noted with considerable interest the operation of "simplified" Mallets in road ore service of the Great Northern on its nearby Mesabi Division, and pondered what could be done to improve the performance of his Mallets so that they could be used in road service. The decision was to change them from compound to single-expansion, and No. 210 was selected for rebuilding. The conversion was most complete, including such major new items as Hilastic steel frames, cast steel cylinders, type E superheater, Coffin feed water heater and a Franklin booster on the tender. Mallet No. 210 came out of the Proctor shops a rejuvenated machine, with a 25 percent increase in pulling power. Now easily the heaviest and most powerful engine on the road, she became known as *Madame Queen*. The rebuilding was so successful that four additional Mallets received similar treatment at Proctor during the next seven years.

So ended the 1914-1929 period, one of continued high level traffic, to be succeeded by a period of unimaginable depression, followed by a second World War and even higher traffic volumes.

113

Ponderous Yellowstone No. 236, bound for the Mesabi Range, leaves Two Harbors with 120 empties straining back of her centipede tender. In the next 13 miles she will climb over 1,000 feet above the elevation of Lake Superior. The track passing under the bridge is the main line between Two Harbors and Duluth. — FRANK A. KING

9

DEPRESSION
THIRTIES AND
WARTIME FORTIES

THE great economic depression of the 1930's that was heralded by the sharp decline in stock prices in late October of 1929 did not hit the Range immediately. Traffic handled by the DM&N and D&IR in 1930 dropped about seven million tons below the 1929 high, but, even so, stood at slightly more than 20 million tons, which was still a good figure. The big pinch did not come, and then with a vengeance, until 1932, when ore traffic sank below a million and a half tons.

Meanwhile, the chief event in 1930 was the culmination of long deferred plans for unifying the operations of the DM&N and the D&IR. The first step, which was to lead to complete consolidation in 1938, was the leasing by the DM&N of the properties of the D&IR. The application for approval was filed with the Interstate Commerce Commission in July of 1929, and may not therefore be said to have been brought on by the economic depression, but the granting of the application in December of 1929 permitted the lease to take effect early in 1930 and yield economies at a time when they were especially needed.

The lease was by the stronger DM&N of the property of the weaker carrier, the D&IR, considered to be weaker because of the downward trend in its tonnages and its lower traffic density. The initial term of the lease was 15 years, continu-

ing thereafter from year to year, subject to termination by either party on one year's notice. It included all the D&IR's real estate except certain lands received under its early swamp land grant.

Economies in the range of $500,000 per year were projected from the unification, including savings from joint use of equipment, elimination of some duplicate facilities and services, and especially savings from common use of the ore docks. In respect to the latter, there appeared to be the necessity, in view of its high traffic volume in the period preceding the lease, for the DM&N to build a new ore dock at Duluth. However, if the unification could be effected, then the DM&N could use as its own the D&IR's reserve capacity at Two Harbors and not have to build a new dock at Duluth. As it turned out, which could not of course have been foreseen, there would soon be ample dock capacity at Duluth to handle all available traffic without having to undertake the new construction, but the point was proved good when war-generated traffic materialized a few years later. Cost reductions at the management level were also possible, particularly because some of the top officers of the D&IR were near retirement age.

As president of the DM&N, the leasing and controlling road, McGonagle immediately became re-

sponsible for the entire operation, and Horace Johnson continued for the time being as titular head of the D&IR, with direct supervision only of real estate outside the scope of the lease. He retired on July 1, 1930, and shortly thereafter McGonagle became president of the D&IR also. He was now both the operating and corporate head of the road he once helped to survey through the wilderness. However, the arduous preparations for the leasing, and the changeover, seemed to place a severe strain on his health. Just as he was planning to take a long-needed rest away from the job, he suffered a fatal heart attack and died on August 2, 1930, almost half a century after he first became involved in Charlemagne Tower's *Vermilion Encounter* (Chapter 1) and the D&IR. Although his roots were in the D&IR where he grew up, McGonagle took great pride in his long tenure as president of the DM&N and the fact that his name had become synonymous with it. McGonagle's successor to the DM&N-D&IR presidency was Charles E. Carlson, who had been vice president prior to his promotion. He liked to date his railroad career from 1882, when at the age of eight he was water boy for his uncles, John and Charles

Prior to the unification of DM&N and D&IR operations during 1930, plans were afoot to construct a third steel ore dock at Duluth. The new dock was to have been higher and have greater capacity than the existing docks at that location. In this late 1920's aerial view, wooden Dock No. 4, second from the right, is being dismantled as a first step to make way for the proposed new dock. — DM&IR COLLECTION (BELOW) During the winter months when ore hauling was at a standstill, it was normal on the DM&N and D&IR to have unneeded locomotives standing outside on the dead line. — AUTHOR'S COLLECTION

Carlson, when they were building the Soudan Hill track for the Minnesota Iron Company. He was to hold the office of president until retirement on May 31, 1944.

The seriousness of the depression became evident in the year 1931 when, at 10,594,677 tons, the combined tonnage handled by the two roads was but half of the 1930 figure. But in 1932 the tonnage was an abysmal 1,485,711 tons, not even five percent of the 1929 figure, and less than for any single year since 1893 when the DM&N first began to operate to its own docks. Ore movement was so infrequent that no ore trains at all were operated that year; the few carloads of ore that moved were handled in local freights. Most of the engines just rusted on the dead line.

During Charles E. Carlson's years as president of the Missabe, ore tonnages fluctuated greatly, plummeting to an all-time low during 1932 and then climbing to record highs 10 years later during World War II. — DM&IR COLLECTION

During the 1930's the DM&N shifted many locomotives of the 0-10-0, 2-10-2, and 2-8-8-2 types to the D&IR, thereby effecting substantial operating cost savings. This scene shows one of the DM&N's powerful 0-10-0 switchers shoving a cut of cars up to Dock No. 1 at Two Harbors. — AUTHOR'S COLLECTION

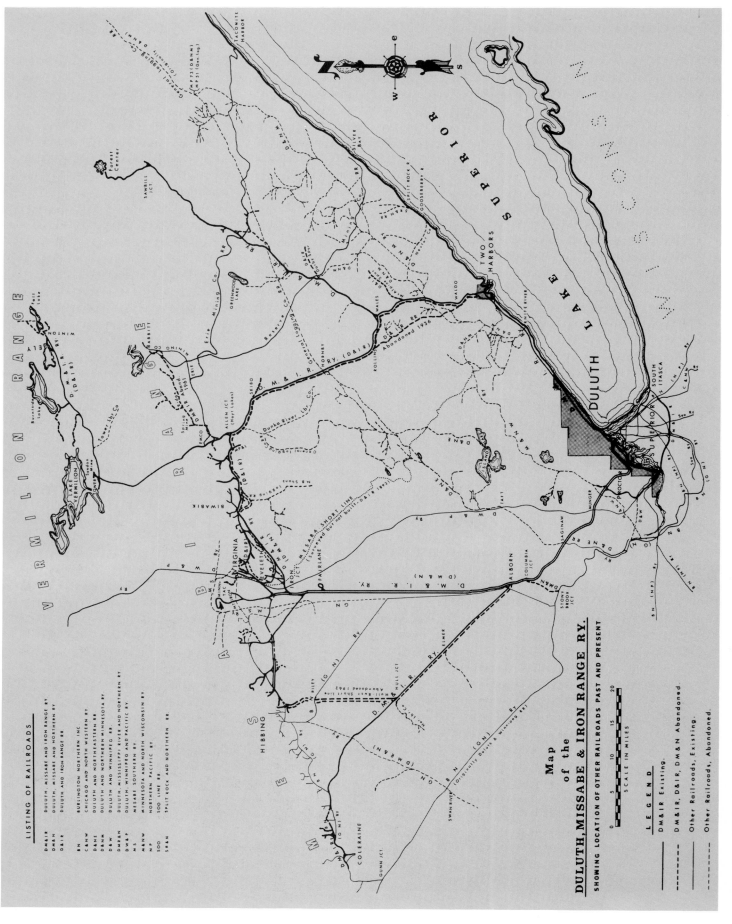

DRAWN BY GLENN W. BURKE

LISTING OF RAILROADS

DM&IR   DULUTH, MISSABE AND IRON RANGE RY.
DM&N   DULUTH, MISSABE AND NORTHERN RY.
D&IR   DULUTH AND IRON RANGE RR.

BN   BURLINGTON NORTHERN INC.
C&NW   CHICAGO AND NORTH WESTERN RY.
D&NE   DULUTH AND NORTHEASTERN RR.
D&NM   DULUTH AND NORTHERN MINNESOTA RY.
D&W   DULUTH AND WINNIPEG RR.
DMR&N   DULUTH, MISSISSIPPI RIVER AND NORTHERN RY.
DW&P   DULUTH, WINNIPEG AND PACIFIC RY.
MS   MESABE SOUTHERN RY.
M&NW   MINNESOTA AND NORTH WISCONSIN RY.
NP   NORTHERN PACIFIC RY.
SOO   SOO LINE RR.
SR&N   SPLIT ROCK AND NORTHERN RR.

Map
of the

DULUTH, MISSABE & IRON RANGE RY.

SHOWING LOCATION OF OTHER RAILROADS PAST AND PRESENT

SCALE IN MILES

0   5   10   15   20

L E G E N D

——————— DM&IR Existing.
- - - - - DM&IR, D&IR, DM&N Abandoned.
——————— Other Railroads, Existing.
- - - - - Other Railroads, Abandoned.

As Appendix A shows, iron ore traffic picked up in 1933 and stayed near the 10 million ton mark, which is to say at the 1902 to 1905 level, through 1935. It went above 17 million in 1936, and to almost 28 million during the false recovery of the year 1937, only to fall back to a dismal 8 million tons during the renewal of the depression in the year 1938. From this point war fever again took over, and new and higher levels of traffic were soon attained.

Meanwhile, corporate developments of note were occurring. First was the consolidation on July 1, 1937, of the DM&N and the Spirit Lake Transfer Railway Company to form the Duluth, Missabe and Iron Range Railway Company (DM&IR), the present company. It will be recalled that the Spirit Lake was organized to form a connection between Adolph on the DM&N and the line of the Interstate Transfer Railway Company at Oliver Bridge. The next step was for the Duluth, Missabe and Iron Range to acquire ownership of the D&IR and the Interstate Transfer Railway Company through exchange of DM&IR bonds for stock of the two companies, which was authorized by the Interstate Commerce Commission on December 28, 1937. The final step, authorized by the Commission on March 18, 1938, and effective four days later, was accomplished through transfer of property and assets of the D&IR and Interstate Transfer to the Duluth, Missabe and Iron Range. Dissolution of Interstate Transfer and

D&IR was approved by their stockholders on June 28 and July 7, 1938, respectively. Only the new corporation, the Duluth, Missabe and Iron Range, survives. It has two operating divisions, the *Missabe* and the *Iron Range*, thus preserving to some extent the old identities.

World War I had cast little of its shadow before it. America was largely unprepared for a land war and did not expect to be drawn into the conflict. World War II was different. Its shadow was cast some'time before the war broke out in 1939. The United States began, somewhat late, to prepare for it and when it did come there was every likelihood of being drawn into it. When the western European nations began to prepare feverishly for war in 1938 and 1939, they turned to United States industry, and especially to its steel industry, for help. It is therefore understandable that the 1939 tonnage moving over the Missabe docks at Duluth and Two Harbors was more than double that of 1938, exceeding 18 million tons, and that the 1940 tonnage leaped to almost 28 million tons. Even though the United States did not become involved in the war until December of 1941, too late to affect the ore traffic in that year, the tonnage had already attained the unprecedented figure of almost 37.5 million tons.

With tonnage at these high levels, it was apparent that additional locomotives should be acquired to handle the even higher volumes being projected. President Carlson looked to his mechanical

By 1940 passenger service over the DM &IR was down to one train daily in each direction over the two divisions. President Carlson greets a veteran Iron Range Division engineer upon completion of his last run on train No. 6. — DM&IR COLLECTION

A Class C-3 Consolidation switches ore empties at the giant Trout Lake Washing Plant near Coleraine on the far western end of the Mesabi Range. — DM&IR COLLECTION

A southbound ore extra departs from the Rust Crusher Yard near Hibbing with 180 loads for Proctor. Conductor on top of the caboose is giving the "highball" to the engineer. Once one of the busiest North End yards on the railroad, this facility is now abandoned, as the giant Hull-Rust pit no longer produces ore. — DM&IR COLLECTION

This old dilapidated engine house at Virginia was replaced by a large, concrete building during 1940. — AUTHOR'S COLLECTION

engineer, George W. Bohannon, to work out the design requirements for new locomotives for use on the Iron Range Division, locomotives capable of handling at least 25 percent more than the simplified Mallets then in use. There was no question but that they would be far bigger than anything yet seen on the Missabe Road. When the specifications for the new locomotives were complete they called for a mammoth machine weighing, with tender, well over a million pounds. They were of the Yellowstone type (2-8-8-4) capable of exerting a tractive effort of 140,000 pounds. The order was placed with the Baldwin Locomotive Works in 1940. The specifications called for 70,000-pound axle loading, 240 pounds of steam pressure, 26x32-inch cylinders cast integral with the frames, 63-inch diameter disc drivers, roller bearings on all locomotive and tender axles, and all the extras associated with modern steam power. They would represent Baldwin's finest.

Arrival of the big engines at Two Harbors in the spring of 1941 aroused great public interest. Local newspapers featured photos of the new giants alongside old *Three Spot*, the original D&IR engine, and it was not unusual for several hundred

Missabe Yellowstone No. 221 is wyed at Hudson, Wisconsin, en route from the Baldwin Locomotive Works to Duluth. — HAROLD VAN HORN

people to gather along the route to watch the big locomotives on their break-in trips. This interest arose partly out of the fascination that new steam locomotives always have, but also out of the feeling that new and bigger locomotives indicated good prospects and greater prosperity for the iron ore country.

The big Yellowstones broke in under practically full tonnage, steamed perfectly and exceeded fuel performance expectations. Incorporating every known labor-saving device, they were easy to handle, rode like Pullmans, and were well-liked by all the enginemen who operated them, some of whom had run old *Three Spot* in its heyday. All eight of the new locomotives, Nos. 220 to 227, were assigned to the Iron Range Division, taking over practically all main line ore haulage. The big engines were rated at better than 9,000 trailing tons over the division's saw-toothed profile where the most severe adverse grade against the loaded movement was 0.62 of one percent for a distance of three miles. Their rating was 25 percent above the best attained by the rebuilt Mallets. Included in the assignments taken over by the new locomotives were the 80-mile run to Ely on the Vermilion

Range and the 75-mile run to Rainy Junction (Virginia) on the Mesabi Range. The round trip to and from Ely took about 12 hours and that to Rainy Junction about 10 hours, but the Yellowstones, with their huge tenders holding 25,000 gallons of water and 26 tons of coal, could make the trips in each direction without intermediate fuel or water stops. The rebuilt Mallets, along with the Santa Fe's, were shifted to main line ore service on the Missabe Division.

The year 1942, with a total ore movement of 44,788,199 tons, proved to be the high point of the war period and the second highest ever attained by the Missabe Road or its components. This tonnage was attained in part from the use of 1,500 new ore cars of 70-ton capacity procured in 500 car lots from Pullman-Standard, General American and American Car and Foundry Company.

The locomotive situation was so critical that the War Production Board permitted the Missabe to order ten more Yellowstones, Nos. 228 to 237, for 1943 delivery. They were built in the winter of 1942-1943, and some of them were sent from Baldwin's Eddystone plant at Philadelphia directly to the Denver and Rio Grande Western for winter

DM&IR No. 225 heads north for Denver during December of 1942. The Rockies can be seen in the background. — R. H. KINDIG COLLECTION

A westbound double header, with Rio Grande Mountain type No. 1516 assisting DM&IR Yellowstone No. 224, is about ready to depart Salida, Colorado. Note dual-gauged trackage for accommodation of narrow gauge trains. — R. H. KINDIG COLLECTION

use and were turned over to the Missabe before the opening of the 1943 shipping season. Such winter use of Missabe's heavy power was not uncommon since the demands of other railroads, especially western roads, were higher in the winter when Missabe's were down. The eight original Yellowstones had been used the previous winter in helper service over the Rio Grande's 10,000-foot Tennessee Pass across the Continental Divide. Other Missabe locomotives also saw wartime service in the west, when Mikado, Santa Fe and Consolidation type engines were used on the Santa Fe, Southern Pacific and Western Pacific railroads during the winter months.

With many of its highly trained personnel called away for military service, the Missabe experienced a critical labor shortage during the war. Apprentices and laborers were hurriedly trained for more skilled positions, and women undertook to perform such roundhouse duties as locomotive fire lighters, engine watchmen, wipers, cinder pit hands and helpers. It was considered men's work, but they did it well and cheerfully.

Distaff roundhouse workers at Proctor pose beneath the ashpan of a Yellowstone. This quartette typifies the many women who served their country by becoming railroaders during the war. — DM&IR COLLECTION

124

The great mines of the Mesabi were continually setting new production records. Hull-Rust at Hibbing, the largest of them all, loaded out 12 million tons in 1944. This location had been a major ore producer during World War I, and its ore was so accessible that it was only natural to use it during the new conflict. But by the war's end its reserves were about exhausted.

Big electric shovel at the Hull-Rust pit drops 17 tons of ore into a Missabe Road car on track 40 feet above. (BELOW) Thousands of cars passed through Proctor Yard daily during World War II shipping seasons. — BOTH AUTHOR'S COLLECTION

"Cross-country" ore drag with single-expansion 2-8-8-2 No. 211 enters CTC territory at Wolf on the main line. (LEFT) Northbound ore extra 224 thunders over the Cloquet River Bridge at 35 mph with 190 empties in tow. — BOTH FRANK A. KING

One device installed on the Missabe to expedite the wartime movement of traffic was Centralized Traffic Control, usually referred to as CTC. It is now fairly common on most railroads, but was then comparatively new. CTC is a system of remote control of power-operated switches that coordinates train movements in such manner as to use track much more efficiently. It was installed in 1943 on five miles of double track and six and a half miles of single track, thereby controlling the junctions at Keenan, Iron Junction and Wolf on the Missabe Division main line and at Spruce and Sparta on the Biwabik Branch. Through the use of CTC, 90 train movements per day were handled through this territory. Almost half of them were on the first eight-hour trick.

Two big Yellowstones meet on the Iron Range Division north of Two Harbors. — DM&IR COLLECTION

With brake shoes smoking a Yellowstone drifts down the 3.0 percent grade into Two Harbors Yard with 100 loads of iron ore. — AUTHOR'S COLLECTION (LEFT) A Yellowstone rounds Pork City Hill as she leaves Two Harbors with a train of empty ore cars bound for the Mesabi Range. — DM&IR COLLECTION

Mikado No. 1303 stands on the turntable at Endion Roundhouse located along the shore of Lake Superior. Duluth may be seen in the background. — AUTHOR'S COLLECTION (LEFT) During P. H. Van Hoven's term as president, the Missabe was happily confronted with sustained high ore tonnages. Included was the all-time record-breaking year of 1953, when just short of 50 million tons were transported. — DM&IR COLLECTION

Although the tonnages handled peaked in 1942, during the next three years they remained at a level in excess of 40 million tons a year, a truly awesome amount of iron ore for one railroad to haul out of the limited area served by the Missabe.

President Carlson, during whose term of office annual tonnages varied from one and one-half to 44 and three-quarter million tons, retired in May of 1944. He was succeeded by Paul H. Van Hoven, who had entered the service of the DM&N in 1911 as chief clerk to the auditor. He was vice

A Class C-3 Consolidation undergoes repairs at Proctor Roundhouse during 1948. (BELOW) A busy shop scene at Two Harbors during the late 1940's. Note how the giant Yellowstone hardly clears the shop building structure. — BOTH DM&IR COLLECTION

IRON ORE TRANSFER
ORE CAR TO ORE BOAT

The handling of natural ores (other than taconite pellets) presents many considerations which are not immediately apparent to the layman. The importance of maintaining uniformity in raw materials, requisite to quality and cost control within the steel industry, is fully recognized by the railways servicing the mines. It is necessary that the railway carefully follow the instructions outlined by mining companies in order that ore within specified limits of silica, manganese, phosphorous and iron be in proper quantity and available for a specific block or vessel. An accurate record is kept of each individual car of ore, showing from what mine it is received and into what ore boat it is to be loaded.

To further facilitate this, the Missabe, in 1965, installed the first automatic car identification (A.C.I.) system to be used in daily operation on a railroad. The car number and empty car weight are read by the scanner as the car passes over automated track scales and the individual car weight information is transmitted to yard and dock offices. After a train is sorted, the cars are reassembled in proper order for movement to the docks.

To expedite vessel loading, the ore is usually brought to the docks in advance of the ore boat's arrival. The cars are dumped mechanically by means of mobile "trapping" machines, and the ore is then discharged into the pockets below the car. The

pockets hold 4 to 5 cars of ore each, or 300 to 350 long tons of ore, depending upon the dock. A specific number of pockets are assigned to each cargo or boat in accordance with its capacity. Since the named ore boat's scheduled arrival is known in ad-

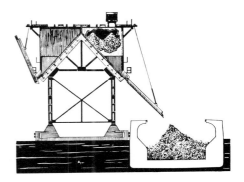

vance, ample time is usually afforded for placement of ore in the dock pockets.

Care is taken to load each vessel evenly to avoid undue strain on its structure; by the raising and lowering of the dock spouts the ore is trimmed and listing of the vessel prevented. The loading usually commences shortly after the vessel's arrival, either day or night, and the average dispatch is about 4.5 hours.

Baldwin built eight-coupled switcher No. 87 prepares to shove some 80 loaded ore cars out onto Dock No. 5 at Duluth. — WAYNE OLSEN

Mobile machines are used to unlatch the car doors when dumping at the docks. The same machine also closes the doors. — DM&IR COLLECTION

Some grades of natural ore, being wet and sticky, were extremely difficult to discharge from the cars, requiring considerable manual assistance. Mobile mechanical carshakers are now used for this purpose. Note cable attached to each man to prevent him from falling into ore dock pockets. — DM&IR COLLECTION

Workers poling sticky ore out of dock pockets at Two Harbors. — DM&IR COLLECTION

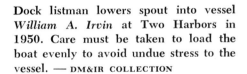

Dock listman lowers spout into vessel *William A. Irvin* at Two Harbors in 1950. Care must be taken to load the boat evenly to avoid undue stress to the vessel. — DM&IR COLLECTION

Ore rushes into the hold of a vessel. Note the "doorman" stationed on the poker deck of the dock. — DM&IR COLLECTION

A typical ore carrier, the *William A. Irvin*, taking on its cargo at Two Harbors.
— DM&IR COLLECTION

president before becoming president.

The termination of World War II caused no change in the operations of the Missabe, since traffic continued at a high level for a number of years, but it was a different world after 1945. This was true not only because of the atomic bomb and developments of nuclear power but, as far as the Missabe was concerned, because of the threat of exhaustion of its high-grade soft iron ore. There was also competition and threat of competition from other newly discovered sources of high-grade ore in other parts of the world, such as Ontario, Quebec, Labrador, Liberia, and Venezuela. World War II hastened the coming of the day, which some had long feared, when the American steel industry no longer would depend so heavily upon the Mesabi for its iron ore. An effort to preserve a competitive position in the iron ore market became a dominant concern of the Minnesota Ranges in the post-World War II period. The year 1945, which marked the end of the war, is thus a good place to end this chapter of Missabe history.

But before reviewing the post-war period and taconite development there will be an interlude chapter, largely pictorial, describing how mining operations were conducted on the Mesabi and Vermilion Ranges. With the coming of the taconite era, in which the most spectacular aspect is the huge plants for crushing rock and making pellets, the mining of natural ores will gradually fade away. The next chapter is a tribute to the enduring fascination of the older methods.

A steam shovel with a four-yard dipper drops eight tons of direct shipping ore into a waiting D&IR 50-ton ore car. This photo, taken during 1936 at the Burt-Day-Sellers open pit at Hibbing, depicts the great days on the Mesabi when much of the ore was loaded directly into cars without beneficiation. The locomotive spotting the cars for loading was an Oliver Iron Mining 600-Class 0-8-0. — MINNESOTA ORE OPERATIONS, U.S. STEEL

10

OF IRON MINES
AND
MINING OPERATIONS

MINNESOTA, famous for its 10,000 lakes and verdant forests and for its fertile farming lands to the west and south was further blessed by nature with the nation's largest deposits of iron ore. For almost nine decades, northeastern Minnesota has provided the bulk of the iron ore used by the nation as it has grown and prospered.

The state was endowed with three sizable iron ore deposits known as the *Vermilion, Mesabi,* and *Cuyuna* Ranges. Commercially acceptable iron ore was discovered first on the Vermilion Range, from which initial shipments were made in 1884. High-grade ore was discovered in 1890 at Mountain Iron on the Mesabi Range, which was destined to become the world's greatest producer, and the first shipments were made two years later. The Cuyuna Range in the midwestern part of the state did not come into production until 1911.

Most of the iron ore from the Vermilion Range was removed by underground mining, though some of the operations started as open pits on surface outcroppings of ore that extended to much deeper levels. The ore was very hard and for the most part had to be blasted out of place whether on the surface or deep down. The Vermilion Range, never a large producer as compared with the Mesabi, is now depleted in the sense that commercial mining there is no longer economically feasible, though good ore is still to be found at lower levels. Some geologists believe that the Minnesota ore deposits extend down under Lake Superior, forming at great depths a connection with the deposits in Michigan and Wisconsin.

The Tower-Soudan Mine that Charlemagne Tower opened up on the Vermilion at Soudan in 1882 was one of the most spectacular of the deep mine operations. For about the first eight years it was an open-pit mine, and from 1890 until 1962 a shaft was employed to reach ever-deepening levels. During the 80-year period of its operation about 15.5 million tons of ore were shipped from the mine. When commercial operations were terminated in December of 1962 the mine was given, along with about 1,000 acres of land, to the State of Minnesota for park purposes. A 600-horsepower motor moves the skip up and down the shaft, winding and rewinding the wire cable around a steel drum 39 feet in diameter. It takes three minutes to lower the skip 2,500 feet to the 27th level where the last mining was done. Tourists may then ride by electric train for about a mile to see an ore face that was being worked when mining ceased.

Many considerations enter into the choice of a mining method, the cost element being generally the controlling factor. The open pit method, which permits maximum use of mechanical devices and

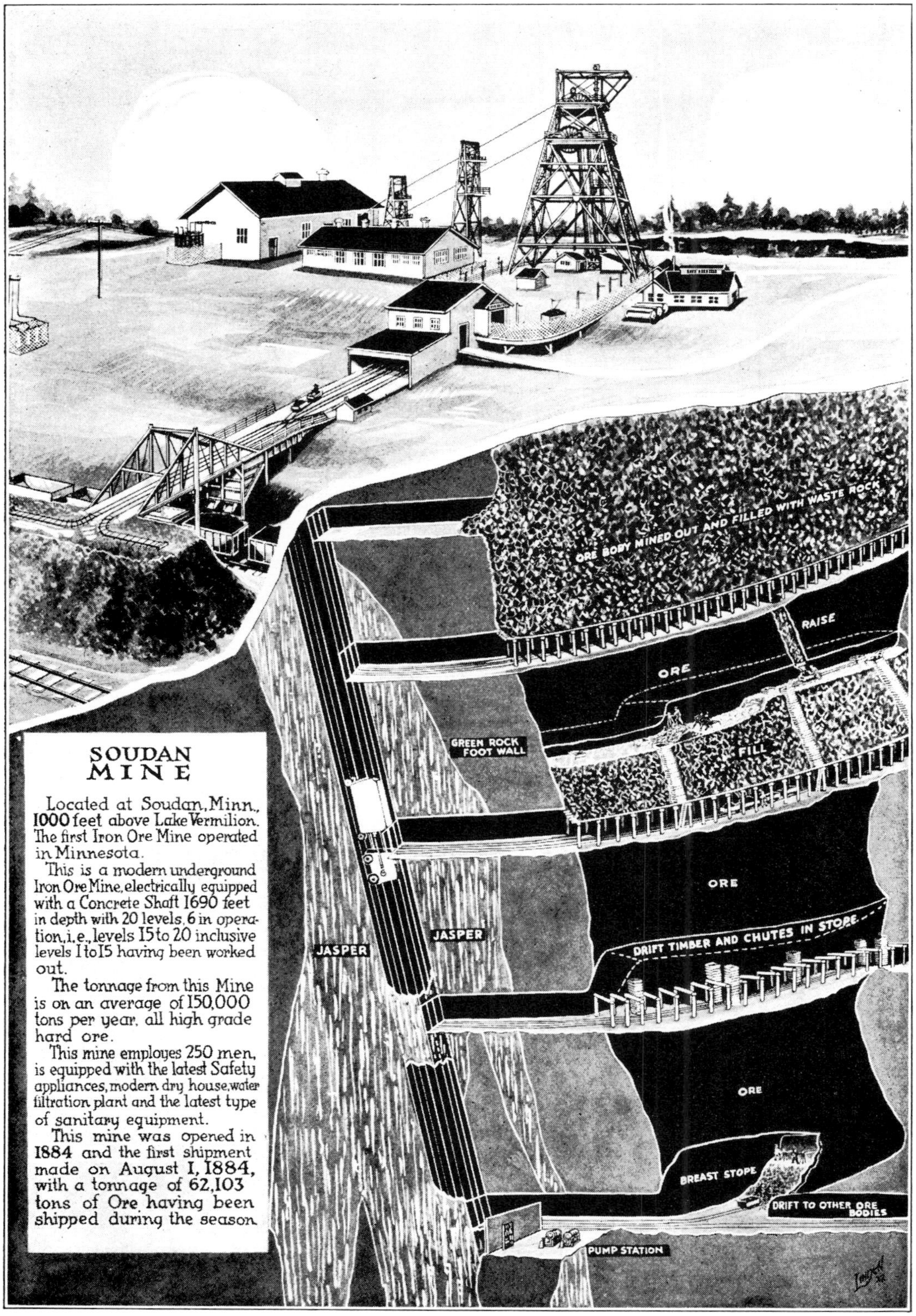
SOUDAN MINE
Located at Soudan, Minn., 1000 feet above Lake Vermilion. The first Iron Ore Mine operated in Minnesota.
This is a modern underground Iron Ore Mine, electrically equipped with a Concrete Shaft 1690 feet in depth with 20 levels, 6 in operation, i.e., levels 15 to 20 inclusive levels 1 to 15 having been worked out.
The tonnage from this Mine is on an average of 150,000 tons per year, all high grade hard ore.
This mine employes 250 men, is equipped with the latest Safety appliances, modern dry house, water filtration plant and the latest type of sanitary equipment.
This mine was opened in 1884 and the first shipment made on August 1, 1884, with a tonnage of 62,103 tons of Ore having been shipped during the season.
ORE BODY MINED OUT AND FILLED WITH WASTE ROCK
RAISE
ORE
FILL
GREEN ROCK FOOT WALL
ORE
DRIFT TIMBER AND CHUTES IN STOPE
JASPER
JASPER
ORE
BREAST STOPE
DRIFT TO OTHER ORE BODIES
PUMP STATION

SOUDAN MINE

Cross-section drawing showing how underground mining was conducted in the Vermilion Range. The Soudan Mine, opened in 1884, was the first iron ore mine in Minnesota. Its first shipment was made on August 1 of that year, and 62,103 tons of ore were dispatched during the first season of operation. — DM&IR COLLECTION

Where it all began in Minnesota. Turn of the century scene of the famed Soudan Mine, high atop the hill overlooking the community of Soudan. Slightly below and to the right of the mine buildings, a D&IR 0-4-0 switcher spots four cars for steam shovel loading at the stockpile. The D&IR's Tower Junction Yard is in the left foreground. Note the mixture of wooden and steel ore cars. (LEFT) The steel headframe of the Sibley underground mine was typical of those in the Ely area. The Sibley, which opened in 1899, produced a total of 9,808,202 tons of high-grade ore during its 55 years of operation. (LOWER LEFT) A group of underground miners stop work long enough to have their picture taken at the Fayal Mine in Eveleth during 1915. Today, there are no underground iron mining operations in Minnesota. — ALL AUTHOR'S COLLECTION

139

Union Mine, Iron Ore
Virginia, Minn. 1915

Photo, by Poliff.
Two Harbors, Minn.

The Union Mine at Virginia worked a long and narrow ore body, unlike the expansive pits in the Hibbing area. In this scene, a steam shovel loads an Oliver Iron Mining Co. train. (LEFT) A big 700-Class 0-8-0 type locomotive spots dump cars for loading at the Hull-Rust pit. These powerful engines were built by the Lima Locomotive Works. — BOTH AUTHOR'S COLLECTION

requires no supporting structures, is generally the most efficient and is used wherever possible.

Mining of Mesabi ore by open pit methods was largely a transportation problem of moving the dirt out of the way, and then taking out the ore. The entire operation must be laid out in advance, with planning based upon information obtained from closely spaced drill cores that thoroughly outlined the ore body and its characteristics, both physical and chemical.

The greatest concentration of high-grade ore occurred in the Hull-Rust-Mahoning area at Hibbing. The largest open pit iron mine in the world, it extends over 1,600 acres, is over three miles in length, a mile in width, and reaches a depth of 535 feet. To date this giant complex, mined by numerous ore interests serving most of the major steel companies, has produced well over one-half

The Fayal Mine was a combination open-pit and underground operation. In the foreground a shovel is loading lean (low grade) ore into dump cars, while another train waits on the right. — AUTHOR'S COLLECTION

Fayal open pit Mine
250 ft. deep - Iron ore
Eveleth, Minn 1915

The famed Mountain Iron Mine, where the Merritt Brothers first discovered ore on the Mesabi Range, opened in November 1892. By the time this photo was taken, in late 1904, shipments of iron ore totaled almost 10 million tons. It was the first Minnesota mine in which Andrew Carnegie became interested (in 1896), an epoch-marking event in the steel industry. At the time of its closing in 1956, total shipments of ore amounted to nearly 50 million tons. Today, the dormant open pit serves as a water reservoir for the nearby Minntac Taconite Plant. — AUTHOR'S COLLECTION

billion tons of high-grade ore. It is now nearing the end of its production. During its peak period there were almost 100 miles of railroad track spiralling down into its depths. Dozens of steam and electric shovels loaded out vast quantities of high-grade ore directly into ore cars which were pulled out in 10 to 18 car drags and marshalled into long road trains in the nearby Hull-Rust and Mitchell yards of the DM&IR, and the Kelly Lake yard of the Great Northern, now Burlington Northern. Rail equipment used in the pits grew steadily in size with the passing years. Locomotives employed in early day stripping operations were usually small, narrow gauge four-wheeled saddle tankers, weighing about ten tons and commonly called "Dinkeys." Standard gauge steam power ranged all the way from saddle tank 0-4-0's to powerful 0-8-0 switchers. Some of the latter, equipped with tender boosters, were capable of shoving as many as 18 heavily loaded ore cars up the long two percent grade leading out of the Hull-Rust pit.

Steam locomotives used in the open pits varied from small narrow gauge 10-ton tank engines to heavy 0-8-0 switchers of main line proportions. This narrow gauge Porter-built locomotive was used in stripping service during the late 1890's.—AUTHOR'S COLLECTION

Longer pit hauls soon necessitated separate tenders. Baldwin-built Oliver Iron Mining Company No. 56 was typical of the many 0-6-0's used in the open pits during the early 1900's. The young engineer, standing nearest the engine, was the author's father, George R. King. (LEFT) Pittsburgh-built Oliver Mining Company No. 4 was a representative saddle-tank standard gauge mining locomotive just before the turn of the century. (BELOW) Mahoning Ore and Steel Company No. 208 was one of the biggest steamers used in the open pits on the Mesabi.
— ALL AUTHOR'S COLLECTION

Balkan Mining Company 0-6-0 No. 26 was one of the last steam locomotives used on the Mesabi Range, operating until 1964. — FRANK A. KING (BELOW) The Susquehanna pit, being very narrow and deep (450 feet), was converted from conventional rail haulage to a combination electric-rail haulage, skip-hoist operation shortly after this photo was taken in 1929. — AUTHOR'S COLLECTION

A typical underground motor at the Fayal Mine — 1915. (BELOW) An 85-ton General Electric steeple cab spots the loading pocket at Cleveland Cliffs Mining Company's Gross-Marble Mine during 1970. Neighboring Interstate Iron Company's electric haulage system, which is now abandoned, once boasted 21 miles of electrified standard gauge trackage. Note offset trolley wire which was necessary for shovel loading in the pit. —BOTH AUTHOR'S COLLECTION

Electric haulage, though common in underground operations, was not used much in Mesabi Range open pits, in marked contrast to the western copper pits where electric locomotives gained wide acceptance. Rail operations in the iron ore pits became dieselized in due course. Multiple unit diesel locomotives consisting of units ranging from 1,200 to 2,400 horsepower are now used on the heaviest hauling jobs. A large taconite pit operation near Mountain Iron utilizes radio-controlled units with a one-man train crew.

As the ore pits became deeper and the grades more severe, trucks and conveyor belt systems were introduced. Truck sizes have grown from the 15-ton units used in the 1930's to the 135-ton-capacity haulers now in use. Even larger trucks may come to the Mesabi, with 200-ton giants now being tested.

In 1929, this "Diffco" haulage unit replaced the steam operation at the Susquehanna pit. — AUTHOR'S COLLECTION (BELOW) A 100-ton capacity electric drive truck, typical of those which have taken over the haulage in many pits. — MINNESOTA ORE OPERATIONS, U.S. STEEL

Power shovels grew from primitive affairs, such as DM&N's No. 1 shown in ore stockpile loading service during the 1890's. — AUTHOR'S COLLECTION

The 300-ton Marion Steam Shovel, shown at the right, was used in the Hull-Rust Mine at Hibbing during 1918. Many shovels of this type were later electrified. (BELOW) Today's shovels are all crawler mounted and electrically powered. — BOTH DM&IR COLLECTION

The size of the excavating equipment has kept pace. Steam shovels were used on the Mesabi from its very beginning. The first, which were primitive affairs, bucked and snorted as they dug into the bank with their one-cubic-yard buckets. All shovels used in the pits were mounted on railroad tracks until about 1920, by which time capacities had risen to five cubic yards. Some extremely large steam shovels were mounted on a double set of tracks spaced 25 to 30 feet apart. The introduction of crawler treads and electrification during the 1920's ushered in a new era and shovels with bucket capacities of 16 to 20 yards are now common. Draglines like those used in coal stripping operations have been successfully used for stripping, the largest having a capacity in excess of 30 cubic yards.

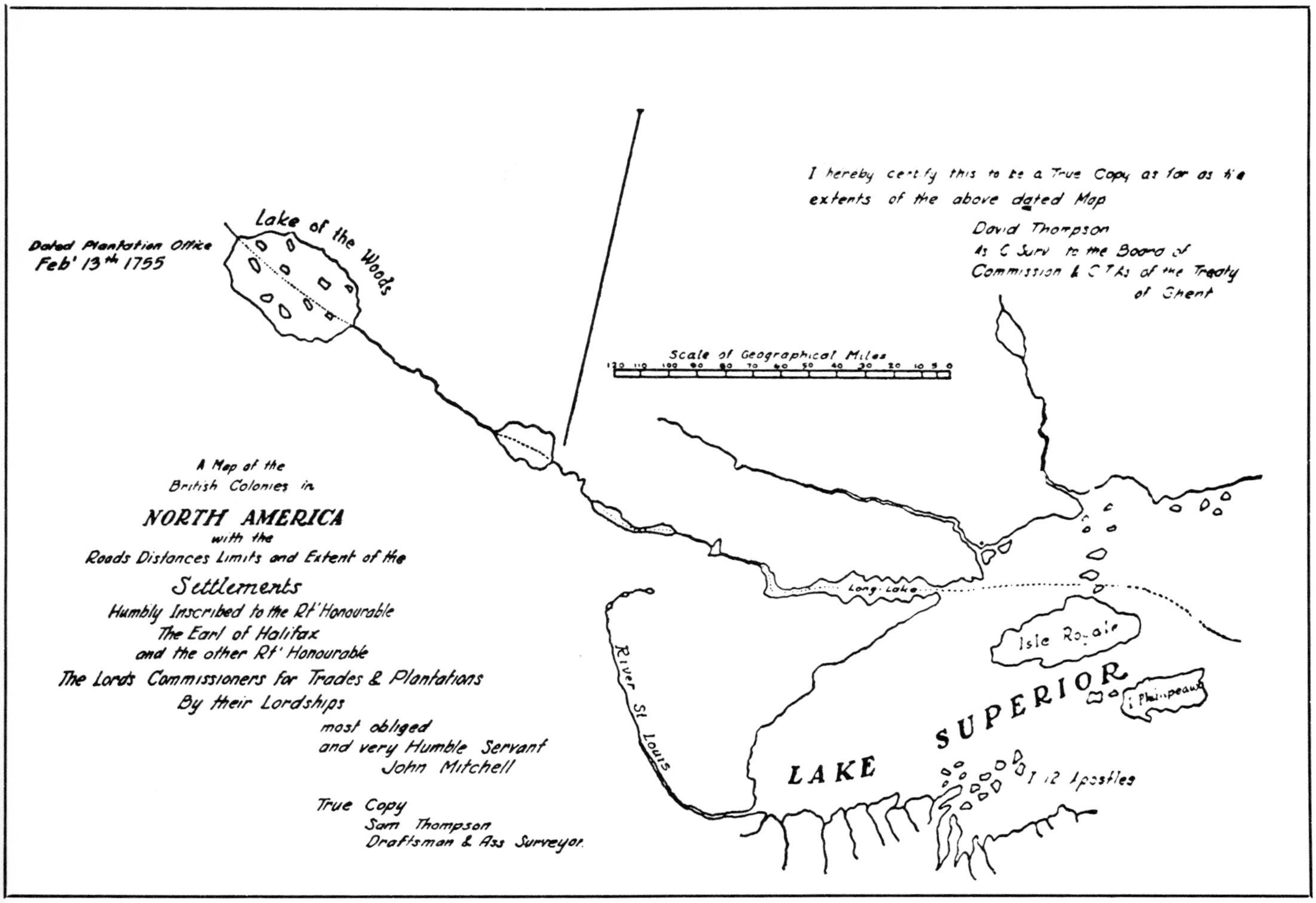

John Mitchell's famous map which was instrumental in placing the vast Minnesota ore deposits within the United States.

The average iron content of soft ores being mined on the Mesabi is now (1972) slightly above 50 percent. Practically all of the soft ore presently mined in Minnesota is beneficiated — treated to bring its iron content up to about 54 percent iron and otherwise improve its quality before shipment. In the early days ore running as high as 65 percent iron content was scooped up and loaded directly into railroad cars for shipment.

Minnesota, still the nation's largest producer, shipped approximately 54,000,000 tons of iron ore in 1970, including taconite concentrates. The high point was attained during 1953, when 81,500,000 tons were produced.

Minnesota in particular, and the United States in general, owe Benjamin Franklin a note of gratitude, for he was instrumental in bringing these valuable deposits within the boundaries of the United States. While the northern boundary of the United States was not accurately defined until the Webster-Ashburton Treaty of 1842, its approximate location was fixed in the 1783 Treaty of Paris. Franklin was one of the commissioners sent to negotiate the treaty. An inaccurate map depicted the Lake of the Woods as flowing into Lake Superior through the Pigeon River, so that water course was established as the international boundary at this point. Had the commissioners been aware that the Pigeon extended only 30 miles to the north, and that most of the vast territory north and west of that area drained into Hudson Bay, it could well have been that the St. Louis River would have been made the boundary, thereby locating the Vermilion Range and the better part of the Mesabi Range in Canada.

Against the backdrop of the imposing north country of Minnesota, ore extra No. 225 approaches Allen Junction en route to Two Harbors during the last days of steam on the Missabe Road. (RIGHT) A Missabe Division southbound ore extra breaks over the grade at Saginaw. This 180-car train contains a mixture of 50 and 70-ton ore cars. Today's trains are made up exclusively of 70-ton cars, all of the old 50-tonners having been phased out. — BOTH FRANK A. KING

LAST OF THE MINNESOTA ORE-HAULING MALLETS

Duluth, Missabe and Iron Range Railway Yellowstone No. 235 heads south for Two Harbors with a heavy ore train during the autumn of the steam locomotive.

11
POST-WORLD WAR II

THE termination of the war in 1945 had little immediate effect on the Missabe Road's traffic, since demand for Mesabi iron ore continued to be strong for several years. Appendix A shows a continuation from 1946 through 1953 of tonnages on the order of those handled in the war years. There is some warrant for calling the years 1951-1953 war years on account of the Korean conflict. Traffic averaged 40.3 million tons per year from 1946 to 1953, reaching an all-time high of 49,317,-625 tons in 1953.

A second traffic plateau appears in Appendix A for the years 1954 to 1957, with average shipments of about 34.5 million tons per year. The sharpest drop, from 1953 to 1954, was an enormous 21 million tons. The traffic came back to 38.4 million tons in 1957, but an air of apprehension began to hang over the Missabe because the end of the abundant supply of high-grade soft ore was in sight and the taconite development, which will be covered in the next chapter, was not yet fully under way.

A third traffic plateau commenced in 1958 and is still continuing in 1972. The year 1958 witnessed another drop of 17 million tons in the Missabe's traffic and ushered in a new low period when movements over the Missabe would average about 20.7 million tons per year.

A good index of what happened to the Missabe Road after World War II may be found in its car fleet. The period witnessed first an expansion, and then a contraction, in the size of the fleet. At the end of World War II many of the old 50-ton ore cars were beyond economical repair and were rapidly being phased out. Their presence in heavy 180-car trains, often grossing over 17,000 tons, became increasingly troublesome. Orders were therefore placed for 2,000 new 70-ton-capacity cars to replace them. Four major car builders shared in the order, and the cars were all in service by 1948. Another 1,000 cars of the 70-ton size were acquired in 1949, which brought the Missabe's ore car roster up to 13,347 units having an aggregate capacity of 807,000 tons. The highest year-end ore car ownership, 14,229 units, was reached on December 31, 1952, from which point it began to decline. As of December 31, 1970, the Missabe owned 8,639 70-ton ore cars, of which 300 were equipped with 20-inch side boards for pellet service.

Passenger service declined gradually after World War II, train by train, first on one portion of the railroad and then on another. Service between Alborn and Coleraine on the western end of the railroad was discontinued in 1951 for lack of patronage, foretelling the day when all passenger

The years following World War II saw considerable upgrading of the Missabe's track. Worn out rail was replaced and many miles of main line resurfaced. An Iron Range Division work train is shown dumping gravel for resurfacing. — AUTHOR'S COLLECTION (RIGHT) Following close behind the work train was the extra gang with their "automatic" tampers. While these machines were a vast improvement over manual tamping, they have long since been replaced by much more sophisticated models. — DM&IR COLLECTION

service would cease for the same reason. The last scheduled run of a steam-powered passenger train over the Iron Range Division was made on January 20, 1953, when a Pacific type engine, No. 1107, pulled two-car train No. 6 from Winton, at the far end of the line, past Ely to Duluth. A Budd-built diesel rail car of the RDC-3 configuration, seating 48 passengers and containing mail and express compartments, took over Iron Range Division passenger service the next day on a stepped-up schedule.

Discontinuing passenger service between Duluth and Hibbing proved to be an ordeal. The service was first discontinued on May 15, 1953, under permission granted by the Minnesota Railroad and Warehouse Commission after a public hearing. Out-of-pocket losses were shown to be at least $200,000 per year and the revenue negligible, so it seemed obvious that no real public interest would be served in continuing the operation. However, less than six months later, after holding a somewhat stormy hearing, the commission issued an order requiring the railroad to restore the service, but on a reverse schedule, i.e., one that required the morning train to originate at Hibbing, instead of Duluth, and the afternoon train to originate at Duluth instead of Hibbing.

There were many empty seats on train No. 2 running between Hibbing and Duluth, shortly before its first discontinuance during May of 1953. — DM&IR COLLECTION (BELOW) Train No. 5, with Pacific type locomotive No. 1107 on the head-end, approaches Duluth. The business car *Northland* is attached to the rear of the daily train. — PETE BONESTEEL COLLECTION

With a clear track ahead, the engineer opens the throttle of locomotive No. 1107, and rolls train No. 5 north through the eastern section of Duluth. — FRANK A. KING

The railroad promptly sought review of the commission's order before the state courts on both procedural and substantive grounds and, for the next three years while the case was being litigated, the original order permitting discontinuance of service was left in effect, and no service was offered. The final decision, rendered by the Supreme Court of Minnesota on February 24, 1956, upheld the order of the commission, which became final on October 8, 1956 when the Supreme Court of the United States dismissed an appeal on the ground that no federal question was involved. It is of interest, not so much in respect to the merits of the case as to show attitudes, to note the following in the opinion of the Supreme Court of Minnesota:

. . . While the loss to the carrier seems out of all proportion to the use made of the service, when the overall operation of the carrier is taken into consideration, we cannot say that the commission went beyond its authority in ordering establishment of the passenger service.

Passenger service between Duluth and the Range was thereupon restored under the commission's schedule that was an hour faster in each direction than the former schedule. In order to keep costs at a minimum the Budd car was used. It was a tight schedule, calling for a run of about 400 miles each day. The forces at Mitchell (near Hibbing) had a tough time servicing the car each night, and an old faithful 400-class Pacific was ready if they could not make it. At Endion (Duluth) a trim Vanderbilt-tanked 1100-class Pacific was on call.

Just minutes out of Duluth, No. 1107 crosses the French River Bridge with southbound train No. 6. — AUTHOR'S COLLECTION

Mikado No. 1336 makes easy work of handling train No. 11 northbound into Eveleth during 1953. — FRANK A. KING

Publicity shot of Budd diesel rail car No. 1, taken along the shore of Lake Superior, with Duluth's famous landmark, the Aerial Bridge, in the background. — DM&IR COLLECTION

Despite the faster schedules, passenger service revenues for operation between Duluth and the Range were less than $7,500 in 1957, and at the end of that year passenger service was discontinued on the Missabe Division, after 63 years of continuous operation. By then even Greyhound was having a hard time of it in the land of its birth. Service between Duluth and Ely via the Iron Range Division continued until July 15, 1961, after which all passenger service ceased on the Missabe Road.

RDC No. 1 heads northbound through Knife River as train No. 5 on March 9, 1958. — WILLIAM D. MIDDLETON

Gas-electric rail motor cars were used quite extensively in the United States from early in the century to the decade of the forties as replacements for unprofitable steam powered passenger trains. While the single car passenger unit saved labor and equipment, thereby cutting railroad operating costs, its major drawbacks were lack of power and constant need of repair.

It was not until 1954 that the first diesel-powered streamlined passenger train appeared and was an immediate success. At this time The Budd Company of Philadelphia studied the possibilities of a new self-propelled diesel car which would overcome the railroads' traditional objections to single unit trains and meet the needs of railroad passengers.

The RDC is the generic name for the diesel self-propelled rail car developed by Budd in four types to provide a single or multiple unit operation with a performance suitable for improving schedules and offering fast service with a minimum of capital, repair and operating costs. As the Missabe Road lost passengers to the highway, the RDC car was a last-ditch effort to provide the riding public with comfortable and convenient service.

In the scene below, RCD No. 1 leaves the classic brick Two Harbors depot en route for Ely.

Dieselization was a post-World War II phenomenon on all railroads. Completion of dieselization took place on the Missabe in the year 1960, somewhat later than on most other railroads. The first step was taken in 1953, while the Missabe was experiencing its all-time tonnage peak, with the acquisition of 15 diesel switching units of 1,200 horsepower, manufactured by the Electro-Motive Division (EMD) of General Motors Corporation. It was quite usual for switching to be the first operation dieselized on a railroad, because the service did not require the sustained use of the power available in a steam engine with its steam up, but did require that power be available in the sudden spurts an internal combustion engine is able to supply. The savings and service advantage to the Missabe in this area of operations were evident and dieselization occurred.

Two of the Missabe's first diesels, Nos. 14 and 19, team up to move a transfer on the Interstate Branch. The Class DS-1 1,200 hp. switchers built by the Electro-Motive Division of General Motors in 1953 were soon displaced by the much heavier SD-9's. — DM&IR COLLECTION

Switcher No. 21 makes up the northbound Ely local freight at Endion Yard during August of 1955. — JIM SHAUGHNESSY

A pair of Fairbanks-Morse Train Master demonstrator units at the head end of an ore extra bound from Ely to Two Harbors during July of 1953. — AUTHOR'S COLLECTION

Diesel units for road service were demonstrated from time to time on the Missabe Road, and studies were made as to the economy of their use, but the 1950 period was one of uncertainty in regard to the future of the railroad. The fact that ore moved on the Missabe for only about eight months of the year, on account of winter conditions, was also a consideration. Then, too, good steam power was available from the other railroads that had already dieselized, such as the Elgin, Joliet and Eastern, the Union and the Bessemer and Lake Erie.

Replacements for the 2-8-8-2 compounds came in the form of nine heavy 0-10-2's from the Union Railroad, one of which is shown on the head end of a long string of empties on Proctor Hill. — DM&IR COLLECTION

Compound No. 201 plods up Proctor Hill with a long string of empties. This photo was taken near the end of her long and useful 43-year career. — AUTHOR'S COLLECTION

During the motive power shortage of 1948, the Rio Grande came to the Missabe's rescue by sending a number of its locomotives to northern Minnesota. Mikado No. 1205 was used in commercial switching service at Two Harbors. — FRANK A. KING

Early in the post-war period, the old work horse C-3 Consolidations were nearing the end of the line, and replacements were needed for them. The Missabe first leased Mikado and Mountain type locomotives from the Rio Grande, then, during 1948, bought 26 diesel-displaced Mikados from the Elgin, Joliet and Eastern.

The Missabe's old 1910 Mallets, which had rendered such excellent service on the Hill between Proctor and the Duluth ore docks for almost 40 years, were now exhibiting fatigue. Main frames continually required welding to keep them intact, and boiler and firebox repairs were troublesome. Thus it came about that during 1949 nine 0-10-2 locomotives were acquired from the Union Railroad and placed in service on the Hill and in Proctor yard. With a tractive effort of 90,900 pounds, they compared favorably with the Mallets. But without the old compounds and the soothing sound of their muffled plodding-like exhaust, the operation was different; the Hill now reverberated to the impatient bark of the ten-drivered replacements.

No. 708 is framed between the bents of Dock No. 5 approach as she pulls a string of empties from Dock No. 6. Low trestle in background is the main line into Duluth. — JIM SHAUGHNESSY

In the spring of 1951 the Missabe procured from the Bessemer and Lake Erie 18 of its big Texas type (2-10-4) locomotives that had been rendered surplus by a fleet of F-7 diesels. These big Texas engines, the world's most powerful two cylindered steam engines, were among the most handsome ever produced. Although they helped the Missabe Road attain peak tonnages in 1953, they exerted 30 percent less drawbar pull than the big Yellowstones and were assigned to main line ore runs only as a last resort. For the most part, they were used in Proctor and Steelton Hill service and in the "Cross-Country" ore haul between the Hibbing district and Biwabik. On occasion they were used for ore sorting and switching in Proctor and Two Harbors yards. Counting the 18 Texas type locomotives, the Missabe's steam locomotive roster reached an all-time high of 172 units in 1951.

The unforgettable pungency of coal smoke, hot metal and valve oil fills the air as No. 714, a Texas type 2-10-4, shakes the ground while leading a string of empty ore cars from the Duluth docks to Proctor Yard. — JIM SHAUGH-NESSY

Alco-built No. 706, its tender heaped with coal, prepares to leave Two Harbors on an ore extra. — DM&IR COLLECTION

Mikado type No. 1321 was one of 26 steam locomotives purchased from the Elgin, Joliet and Eastern during 1948. In this scene, No. 1321 was in service at Virginia. — FRANK A. KING (LEFT) Bound for Steelton with a train of loaded ore cars, husky Union type engine No. 607 defiantly hurls her exhaust skyward on the heavy pull out of Proctor. — FRANK A. KING

Biwabik-bound cross-country ore drag snakes through Sparta during 1955 behind 2-8-8-2 type engine No. 211. Originally a compound Mallet, the 211 was rebuilt to single expansion at the Proctor Shops in 1931. — FRANK A. KING

The final ore season for Missabe steam power, the last great steam operation in North America, came in 1960. In this typical Missabe Road scene, Yellowstone No. 221 nears the end of its ore run at Proctor. — JOE G. COLLIAS

Yellowstone engineer Ed App looks back from his cab for a "highball" before leaving Fraser Yard for Proctor with 190 loads. Gross weight of the train was just under 18,000 tons. — WILLIAM D. MIDDLETON

At Fraser, a big drink is required to fill the 25,000 gallon centipede tank of Yellowstone No. 228. Behind engineer App can be seen some of the 200 empties which his engine had just brought in from Proctor. — WILLIAM D. MIDDLETON

The DM&IR was a pioneer in the use of radio communications for train operation. In the view above, the engineer of Yellowstone No. 231 makes contact with the train conductor. — DM&IR COLLECTION (RIGHT ABOVE) Fireman John Shovein checks his fire prior to leaving Fraser Yard for Proctor. While working hard on the road, the big 2-8-8-4 could consume 500 pounds of coal per minute. — WILLIAM D. MIDDLETON

THE MISSABE AT NIGHT

After the sun slips away and night drapes its darkcloth, even the commonplace on the Missabe Road assumes an air of mystery and drama. Stirring in daylight, the railroad at night furnishes added excitement for the cameraman. (ABOVE) A busy night at Rainy Junction Yard (Virginia) during the Korean conflict. The structure on the left is the Rouchleau Ore Crushing Plant. — DM&IR COLLECTION (LEFT) Mikado No. 1303 being coaled at Endion preparatory to taking out the Ely local freight. — WILLIAM D. MIDDLETON

Late on a May night in 1959 Yellowstone No. 228 waits to cross the scales at Proctor Yard with a just arrived 190-car ore train. (BELOW) Lit up like a giant Christmas tree, the Duluth Ore Docks present a startling picture at night. Here Shenango Furnace Company's steamer *Schoonmaker* takes on her cargo at Dock No. 6 during a clear evening during May of 1959. — BOTH WILLIAM D. MIDDLETON

The caboose in the pale light seems square, compact, and the arch of the cupola appears uncomprisingly high and old fashioned. Across the track, Santa Fe type No. 502 picks up a few additional cars at Missabe Junction before leaving for Proctor with the transfer. — JIM SHAUGHNESSY

171

Four SD-9 units, totaling 7,000 hp., prepare to leave Biwabik with 170 loads for Two Harbors in 1958. By this time, Missabe Road operations were largely dieselized. — FRANK A. KING

Nos. 101 and 102, moving a dock-bound Proctor Hill ore train, were two of the ten original General Motors EMD road diesels received in 1956. — DM&IR COLLECTION

Dieselization of the Missabe's road service commenced with the opening of the 1956 ore season when ten 1,750-horsepower, six-motor EMD (SD-9) units were placed in service. The program was completed with EMD's in 1959. By that time the traffic was down to about 19 million tons per year, and the 95 diesel units then owned, together with a number under lease, were sufficient to handle all road and switching service.

The Missabe had built a modern, well-equipped shop at Proctor for repairing and servicing diesel units, and in 1960 announced plans for the construction of a comparable facility at Two Harbors. In view of the uncertainty prevailing at that time regarding the future of the railroad, the Two Harbors facility was not built. This was fortunate because experience soon proved that one such facility was all that was needed on the railroad. Unlike steam engines, diesels need not remain very long in a shop. Their motors and many other parts are interchangeable and little time is required to remove a defective component and install a replacement.

The transition period prior to total dieselization saw leased diesels on the Missabe from time to time. In this scene, two B&LE F-7 units lug a 180-car ore drag over Saginaw Hill. Diesels were also leased from the Great Northern. — FRANK A. KING

During the long twilight of a Minnesota summer evening, a mighty Yellowstone pumps up its train line prior to departure from Fraser Yard for Proctor. The three diesel units throbbing at the right are bound for Biwabik with ore for Two Harbors. — WILLIAM D. MIDDLETON (LEFT) The Missabe's diesel facilities at Proctor are the finest in the country for a road of its size. This photograph shows the sanding and fueling facility. — DM&IR COLLECTION

Each winter saw many of the Missabe's steam locomotives in temporary storage. This time it was different, as most of the locomotives shown in this 1958 scene at Proctor were replaced by diesels and never again turned a wheel except on their final journey to be scrapped. — FRANK A. KING

Dock 6 at Duluth is bathed in bright lights as SD-9 No. 158 throbs away while waiting on the lead track between spotting assignments. — WILLIAM D. MIDDLETON (BELOW) The diesel repair facilities of the Missabe Road are located at Proctor. During the steam era, the railroad maintained two complete service facilities, one at Proctor and one at Two Harbors. With the coming of the diesel locomotive, the road has combined its repair and maintenance plant into this complete and compact facility. — DM&IR COLLECTION

A 32-mile extension of the Wales Branch into heavy timber lands was the last major line construction by the Missabe. Much of the line passed through swampy areas which presented many unique problems. Dynamite was sometimes used to blast out muskeg prior to dumping fill. This photo shows a dynamite charge clearing out a drainage ditch. — DM&IR COLLECTION

The final curtain call for old Missabe Road Class F 10-Wheeler No. 21 was the handling of work trains during construction of the Wales Branch extension. The last of the 10-Wheelers, No. 21, was the only locomotive light enough to negotiate the spongy track encountered during the construction period. — FRANK A. KING (RIGHT) The pulpwood storage and loading area at Forest Center is located at the end of the Wales Branch extension. — AUTHOR'S COLLECTION

In addition to operational and equipment changes, there have also been a number of changes in leadership during the post-war years.

At the outset of the period Paul H. Van Hoven was president of the Missabe. He had become the chief officer in May of 1944 and retired almost 10 years later, in December 1953. During all of Van Hoven's term as president the traffic volume was high, creating problems of the kind that management prefers to deal with, rather than problems associated with declining volume when facilities have to be shut down and men laid off. In 1947, during his tenure, the Missabe completed its last major extension of line. Essentially a logging railroad, this 32-mile extension of the Wales Branch went from Whyte to Forest Center in the Superior National Forest timberlands. It opened up a large timber area to rail service, and averaged 5,000 carloads per year during the first six years of its operation. Forest products loadings on the Wales Branch are now (1971) down to a steady 2,500 cars per year.

Van Hoven was succeeded as president by Fred J. Voss on April 7, 1954. Although his term was relatively short, lasting only until his untimely death on July 3, 1961, from heart failure, it was one of great change. During his seven-year tenure the Missabe suffered a severe decline in traffic volume, converted from steam to diesel power and discontinued its passenger service to the accom-

Fred J. Voss became president during 1954, following the Missabe's record tonnage year of 1953. Eight years later, ore traffic plunged to 18.5 million tons. — DM&IR COLLECTION (BELOW) A pair of Alco 2,400 horsepower units pick up pulpwood loads at Isabella on the Wales Branch extension. — AUTHOR'S COLLECTION

paniment of protracted litigation. Voss had become a member of the DM&N engineering department soon after graduating from Purdue University in 1926. He left the railroad two years later to be field engineer for the Portland Cement Association but returned to the DM&N in 1936. He was vice president and chief engineer immediately prior to becoming president.

Speaking at the Missabe Veterans dinner in January 1960, Voss had alluded to the necessity of facing reality concerning future prospects of the Missabe. "We must run fast in northern Minnesota to stay where we are," he said, pointing out that Canada was then producing 17 million tons of ore annually and that this figure could double within the next five years. He mentioned that South American imports, running at 20 million tons annually, could readily be doubled and that much of this foreign production would be at the expense of the Mesabi Range. Voss was positive, however, that by improving operations and effecting all possible economies, the Missabe would be able to retain a substantial volume of business.

The situation that Voss would have had to face had death not removed him from office would have been a very difficult one for him. Traffic dropped to 18.5 million tons in 1961 and was to remain very close to that level for the next three

years. Voss was an old-time employee, who knew all the men by name, and he would have disliked to tell many of them that their jobs had been lost because of low traffic volume.

Daniel J. Smith became president on August 1, 1961. He had previously been president of the Lake Terminal Railroad, Newburgh and South Shore Railway, McKeesport Connecting Railroad, Northampton and Bath Railroad, Hannibal Connecting Railroad and Donora Southern Railroad, all small companies headquartered in Pittsburgh.

A major change made in 1961 was the reorganization of the transportation department soon after Smith became president. A new operations center, planned under the Voss regime, was established at Iron Junction to control all north-end train movements on both the Missabe and Iron Range Divisions. Iron Junction had been the operating headquarters for the Merritt brothers' DM&N 70 years before, and the new building is within sight of their original station building, which still stands. The new headquarters houses the CTC console and all information gathering and dispersing activities.

Unloading a coal cargo at the Limestone Dock at Duluth. (BELOW) Loading steel billets at the Limestock Dock. — BOTH DM&IR COLLECTION

Daniel J. Smith became president on August 1, 1961, following Fred J. Voss's untimely death a month earlier. He retired early in 1964. — DM&IR COLLECTION

Santa Fe type engine No. 514 pulled the last steam train over the Missabe Road on September 29, 1962. The six car special, operated on the 70th anniversary of the opening of the DM&N, stands on the Sliver Branch at Virginia while disembarking its 325 passengers.
— FRANK A. KING

The 70th anniversary of the beginning of the Missabe was celebrated on September 29, 1962 by the running of a special train carrying 325 passengers. The trip was sponsored by the St. Louis County Historical Society to mark the opening of the DM&N from Stony Brook to Mountain Iron, and the first commercial shipment of iron ore from the Mesabi. It commemorated the gay excursion of October 15, 1892 that the Merritt brothers arranged to provide family and friends with a first look at their new railroad and ore mine and to honor their mother on her 80th birthday. The 1962 trip was also an historical event in its own right, since it was the last run of steam on the Missabe; a Santa Fe type locomotive, No. 514, pulled the six-car special train.

One of the hard decisions that Smith had to make a year after he came to Duluth was to close the Missabe's port facilities at Two Harbors for the 1963 ore season. There was not enough traffic in prospect to warrant keeping both Two Harbors and Duluth open. One reason for this decision was the closing of the historic Soudan Mine the year before. Only one operating mine was now left on the Vermilion Range, the Pioneer Mine at Ely, and it closed in 1963. There was a movement from stockpiles at both the Soudan Mine and from the closed Zenith Mine, but for practical purposes the Vermilion Range, which had been deep mining from almost the beginning, was done. Total shipments from the Vermilion Range, during its productive period, were just over 100 million tons.

In a press release issued on January 18, 1963, President Smith pointed out that Missabe Road customers were planning to move less than 15 mil-

During 1962 the historic Soudan Mine ceased operations. The mine on the hill overlooking the community of Soudan is now a State Park.
— FRANK A. KING

179

lion tons of ore during the 1963 shipping season, down from more than 49 million tons just ten years previously. He said that concentrating shipments at Duluth would give shippers better service, since most of the ore would originate in the central and western portions of the Mesabi Range. Duluth's docks, he explained, were adjacent to connecting railroads, giving iron ore shippers the necessary flexibility for grading and blending of ores.

More than 150 Iron Range Division men were transferred to the Missabe Division, and over 100 former employees were hired by Reserve Mining Company. The former locomotive repair shop at Two Harbors was taken over by Universal Fiberglass Corporation which for a time provided jobs to furloughed employees. The idle car repair shop was acquired by Abex Corporation and converted into a foundry to produce castings for the local taconite industry.

Two Harbors' docks were not re-opened until the 1966 shipping season. With deep water close at hand, and with the coming of bigger ore-carrying vessels, Two Harbors may in the future have advantages not previously apparent.

Lake ore carriers have increased in size over the years, the larger vessels of the older class eventually attaining a length of 730 feet, a breadth of 75 feet, and cargo capacity of about 25,000 tons. This seemed to be about the maximum practical size.

However, completion in 1968 of the new Poe Lock at the Soo permits the handling of vessels up to 1,000 feet long and 105 feet wide. The United States Steel Corporation and Bethlehem Steel Corporation both have super-carriers under construction. The United States Steel vessel, the *Roger Blough*, will have an overall length of 805 feet, a beam of 105 feet, and a pellet cargo capacity of 45,000 tons. Bethlehem's new vessel, the *Stewart Cort*, will be 1,000 feet in length, with a beam of 105 feet, and have a cargo capability of 52,000 tons. Both vessels will be self-unloaders, making them independent of land-based unloading systems at ports on the lower lakes.

The new super-carriers are expected to lengthen the traditional iron ore shipping season, and ten or eleven month operations are considered within reach. The federal government is making a study of means to extend the length of the shipping season, with the ultimate aim of year around shipping on the entire Seaway system. The length of the 1970 shipping season turned out to be a record breaker. The last vessel, the *Philip R. Clarke*, was dispatched from Two Harbors on January 27, 1971.

President Smith retired on January 31, 1964, ending a railroad career that he began as a messenger boy on the Baltimore and Ohio Railroad at the age of 15. On February 1, 1964, Fred W. Okie became president of the Missabe. Okie's induction into railroad service was with the Southern Rail-

Great Lakes ore boats have increased in size over the years. The United States Steel vessel, the *Roger Blough*, will have a pellet cargo capacity of 45,000 tons. — U.S. STEEL

Fred W. Okie, who began his railroad career on the Southern Railway in 1930, is the Missabe Road's current president, having been elected to that post February 1, 1964. He became the 17th president to head the Missabe and its predecessor companies.

Donald B. Shank, who joined the DM&IR in 1940 as a locomotive fireman, worked his way up through the ranks, holding numerous official positions in the Equipment and Transportation Departments. He was named vice president and general manager in 1964 and is the Duluth executive in charge of local operations.

way shortly after his graduation from Virginia Military Institute in 1929. Advancing through various assignments on the Southern, interrupted by three years of military service in the African and European theaters during World War II where he attained the rank of colonel, he was promoted to general manager, western lines, in March of 1946. In August of that year he left the Southern to become president of the Union Railroad at Pittsburgh, and three years later was also elected president of the Bessemer and Lake Erie Railroad. One month before becoming president of the Missabe, Okie took on the additional responsibilities of president of the Elgin, Joliet and Eastern Railway.

Donald B. Shank, who began railroading as a locomotive fireman on the DM&IR in 1940, is the local Duluth executive in charge of Missabe Road operations. Shank served in the European theater during World War II, attaining the rank of captain. Following his return to railroad service in 1947, he worked as locomotive engineer and held various positions in the motive power department before being appointed assistant superintendent of

motive power and cars. He subsequently moved to the transportation department as assistant superintendent, was promoted to superintendent in 1955, and two years later became general superintendent. In June of 1959 Shank was appointed general manager, and on February 4, 1964, he was elected to his present position of vice president and general manager.

Under the guidance of President Okie, the Missabe Road has successfully emerged from the period when its future was clouded with uncertainty. Instrumental in effecting the turn-around were Vice President and General Manager Shank and the loyal employees of the Missabe, with great assistance from the innovative ideas of Glenn A. Squibb, who served as vice president of marketing during the critical years. With the development of new techniques for utilization of taconite, and with the construction of huge plants for turning Minnesota's abundant resources of this ore into high-grade iron ore pellets, the people of the Missabe are looking forward with confidence to the vital role their railroad will play in the new Taconite Era.

Late afternoon shadows cast by ore cars create an interesting pattern in this 1971 Proctor Yard scene. A considerable number of track changes have recently been made in the yard to better adapt its function to present-day and anticipated future requirements. On the extreme left can be seen the ore car repair shop while on the extreme upper right is the diesel locomotive repair facility and roundhouse. A unit train, carrying taconite pellets, can be seen on the next to the outside track on the left side of the yard. — EARL E. JOHNSON, DULUTH HERALD AND NEWS-TRIBUNE

12

BEGINNING
OF THE
TACONITE ERA

THE possibility of exhaustion of the road's primary source of traffic, the soft, high-quality ore of the Mesabi Range, became of increasing concern to Missabe people after the traffic peak of 1953. The demands of two world wars had materially depleted the reserves of natural ores, and iron mining technology was changing rapidly. It was a time of gloom on the Range because its future was by no means assured, and the continued high volume of iron ore production seemed only to be hastening the day when the good ore would be gone. Not that the high-grade soft ore was completely exhausted, but it was becoming localized or limited, and there was no expectation of finding more. Added to this was the discovery of new sources of iron ore in other places throughout the world. Pit after pit closed down on the Mesabi because the ores could no longer compete, and reserves that had formerly been considered valuable were being written off as unmineable under the changed circumstances.

Development of Minnesota's vast reserves of taconite had been hampered by the lack of a practical method of crushing the hard taconite and recovering the pure ore. The development of a technique for processing taconite is a long and interesting story that need be covered here but

briefly. It began in the Mines Experimental Station of the University of Minnesota as far back as 1913, with countless experiments being conducted in crushing, screening and washing the taconite in an effort to isolate the pure ore by mechanical, chemical and electrical means.

Between 1915 and 1920, further experimentation was done by a Duluth group headed by Daniel C. Jackling, of Utah copper mining fame, and Dr. Edward W. Davis of the Mines Experimental Station. They felt ready to try commercial production in 1919, and formed the Mesabi Iron Company to construct a plant near Babbitt at the eastern end of the Range. The site was served by the D&IR. The plant commenced operations on June 21, 1922, producing an irregularly shaped sintered product at the rate of about 350 to 400 tons a day. While it was a fairly good product, it was not sufficiently superior to the high-grade, low-cost ore of the Mesabi Range to command the premium price necessary to sustain the operation and, as a consequence, the Mesabi Iron Company ceased operations in May 1924 and commercial exploitation of taconite languished for almost 20 years. Meanwhile, laboratory work continued, resulting in improved techniques that permitted commercial operations to be resumed on a profit-

The 1960's saw mine after mine close down. Usually the first to go were the high cost underground operations. Typical was the Godfrey Mine near Chisholm, which made its last shipment in 1962. (BELOW) Even the big open pits, in spite of beneficiation of their product, were finding it hard to compete with higher grade ores from other sources.
— BOTH DM&IR COLLECTION

able basis when the time came.

When the soft ore was giving out, owners of the deposits were considering the advisability of spending hundreds of millions of dollars on new taconite extracting facilities. Many people felt it was necessary to have some assurance that discriminatory taxes would not be placed on such plants in the future if the expenditures were to be induced. A block to giving assurances in respect to the future was that one legislature could not bind a future legislature not to change the law; such a restriction on legislative power could be conferred only by an amendment to the State Constitution.

The upshot was that after considerable public discussion and education and great debate, the Minnesota legislature passed laws prohibiting inequitable increases in occupation, royalty and excise taxes on taconite in relation to taxes on manufacturing corporations, and by popular vote a constitutional amendment was adopted on November 3, 1963, prohibiting changes in the relationships for a period of 25 years.

Some years before the Taconite Amendment was finally adopted, a group that had faith in the newly developed processes for handling taconite organized Reserve Mining Company. Reserve went ahead with plans to mine its taconite from the eastern end of the Range near Babbitt, near where Mesabi Iron Company had operated a generation before. The plan involved transporting the crude

One of the many pamphlets used to generate grass roots support for the Taconite Amendment.

184

Mesabi Iron Company's taconite operation at Babbitt came 30 years too soon! This 1922 scene shows a steam shovel loading the hard rock into dump cars for movement to the crusher. The big physical obstacle at the time was drilling through the hard taconite prior to blasting. The conventional diamond drills used wore out within a disappointingly short time. Blast holes are no problem today, as special jet machines are able to pierce the rock swiftly and economically. — J. H. HEARDING JR.

Reserve Mining Company moves over 30 million tons of taconite each year over its 47-mile double-tracked railroad. Shown here are three SD-18's drifting downgrade near Silver Bay with 135 cars, each carrying some 85 long tons of crushed taconite. — FRANK A. KING

Eveleth Taconite Company's Fairlane Pellet Plant near Forbes is an important Missabe Road shipper. Taconite crude ore is mined at the Thunderbird Mine situated near Eveleth, and processed at this plant. — EVELETH TACONITE CO.

The first taconite crude ore from Thunderbird Mine is loaded as train is pulled through the tunnel beneath the surge pile. — DM&IR COLLECTION

ore over its own 47-mile private railroad to Silver Bay, a new port on Lake Superior, where its processing plant would be built. Permission was obtained to use water from Lake Superior and to dump tailings in restricted areas along its shore. The whole complex was built between 1951 and 1955 and started operation the summer of 1955. The first pellets were produced in October of that year, and published statistics indicate that Reserve has a current annual production capacity of approximately ten million tons.

A similar plant owned by Erie Mining Company, with Pickands, Mather & Company as operating agents, went into production near Hoyt Lakes on the eastern end of the Range late in 1957. It uses its own 74-mile private railroad to haul pellets to another new port on Lake Superior, located somewhat north of Silver Bay and called Taconite Harbor. The Erie Mining operation similarly has an annual production capability

of approximately ten million tons, according to trade publications.

Passage of the Taconite Amendment in 1963 was the green light for the construction of additional taconite plants. The next plant was that of Eveleth Taconite Company. Taconite is produced at the Thunderbird Mine, near Eveleth, and processed at its Fairlane plant near Forbes. Both the mine and plant are served by the Missabe Road, and current pellet production is reported to be approaching two million tons annually.

On April 8, 1966, the steamer *Edmund Fitzgerald* of the Oglebay-Norton fleet took on the first cargo of Eveleth pellets, totalling about 23,000 tons, in only one hour and fifteen minutes. Quite appropriately, Oglebay-Norton was the same company that had received the first Mesabi ore shipment, the one made by the Merritt brothers over the DM&N almost three-quarters of a century earlier.

Shipment from Eleveth Taconite's Thunderbird Mine heralded a new era for the Missabe Road. High atop the first load was the traditional pine tree. — DM&IR COLLECTION

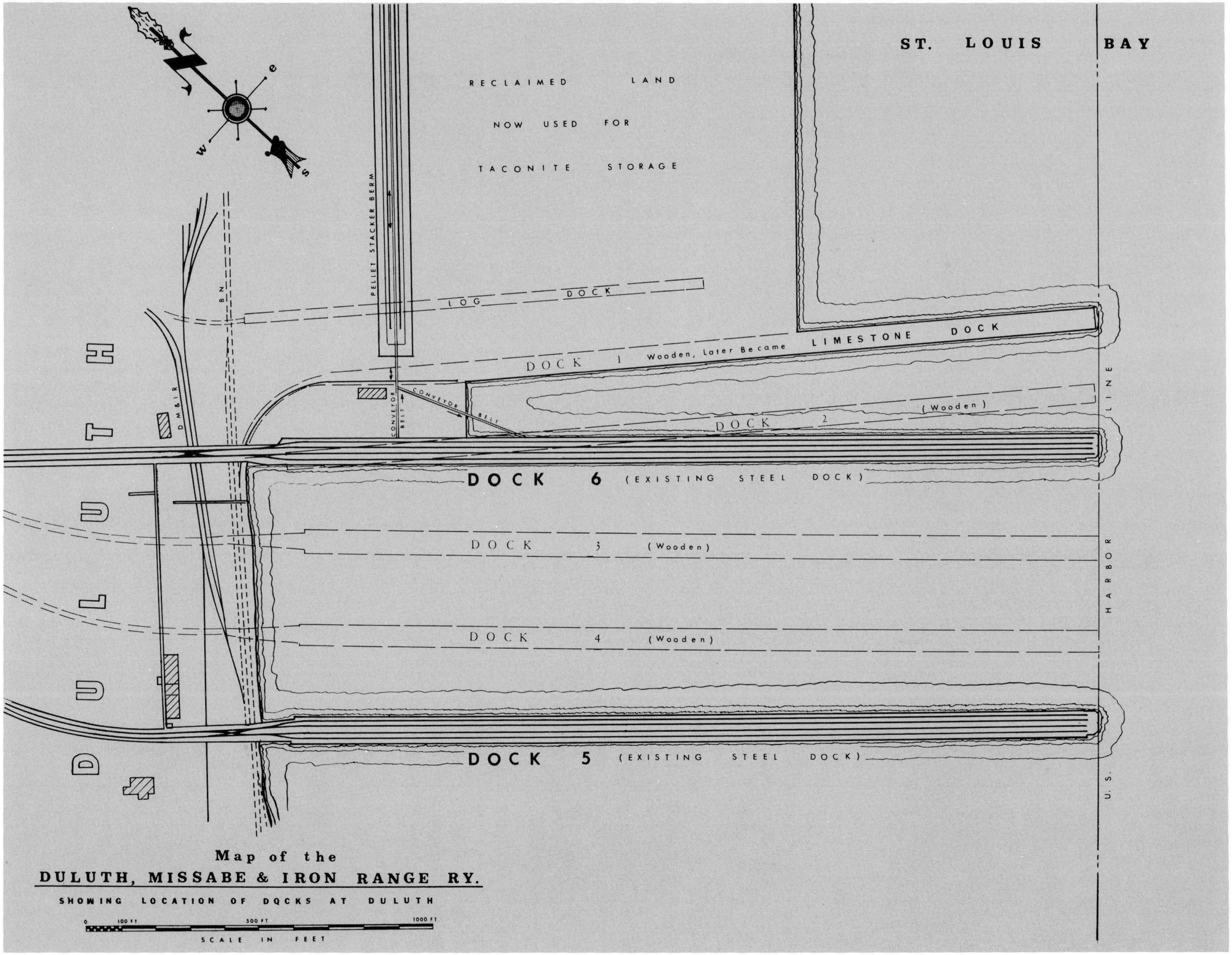
ST. LOUIS BAY
RECLAIMED LAND
NOW USED FOR
TACONITE STORAGE
PELLET STACKER BERM
LOG DOCK
LIMESTONE DOCK
DOCK 1 Wooden, Later Became
DOCK 2 (Wooden)
CONVEYOR BELT
CONVEYOR BELT
DOCK 6 (EXISTING STEEL DOCK)
DOCK 3 (Wooden)
DOCK 4 (Wooden)
DOCK 5 (EXISTING STEEL DOCK)
U.S. HARBOR LINE
B N
D M & I R
D U L U T H
w
e
s
Map of the
DULUTH, MISSABE & IRON RANGE RY.
SHOWING LOCATION OF DOCKS AT DULUTH
0
100 FT
500 FT
1000 FT
SCALE IN FEET

DRAWN BY GLENN W. BURKE

Plans were announced by the Missabe Road in the latter part of 1964 for construction of a facility at Duluth for the winter storage of pellets, and it was completed the following year. It is located adjacent to Dock No. 6 and extends to the site of the old coal dock. Moving pellets by rail in the winter not only avoids the necessity of providing storage facilities at the plants, but also permits year around rail movement, which, in turn, stabilizes employment and uses cars and locomotives more efficiently.

Missabe's Lakehead Taconite Storage Facility at Duluth, which provides winter storage for pellets, has a total capacity of 2.24 million tons. During the winter months, unit trains discharge their loads into 64 specially modified pockets on Dock No. 6 which feed onto a belt conveyor system carrying the pellets to the stockpile area. During the shipping season the process is reversed, the pellets being reclaimed off the ground onto the belt system for movement to the top of the dock and into the dock pockets from which vessels are loaded in the conventional manner. — DM&IR COLLECTION

Pellets are deposited onto the stockpile by a huge rail-mounted stacker. During the shipping season the same machine, in conjunction with a bucket-wheel reclaimer, is used to reclaim the pellets. — DM&IR COLLECTION

An elaborate conveyor system serves the Missabe Road's pellet storage facility. — DM&IR COLLECTION

A new bucket-wheel pellet reclaimer, which was received during 1971, increased storage capacity by 300,000 tons. — EARL E. JOHNSON, DULUTH HERALD & NEWS-TRIBUNE

The huge taconite plant which the United States Steel Corporation built is located at Mountain Iron, only a short distance from the spot where the Merritts discovered and mined the first ore on the Mesabi. It is called "Minntac."

The plant, which was three years in the building, commenced operations on October 25, 1967. Construction now in progress will double its present annual capacity of six million tons, making it the largest facility of its kind. The plant is located on a ridge 1,775 feet above sea level on the Laurentian continental divide and has a large supply of taconite available nearby. The crude ore is blasted out of place and is moved about three miles by a plant-operated rail system to a giant crusher.

United States Steel Corporation's Minntac Pellet Plant at Mountain Iron. Completion of an expansion program in 1972 will make it the largest pellet plant in the United States.
— MINNESOTA ORE OPERATIONS, U.S. STEEL

Taconite processed at the Minntac Plant originates at this mine, which is identified as the West Taconite Pit. An East Pit is currently under development to provide the additional ore that will be required in the near future when Minntac expands its production capacity. (BELOW) Electric shovel loading taconite into 100-ton capacity side-dump cars. All crude ore is handled to the Minntac Plant by rail. — BOTH MINNESOTA ORE OPERATIONS, U.S. STEEL

Giant electric-drive trucks are employed at Minntac to handle overburden. This one is rated at 120 tons. — MINNESOTA ORE OPERATIONS, U.S. STEEL

Rod and ball mills are used to grind hard taconite rock to talcum powder fineness. —GRAND RAPIDS HERALD-REVIEW (BELOW) Locomotive units Nos. 176 and 174 depart Minntac for Proctor with the first train of pellets. — DM&IR COLLECTION

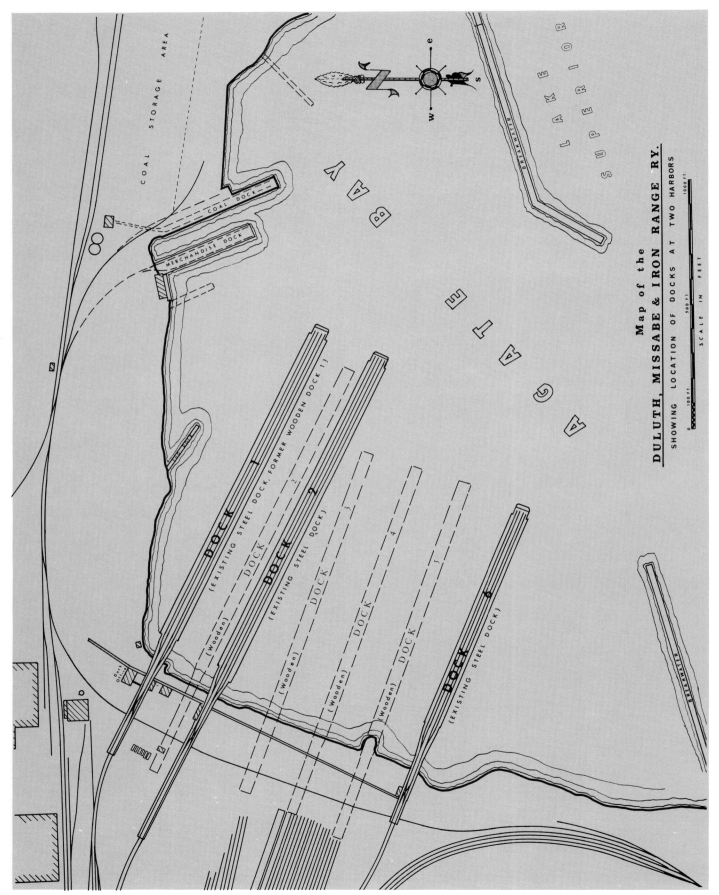

Map of the
DULUTH, MISSABE & IRON RANGE RY.
SHOWING LOCATION OF DOCKS AT TWO HARBORS

SCALE IN FEET

DRAWN BY GLENN W. BURKE

Minntac's pellets are shipped out twice daily in Missabe Road unit trains. By chance, the first car of the initial trainload of pellets that moved from Minntac on October 25, 1967, was loaded one week earlier on exactly the 75th anniversary of the first shipment of Mesabi ore from the original Mountain Iron Mine. Like DM&N wooden car No. 342, this car, which was Missabe high-side car No. 52497, carried the traditional pine tree perched high atop its load.

The effect of the pellet revolution on the Missabe has been profound. Pellet production is uniquely adapted to unit train operation because the shipment originates at one point and travels without intermediate yarding to one destination, which can be either the dock or the stockpile.

Soft ore must be held at yards so cars can move to the dock in proper order to meet vessel cargo requirements. Since pellets are uniform to start with, holding in cars or stopping trains at Proctor for the mixing of vessel cargo is normally not required.

Unless unduly wet, pellets do not freeze together at low temperatures, and tend to run easily at all times. With the thawing problem largely eliminated, both production and movement can be and now are year around; the Missabe is no longer an eight-month ore carrier with operations limited by inability to mine and transport iron ore in winter. Pellets can be stockpiled in the winter and removed during the shipping season at will.

That pellets handle better than natural ore on belts raises interesting possibilities. This characteristic has already dictated that the new docks of Reserve Mining Company at Silver Bay and Erie Mining Company at Taconite Harbor be at land-

Steam was used to thaw cars of frozen natural ore during the steam locomotive era. With pellets, the freezing problem is largely eliminated. — CHARLES STEINHEIMER (BELOW) Laborer inserts a steam lance into a car of frozen ore. — DM&IR COLLECTION

A 36-car capacity, gas-fired, infrared ore thawing plant was constructed at Two Harbors in 1960. With steam locomotives no longer available to thaw frozen ore, this modern alternative became necessary. — FRANK A. KING

side, and not jut into the water as previous ore docks have done. Docks no longer have to be built for storage as well as loading. The storage can be on land, and belts can accomplish the loading in a short time. While the Missabe's present docks handle pellets very well, any new docks that may be required will likely be of a different type.

Natural ore will continue to move on the Missabe for some time to come. The competition of the taconite pellet is being met to some extent by mixing and sintering natural ores en route or near to points of consumption.

The iron ore pellet produced from low-grade ore is here to stay, even though its reign may not be absolute. Clearly, there is now no shortage of iron ore in the United States nor, apparently, any shortage of human ingenuity to overcome what was once thought to be a shortage.

The Missabe Road intends to stay in business and remain competitive in the transportation of natural ore and taconite pellets, which constitute its life blood. Additionally, it is vitally interested in attracting new business to the region it serves and thereby broadening its traffic mix. It will continue to explore its role as a transportation agency and will employ any new concept or mode that proves to be feasible and has economic justification.

No account of the Missabe Road would be complete without referring to the influence of Lake Superior, the great lake to which the railroad carries most of its freight. More like a fresh-water ocean than a lake, with a bottom well below sea level and a constant lower level temperature of 36 degrees, Lake Superior both controls the area's climate and creates its moods.

Most railroads either deliver their loaded cars to industries on their rails or pass them on to other railroads for delivery, but the Missabe drops its carloads of iron ore into deep pockets in a special kind of dock for release into boats that on clear days can be seen coming out of or disappearing into the far eastern horizon. The closing of the navigation season in early winter is not apt to be abrupt, but the opening of the season in the spring, signaled by the arrival of the first boat from down below, is a notable event. When it comes, activity quickens on both the railroad and in the port communities.

Lake Superior is always there, reflecting on its surface the sunlight of summer and the dark clouds of winter, though deep down it never changes.

As for the Missabe Road, it carries on, and hopefully on and on, as long as men make steel out of iron ore.

ORE TONNAGE HAULED TO DOCKS AND ALL-RAIL

Year	MISSABE DIVISION		IRON RANGE DIVISION		TOTAL		GRAND TOTAL
	All-Rail	Docks	All-Rail	Docks	All-Rail*	Docks	
1884	--	--	--	62,122	--	62,122	62,122
1885	--	--	--	227,075	--	227,075	227,075
1886	--	--	--	307,949	--	307,949	307,949
1887	--	--	--	394,911	--	394,911	394,911
1888	--	--	56,543	452,111	56,543	452,111	508,654
1889	--	--	11,304	825,786	11,304	825,786	837,090
1890	--	--	1,107	879,125	1,107	879,125	880,532
1891	--	--	2,644	893,703	2,644	893,703	896,347
1892	4,245	--	1,915	1,166,016	6,160	1,166,016	1,172,176
1893	80,763	436,938	18,285	900,167	99,048	1,337,105	1,436,153
1894	--	1,365,296	137	1,382,008	137	2,747,304	2,747,441
1895	--	1,596,993	3,071	2,130,636	3,071	3,727,629	3,730,700
1896	--	1,994,868	--	1,814,187	--	3,809,055	3,809,055
1897	--	2,374,499	--	2,651,275	--	5,025,774	5,025,774
1898	--	2,626,403	25	2,694,969	25	5,321,372	5,321,397
1899	10,875	3,509,944	13,221	3,972,010	24,096	7,481,954	7,506,050
1900	14,434	3,888,941	28,804	4,014,375	43,238	7,903,316	7,946,554
1901	--	3,437,158	20,186	5,008,578	20,186	8,445,736	8,465,922
1902	--	5,610,407	17,995	5,604,768	17,995	11,215,175	11,233,170
1903	--	5,344,635	1,024	5,124,317	1,024	10,468,952	10,469,976
1904	1,168	4,649,604	498	4,562,903	1,666	9,212,507	9,214,173
1905	1,419	8,821,673	78	7,781,687	1,497	16,603,360	16,604,857
1906	--	11,206,719	26,945	8,178,048	26,945	19,384,767	19,411,712
1907	390	13,445,219	19,684	8,188,904	20,074	21,634,123	21,654,197
1908	385	8,808,167	17,788	5,702,691	18,173	14,510,858	14,529,031
1909	--	13,470,641	11,449	9,180,677	11,449	22,651,318	22,662,767
1910	627	13,609,017	17,851	8,271,167	18,478	21,880,184	21,898,662
1911	--	6,940,743	28,454	6,389,067	28,454	13,329,810	13,358,264
1912	--	10,491,298	34,979	9,349,435	34,979	19,840,733	19,875,712
1913	7,848	12,328,930	36,035	10,075,879	43,883	22,404,809	22,448,692
1914	--	6,319,523	27,038	5,610,137	27,038	11,929,660	11,956,698
1915	52,905	15,436,186	80,768	8,642,942	133,673	24,079,128	24,212,801
1916	602,519	21,838,056	158,497	10,735,853	761,016	32,573,909	33,334,925
1917	682,908	20,567,212	118,255	9,993,923	801,163	30,561,135	31,362,298
1918	520,122	20,569,958	80,123	8,723,944	600,245	29,293,902	29,894,147
1919	512,406	16,819,068	100,136	6,423,848	612,542	23,242,916	23,855,458
1920	768,537	15,478,805	59,881	9,278,463	828,418	24,757,268	25,585,686
1921	468,252	9,165,067	1,312	3,286,338	469,564	12,451,405	12,920,969
1922	453,851	13,044,507	66,219	5,961,141	520,070	19,005,648	19,525,718
1923	784,837	20,163,619	137,435	6,409,762	922,272	26,573,381	27,495,653
1924	395,244	12,882,082	44,542	4,817,494	439,786	17,699,576	18,139,362
1925	108,254	17,707,978	296,006	6,016,200	404,260	23,724,178	24,128,438
1926	75,362	18,638,395	376,010	6,266,548	451,372	24,904,943	25,356,315
1927	141,964	15,432,188	492,573	5,703,919	634,537	21,136,107	21,770,644
1928	100,582	17,454,063	434,712	5,732,741	535,294	23,186,804	23,722,098
1929	341,375	20,562,705	298,594	6,601,736	639,969	27,164,441	27,804,410
1930	268,492	14,001,327	53,972	6,308,245	322,464	20,309,572	20,632,036
1931	2,681	7,267,023	--	3,324,973	2,681	10,591,996	10,594,677
1932	--	1,047,997	--	410,714	--	1,458,711	1,458,711
1933	52,502	5,839,523	--	3,277,941	52,502	9,117,464	9,169,966
1934	95,999	6,015,630	--	3,199,696	95,999	9,215,326	9,311,325
1935	158,926	6,995,980	5,770	3,234,171	164,696	10,230,151	10,394,847
1936	228,483	11,738,528	34,748	5,546,040	263,231	17,284,568	17,547,799
1937	659,275	16,721,205	40,484	9,743,476	699,759	26,464,681	27,764,490
1938	484,816	3,920,961	26,841	3,833,114	511,657	7,754,075	8,265,732
1939	690,518	9,081,476	54,271	8,663,503	744,789	17,744,979	18,489,768
1940	896,203	16,267,848	136,390	10,705,000	1,032,593	26,972,848	28,005,441

NOTE: * All-Rail denotes tonnage delivered to connecting railroads and local industry. Tonnages represent long tons of 2.240 lbs. each.

Year	MISSABE DIVISION		IRON RANGE DIVISION		TOTAL		GRAND TOTAL
	All-Rail	Docks	All-Rail	Docks	All-Rail*	Docks	
1941	1,856,150	20,498,778	81,507	15,011,066	1,937,657	35,509,844	37,447,501
1942	1,794,792	23,968,309	212,770	18,812,328	2,007,562	42,780,637	44,788,199
1943	2,041,695	21,373,773	126,906	19,275,591	2,168,601	40,649,364	42,817,965
1944	1,707,208	20,332,214	95,016	19,331,761	1,802,224	39,663,975	41,466,199
1945	2,309,061	20,036,365	83,181	17,625,890	2,392,242	37,662,255	40,054,497
1946	3,018,988	15,695,758	65,091	13,925,588	3,084,079	29,621,346	32,705,425
1947	2,504,470	19,364,852	77,428	16,964,098	2,581,898	36,328,950	38,910,848
1948	3,223,677	19,166,644	80,007	18,747,287	3,303,684	37,863,931	41,167,615
1949	2,971,448	15,751,829	74,804	14,763,497	3,046,252	30,515,326	33,561,578
1950	4,110,960	18,768,161	131,378	17,089,983	4,242,338	35,858,144	46,100,482
1951	7,176,987	21,600,540	291,730	19,730,558	7,468,717	41,331,098	48,799,815
1952	5,143,340	16,495,624	306,012	15,626,220	5,449,352	32,121,844	37,571,196
1953	5,053,930	22,928,898	211,950	21,122,847	5,265,880	44,051,745	49,317,625
1954	2,927,544	12,728,854	44,374	12,864,988	2,971,918	25,593,842	28,565,760
1955	4,724,404	17,394,459	33,074	17,150,987	4,757,478	34,545,446	39,302,924
1956	5,078,492	12,787,902	132,327	14,367,742	5,210,819	27,155,644	32,366,463
1957	3,786,087	17,430,495	41,516	17,143,168	3,827,603	34,573,663	38,401,266
1958	3,230,951	7,679,969	22,074	10,636,004	3,253,025	18,315,973	21,568,998
1959	3,189,812	7,333,896	4,106	8,262,737	3,193,918	15,596,633	18,790,551
1960	3,273,421	10,879,453	49,825	14,785,457	3,323,246	24,664,910	27,988,156
1961	3,715,566	4,208,287	13,423	10,481,676	3,728,989	14,689,963	18,418,952
1962	3,061,315	3,781,242	43,735	11,771,209	3,105,050	15,552,451	18,651,501
1963	3,371,909	13,293,142	--	--	3,371,909	13,293,142	16,665,051
1964	3,824,175	14,678,455	--		3,824,175	14,678,455	18,502,630
1965	3,768,465	15,764,680	--		3,768,465	15,764,680	19,533,145
1966	3,964,058	15,822,344	--	2,793,813	3,964,058	18,616,157	22,580,215
1967	3,012,172	14,098,255	--	2,352,818	3,012,172	16,451,073	19,463,245
1968	3,737,222	14,229,187	--	2,565,876	3,737,222	16,795,063	20,532,285
1969	3,073,500	15,838,402	--	4,801,767	3,073,500	20,640,169	23,713,669
1970	2,055,591	16,505,458	--	4,813,377	2,055,591	21,318,835	23,374,426
1971	2,158,560	14,222,073	--	4,405,363	2,158,560	18,627,436	20,785,996
Totals	114,535,117	981,543,301	5,716,833	652,862,104	120,251,950	1,634,405,405	1,754,657,355

NOTE: * All-Rail denotes tonnage delivered to connecting railroads and local industry. Tonnages represent long tons of 2,240 lbs. each.

STEAM LOCOMOTIVES

DULUTH & IRON RANGE RAIL ROAD

Orig. No.	2nd No.	3rd No.	Type	Class	Builder and Construction No.		Date Built	Dimensions Dr.–Cyls.–Wt.	Tractive Effort	Date Retired	Final Disposition and Remarks
1			4-4-0	A	Baldwin	7258	1884	63-17x24- 83,900	13,600	1911	Deer Park R.R. 2
2			4-4-0	A	Baldwin	7259	1884	63-17x24- 83,900	13,600	1911	
3			2-6-0		Baldwin	6649	1883	52-16x24- 75,000	15,075	1899	On exhibit at Two Harbors
4			0-4-0	B	Baldwin	7252	1884	51-16x24- 69,000	14,300	1912	Section 30 Mining Co.
5			0-4-0	B	Baldwin	7358	1884	51-16x24- 69,000	14,300		
6	36	136	2-8-0	G	Baldwin	6874	1883	51-20x24-110,000	24,000	1933	Sold for Scrap
7	37	137	2-8-0	G	Baldwin	6937	1883	51-20x24-110,000	24,000	1933	Sold for Scrap
8	38	138	2-8-0	G	Baldwin	7347	1883	51-20x24-110,000	24,000	1933	Sold for Scrap
9	39		2-8-0	G	Baldwin	7354	1884	51-20x24-110,000	24,000	1916	Sold for Scrap
10	40		2-8-0	G	Baldwin	7374	1884	51-20x24-110,000	24,000	1916	Sold for Scrap
11	41	141	2-8-0	G	Baldwin	7381	1884	51-20x24-110,000	24,000	1939	Sold for Scrap
12	42	142	2-8-0	G	Baldwin	7921	1886	51-20x24-110,000	24,000	1933	Sold for Scrap
13			0-4-0	B	Baldwin	7964	1886	51-16x24- 69,000	14,300	1912	P. Meagher
14			0-4-0	B	Baldwin	8646	1887	51-16x24- 69,000	14,300	1914	P. Meagher
15			0-4-0	B	Baldwin	8647	1887	51-16x24- 69,000	14,300	1899	Loraine Steel Co.
16	43	143	2-8-0	G	Baldwin	8633	1887	51-20x24-110,000	24,000	1933	Sold for Scrap
17	44	144	2-8-0	G	Baldwin	8634	1887	51-20x24-110,000	24,000	1933	Sold for Scrap
18	45	145	2-8-0	G	Baldwin	9261	1888	51-20x24-110,000	24,000	1933	Sold for Scrap
19	46	146	2-8-0	G	Baldwin	9257	1888	51-20x24-110,000	24,000	1933	Sold for Scrap
20	47	147	2-8-0	G	Baldwin	9265	1888	51-20x24-110,000	24,000	1933	Sold for Scrap
21	48	148	2-8-0	G	Baldwin	9266	1888	51-20x24-110,000	24,000	1933	Sold for Scrap
22	49	149	2-8-0	G	Baldwin	9273	1888	51-20x24-110,000	24,000	1933	Sold for Scrap
23			4-4-0	C	Baldwin	9272	1888	63-18x24- 96,600	15,700	1920	Sold for Scrap
24			4-4-0	C	Baldwin	9277	1888	63-18x24- 96,600	15,700	1916	Sold for Scrap
25			4-4-0	C	Baldwin	9278	1888	63-18x24- 96,600	15,700	1916	J. H. Kaiser Lbr. Co.
	DM&IR No.										
26			0-4-0	B	Baldwin	9274	1888	51-16x24- 69,000	14,300	1899	Loraine Steel Co.
27	127		0-6-0	D	Schenectady	2838	1889	51-18x24- 94,400	20,090	1940	Sold for Scrap
28			2-8-0		Schenectady	2832	1889	51-20x24-120,400	24,480	1892	Chicago & Eastern Illinois 111-810
29			2-8-0		Schenectady	2833	1889	51-20x24-120,400	24,480	1892	Chicago & Eastern Illinois 112-811
30			2-8-0		Schenectady	2834	1889	51-20x24-120,400	24,480	1892	Chicago & Eastern Illinois 113-812
31			2-8-0		Schenectady	2835	1889	51-20x24-120,400	24,480	1892	Chicago & Eastern Illinois 114-813
32			2-8-0		Schenectady	2836	1889	51-20x24-120,400	24,480	1892	Chicago & Eastern Illinois 115-814
33			2-8-0		Schenectady	2837	1889	51-20x24-120,400	24,480	1892	Chicago & Eastern Illinois 116-815
28			0-6-0	F	Baldwin	27728	1906	51-20x26-150,000	33,000	1927	
29			0-6-0	F	Baldwin	27729	1906	51-20x26-150,000	33,000	1928	
30			0-6-0	F	Baldwin	27744	1906	51-20x26-150,000	33,000	1928	
31			0-6-0	F	Baldwin	27761	1906	51-20x26-150,000	33,000	1928	
50	150		2-8-0	H	Schenectady	3738	1892	51-20x24-117,000	24,600	1933	Sold for Scrap
51	151		2-8-0	H	Schenectady	3739	1892	51-20x24-117,000	24,600	1938	Sold for Scrap
52	152		2-8-0	H	Schenectady	3740	1892	51-20x24-117,000	24,600	1936	Sold for Scrap
53	153		2-8-0	H	Schenectady	3741	1892	51-20x24-117,000	24,600	1933	Sold for Scrap
54	154		2-8-0	H	Schenectady	3742	1892	51-20x24-117,000	24,600	1934	Sold for Scrap
55	155		2-8-0	H	Schenectady	3743	1892	51-20x24-117,000	24,600	1938	Sold for Scrap
56			2-8-0	H	Schenectady	3744	1892	51-20x24-117,000	24,600	1899	El Paso & Northeastern 51
57	157		2-8-0	H	Schenectady	3745	1892	51-20x24-117,000	24,600	1933	Sold for Scrap
58	158		2-8-0	H	Schenectady	3805	1892	51-20x24-117,000	24,600	1933	Sold for Scrap
59	159		2-8-0	H	Schenectady	3806	1892	51-20x24-117,000	24,600	1933	Sold for Scrap
60			4-8-0	J	Schenectady	4041	1893	54-22x26-174,800	37,600	1928	Sold for Scrap
61			4-8-0	J	Schenectady	4042	1893	54-22x26-174,800	37,600	1927	
62			4-8-0	J	Schenectady	4043	1893	54-22x26-174,800	37,600	1928	Sold for Scrap
63			4-8-0	J	Schenectady	4044	1893	54-22x26-174,800	37,600	1928	Sold for Scrap
64			4-8-0	J	Schenectady	4045	1893	54-22x26-174,800	37,600	1928	Sold for Scrap
65			4-8-0	J	Schenectady	4046	1893	54-22x26-174,800	37,600	1927	
66			4-8-0	J	Schenectady	4047	1893	54-22x26-174,800	37,600	1927	
67			4-8-0	J	Schenectady	4048	1893	54-22x26-174,800	37,600	1928	Sold for Scrap
68			4-8-0	J	Schenectady	4049	1893	54-22x26-174,800	37,600	1927	
69			4-8-0	J	Schenectady	4145	1893	54-22x26-174,800	37,600	1928	Sold for Scrap
70			4-8-0	J	Schenectady	4327	1895	54-22x26-176,400	37,600	1929	Sold for Scrap

NOTE: Dimensions and weights shown for locomotives as originally built.

Orig. No.	2nd No.	Type & Class		Builder and Construction No.		Date Built	Dimensions Dr.—Cyls.—Wt.	Tractive Effort	Date Retired	Final Disposition and Remarks
71	171	4-8-0	J	Schenectady	4328	1895	54-22x26-176,400	37,600	1933	Sold for Scrap
72		4-8-0	J	Schenectady	4329	1895	54-22x26-176,400	37,600	1929	Sold for Scrap
73		4-8-0	J	Schenectady	4330	1895	54-22x26-176,400	37,600	1927	
74		4-8-0	J	Baldwin	14717	1896	54-22x26-176,200	37,600	1923	Illinois Steel Co.
75		4-8-0	J	Baldwin	14718	1896	54-22x26-176,200	37,600	1929	Sold for Scrap
76	176	4-8-0	J	Baldwin	14719	1896	54-22x26-176,200	37,600	1933	Sold for Scrap
77		4-8-0	J	Baldwin	14720	1896	54-22x26-176,200	37,600	1929	Sold for Scrap
78		4-8-0	J	Baldwin	14721	1896	54-22x26-176,200	37,600	1929	Sold for Scrap
79		4-8-0	J	Baldwin	14722	1896	54-22x26-176,200	37,600	1923	Illinois Steel Co.
80	180	4-8-0	J	Baldwin	16747	1899	54-22x26-180,000	37,600	1933	Sold for Scrap
81	181	4-8-0	J	Baldwin	16748	1899	54-22x26-180,000	37,600	1933	Sold for Scrap
82		4-8-0	J	Baldwin	16749	1899	54-22x26-180,000	37,600	1933	Sold for Scrap
83		4-8-0	J	Baldwin	16750	1899	54-22x26-180,000	37,600	1926	Sold for Scrap
84		4-8-0	J	Schenectady	5412	1900	54-22x26-182,600	37,600	1933	Sold for Scrap
85		4-8-0	J	Schenectady	5413	1900	54-22x26-182,600	37,600	1933	Sold for Scrap
86		4-8-0	J	Schenectady	5414	1900	54-22x26-182,600	37,600	1933	Sold for Scrap
87		4-8-0	J	Schenectady	5415	1900	54-22x26-182,600	37,600	1933	Sold for Scrap
88		4-8-0	J	Schenectady	5416	1900	54-22x26-182,600	37,600	1933	Sold for Scrap
89	DM&IR No.	4-8-0	J	Schenectady	5417	1900	54-22x26-182,600	37,600	1933	Sold for Scrap
90	190	2-8-0	K	Baldwin	25465	1905	54-22x28-193,400	42,553	1961	Renumbered 199—Sold for Scrap
91	191	2-8-0	K	Baldwin	25466	1905	54-22x28-193,400	42,553	1957	Sold for Scrap
92	192	2-8-0	K	Baldwin	25467	1905	54-22x28-193,400	42,553	1958	Sold for Scrap
93	193	2-8-0	K	Baldwin	25509	1905	54-22x28-193,400	42,553	1958	Sold for Scrap
94	194	2-8-0	K	Baldwin	25783	1905	54-22x28-193,400	42,553	1956	Sold for Scrap
95	195	2-8-0	K	Baldwin	25805	1905	54-22x28-193,400	42,553	1958	Sold for Scrap
96	196	2-8-0	K	Baldwin	25873	1905	54-22x28-193,400	42,553	1957	Sold for Scrap
97	197	2-8-0	K	Baldwin	25874	1905	54-22x28-193,400	42,553	1958	Sold for Scrap
98	198	2-8-0	K	Baldwin	25885	1905	54-22x28-193,400	42,553	1961	Sold for Scrap
99	2nd No.	4-4-0		Hinkley		1871	54-16x24-			Ex Chicago & Eastern Illinois 12
101	1101	4-6-0	M	Schenectady	5408	1900	58-19x26-150,800	26,125	1933	Sold for Scrap
102		4-6-0	M	Schenectady	5409	1900	58-19x26-150,800	26,125	1929	Sold for Scrap
103	1103	4-6-0	M	Schenectady	5410	1900	58-19x26-150,800	26,125	1933	Sold for Scrap
104		4-6-0	M	Schenectady	5411	1900	58-19x26-150,800	26,125	1929	Sold for Scrap
105	1105	4-6-0	M	Schenectady	5433	1900	58-19x26-150,800	26,125	1933	Sold for Scrap
106	DM&IR No.	4-6-0	M	Schenectady	5434	1900	58-19x26-150,800	26,125	1929	Sold for Scrap
107	1107	4-6-2	A	Baldwin	39861	1913	69-22x28-219,000	33,400	1955	Sold for Scrap
108	1108	4-6-2	A	Baldwin	39862	1913	69-22x28-219,000	33,400	1953	Sold for Scrap
109	1109	4-6-2	A	Baldwin	39863	1913	69-22x28-219,000	33,400	1953	Sold for Scrap
110	1110	4-6-2	A	Baldwin	39864	1913	69-22x28-219,000	33,400	1954	Sold for Scrap
200	1200	2-8-0	K	Baldwin	27722	1906	54-22x28-196,050	42,553	1956	Sold for Scrap
201	1201	2-8-0	K	Baldwin	27738	1906	54-22x28-196,050	42,553	1958	Sold for Scrap
202	1202	2-8-0	K	Baldwin	27739	1906	54-22x28-196,050	42,553	1958	Sold for Scrap
203	1203	2-8-0	K	Baldwin	27740	1906	54-22x28-196,050	42,553	1955	Sold for Scrap
204	1204	2-8-0	K	Baldwin	27755	1906	54-22x28-196,050	42,553	1959	Sold for Scrap
205	1205	2-8-0	K	Baldwin	27773	1906	54-22x28-196,050	42,553	1956	Sold for Scrap
206	1206	2-8-0	K	Baldwin	30311	1906	54-22x28-196,050	42,553	1954	Sold for Scrap
207	1207	2-8-0	K	Baldwin	30322	1906	54-22x28-196,050	42,553	1956	Sold for Scrap
208	1208	2-8-0	K	Baldwin	30323	1906	54-22x28-196,050	42,553	1958	Sold for Scrap
209	1209	2-8-0	K	Baldwin	33308	1909	54-22x28-198,850	42,553	1956	Sold for Scrap
210	1210	2-8-0	K	Baldwin	33309	1909	54-22x28-198,850	42,553	1950	Sold for Scrap
211	1211	2-8-0	K	Baldwin	33310	1909	54-22x28-198,850	42,553	1954	Sold for Scrap
212	1212	2-8-0	K	Baldwin	33311	1909	54-22x28-198,850	42,553	1959	Sold for Scrap
213	1213	2-8-0	K	Baldwin	34740	1910	54-22x28-198,850	42,553	1958	Sold for Scrap
214	1214	2-8-0	K	Baldwin	34741	1910	54-22x28-198,850	42,553	1958	Sold for Scrap
215	1215	2-8-0	K	Baldwin	34742	1910	54-22x28-198,850	42,553	1959	Sold for Scrap
216	1216	2-8-0	K	Baldwin	34743	1910	54-22x28-198,850	42,553	1957	Sold for Scrap
217	1217	2-8-0	K	Baldwin	34744	1910	54-22x28-198,850	42,553	1958	Sold for Scrap
218	1218	2-8-0	K	Baldwin	34745	1910	54-22x28-198,850	42,553	1962	Donated to Tower, Minnesota
219	1219	2-8-0	K	Baldwin	34813	1910	54-22x28-198,850	42,553	1958	Sold for Scrap
220	1220	2-8-0	K	Baldwin	34814	1910	54-22x28-198,850	42,553	1957	Sold for Scrap
221	1221	2-8-0	K	Baldwin	34841	1910	54-22x28-198,850	42,553	1959	Sold for Scrap
222	1222	2-8-0	K	Baldwin	34842	1910	54-22x28-198,850	42,553	1956	Sold for Scrap
223	1223	2-8-0	K	Baldwin	34843	1910	54-22x28-198,850	42,553	1959	Sold for Scrap
224	1224	2-8-0	K	Baldwin	34844	1910	54-22x28-198,850	42,553	1959	Sold for Scrap

Orig. No.	DM&IR No.	Type & Class		Builder and Construction No.		Date Built	Dimensions Dr.–Cyls.–Wt.	Tractive Effort	Date Retired	Final Disposition and Remarks
300	1300	2-8-2	N	Baldwin	39671	1913	58-27x30-287,600	59,250	1958	Sold for Scrap
301	1301	2-8-2	N	Baldwin	39672	1913	58-27x30-287,600	59,250	1962	Sold for Scrap
302	1302	2-8-2	N	Baldwin	39916	1913	58-27x30-287,600	59,250	1962	Sold for Scrap
303	1303	2-8-2	N	Baldwin	39917	1913	58-27x30-287,600	59,250	1959	Sold for Scrap
304	1304	2-8-2	N	Lima	1311	1913	58-27x30-287,600	59,250	1961	Sold for Scrap
305	1305	2-8-2	N	Lima	1312	1913	58-27x30-287,600	59,250	1959	Sold for Scrap
306	1306	2-8-2	N1	Baldwin	43303	1916	58-27x30-294,000	59,250	1958	Sold for Scrap
307	1307	2-8-2	N1	Baldwin	43304	1916	58-27x30-294,000	59,250	1959	Sold for Scrap
308	1308	2-8-2	N1	Baldwin	43305	1916	58-27x30-294,000	59,250	1958	Sold for Scrap
309	1309	2-8-2	N2	Baldwin	56507	1923	58-27x30-321,400	59,250	1959	Sold for Scrap
310	1310	2-8-2	N2	Baldwin	56508	1923	58-27x30-321,400	59,250	1959	Sold for Scrap
311	1311	2-8-2	N2	Baldwin	56509	1923	58-27x30-321,400	59,250	1958	Sold for Scrap

STEAM LOCOMOTIVES

DULUTH, MISSABE & NORTHERN RAILWAY

Orig. No.	DM&IR No.	Type & Class		Builder and Construction No.		Date Built	Dimensions Dr.–Cyls.–Wt.	Tractive Effort	Date Retired	Final Disposition and Remarks
1		4-4-0	A	Pittsburgh	1409	1893	62-17x22- 89,800	15,214	1928	Sold for Scrap
2		4-4-0	A	Pittsburgh	1410	1893	62-17x22- 89,800	15,214	1925	Cazenovia Southern Ry.
5	5	4-6-0	F	Pittsburgh	1427	1983	56-19x26-123,000	23,000	1940	Detroit, Caro & Sandusky Ry.
6		4-6-0	F	Pittsburgh	1428	1893	56-19x26-123,000	23,000	1935	Sold for Scrap
7		4-6-0	F	Pittsburgh	1387	1893	56-19x26-123,000	23,000	1901	Indiana, Illinois & Iowa Ry. 41
8		4-6-0	F	Pittsburgh	1388	1893	56-19x26-123,000	23,000	1901	Indiana, Illinois & Iowa Ry. 40
9		4-6-0	F	Pittsburgh	1389	1893	56-19x26-123,000	23,000	1901	Indiana, Illinois & Iowa Ry. 42
10		4-6-0	F	Pittsburgh	1429	1893	56-19x26-123,000	23,000	1901	Indiana, Illinois & Iowa Ry. 44
11		4-6-0	F	Pittsburgh	1430	1893	56-19x26-123,000	23,000	1933	Sold for Scrap
12	12	4-6-0	F	Pittsburgh	1431	1893	56-19x26-123,000	23,000	1939	Sold for Scrap
13		4-6-0	F	Pittsburgh	1432	1893	56-19x26-123,000	23,000	1937	American Steel & Wire Co.
14		4-6-0	F	Pittsburgh	1433	1893	56-19x26-123,000	23,000	1901	Indiana, Illinois & Iowa Ry. 45
15		4-6-0	F	Pittsburgh	1462	1893	56-19x26-123,000	23,000	1933	American Steel & Wire Co.
16		4-6-0	F	Pittsburgh	1463	1893	56-19x26-123,000	23,000	1937	American Steel & Wire Co.
17	17	4-6-0	F	Pittsburgh	1464	1893	56-19x26-123,000	23,000	1940	Sold for Scrap
18		4-6-0	F	Pittsburgh	1465	1893	56-19x26-123,000	23,000	1901	Indiana, Illinois & Iowa Ry. 43
19	19	4-6-0	F	Pittsburgh	1466	1893	56-19x26-123,000	23,000	1940	Boiler at Virginia Enginehouse
20		4-6-0	F	Pittsburgh	1467	1893	56-19x26-123,000	23,000	1933	American Steel & Wire Co.
21	21	4-6-0	F	Pittsburgh	1840	1898	56-19x26-123,000	23,000	1948	American Steel & Wire Co.
22		4-6-0	F	Pittsburgh	1841	1898	56-19x26-123,000	23,000	1923	Northern Lumber Co. 22
23		4-6-0	F	Pittsburgh	1957	1899	56-19x26-123,000	23,000	1933	Sold for Scrap
24		4-6-0	F	Pittsburgh	1958	1899	56-19x26-123,000	23,000	1923	Northern Lumber Co. 24
25		4-6-0	F	Pittsburgh	1959	1899	56-19x26-123,000	23,000	1933	Sold for Scrap
26		4-6-0	F	Pittsburgh	1960	1899	56-19x26-123,000	23,000	1933	Sold for Scrap
27		4-6-0	F	Pittsburgh	2092	1900	56-19x26-123,000	23,000	1937	American Steel & Wire Co.
28		4-6-0	F	Pittsburgh	2093	1900	56-19x26-123,000	23,000	1933	Sold for Scrap
29		4-6-0	F	Pittsburgh	2094	1900	56-19x26-123,000	23,000	1923	Northern Lumber Co. 29
30	30	4-6-0	F	Pittsburgh	2095	1900	56-19x26-123,000	23,000	1939	
31	31	4-6-0	F	Pittsburgh	2096	1900	56-19x26-123,000	23,000	1940	Detroit, Caro & Sandusky Ry.
32		4-6-0	F	Pittsburgh	2097	1900	56-19x26-123,000	23,000	1928	Sold for Scrap
33		4-6-0	F	Pittsburgh	2098	1900	56-19x26-123,000	23,000	1923	Northern Lumber Co. 33
50		0-6-0	S	Pittsburgh	1455	1893	50-17x24- 84,000	18,866	1918	Chickasaw Shipbldg. Co.
51		0-6-0	S	Pittsburgh	1456	1893	50-17x24- 84,000	18,866	1916	Minnesota Steel Co.
52		0-6-0	S	Pittsburgh	1457	1893	50-17x24- 84,000	18,866	1916	Pittsburg Iron Mining Co.
53		0-6-0	S	Pittsburgh	1458	1893	50-17x24- 84,000	18,866	1916	Universal Atlas Cement
54		0-6-0	S	Pittsburgh	1459	1893	50-17x26- 84,000	18,866	1916	Minnesota Steel Co.
55		0-6-0	S	Pittsburgh	1460	1893	50-17x26- 84,000	18,866	1917	Pittsburg Iron Mining Co.
56		0-6-0	S1	Pittsburgh	2122	1900	50-19x26-120,450	28,721	1920	Minn. Dakota & Western Ry. 8
57		0-6-0	S1	Pittsburgh	2123	1900	50-19x26-120,450	28,721	1920	Minn. Dakota & Western Ry.
58		0-8-0	S3	Baldwin	30487	1907	51-21x28-164,000	41,160	1927	Oliver Iron Mining 800
59		0-8-0	S3	Baldwin	30488	1907	51-21x28-164,000	41,160	1927	Oliver Iron Mining 801
60		0-8-0	S3	Baldwin	30501	1907	51-21x28-164,000	41,160	1927	Oliver Iron Mining 802

NOTE: Dimensions and weights shown for locomotives as originally built.

Orig. No.	DM&IR No.	Type & Class		Builder and Construction No.		Date Built	Dimensions Dr.—Cyls.—Wt.	Tractive Effort	Date Retired	Final Disposition and Remarks
61		0-8-0	S3	Baldwin	30586	1907	51-21x28-164,000	41,160	1927	Oliver Iron Mining 803
62		0-8-0	S4	Baldwin	34754	1910	51-21x28-164,000	41,160	1927	Oliver Iron Mining 804
63		0-8-0	S4	Baldwin	34755	1910	51-21x28-164,000	41,160	1927	Oliver Iron Mining 805
64		0-8-0	S4	Baldwin	34756	1910	51-21x28-164,000	41,160	1927	Oliver Iron Mining 806
80	80	0-8-0	S2	Schenectady	47925	1910	51-21x28-207,500	45,850	1948	American Steel & Wire Co.
81	81	0-8-0	S2	Schenectady	47926	1910	51-21x28-207,500	45,850	1950	American Steel & Wire Co.
82	82	0-8-0	S2	Schenectady	47927	1910	51-21x28-207,500	45,850	1948	American Steel & Wire Co.
83	83	0-8-0	S2	Schenectady	47928	1910	51-21x28-207,500	45,850	1949	American Steel & Wire Co.
84	84	0-8-0	S2	Schenectady	47929	1910	51-21x28-207,500	45,850	1949	American Steel & Wire Co.
85	85	0-8-0	S2	Schenectady	47930	1910	51-21x28-207,500	45,850	1949	American Steel & Wire Co.
86	86	0-8-0	S5	Baldwin	45704	1917	51-24x28-216,000	53,575	1954	Sold for Scrap
87	87	0-8-0	S5	Baldwin	45705	1917	51-24x28-216,000	53,575	1958	Sold for Scrap
88	88	0-8-0	S5	Baldwin	45706	1917	51-24x28-216,000	53,575	1958	Sold for Scrap
89	89	0-8-0	S5	Baldwin	45707	1917	51-24x28-216,000	53,575	1958	Sold for Scrap
90	90	0-10-0	S6	Baldwin	60213	1928	57-28x30-352,250	77,600‡	1955	Sold for Scrap
91	91	0-10-0	S6	Baldwin	60263	1928	57-28x30-352,250	77,600‡	1958	Sold for Scrap
92	92	0-10-0	S6	Baldwin	60293	1928	57-28x30-352,250	77,600‡	1958	Sold for Scrap
93	93	0-10-0	S6	Baldwin	60294	1928	57-28x30-352,250	77,600‡	1958	Sold for Scrap
100		4-6-0	F1	Baldwin	27719	1906	67-20x26-166,200	26,400	1933	American Steel & Wire Co.
101		4-6-0	F1	Baldwin	27727	1906	67-18¾x26-166,200	23,200	1933	American Steel & Wire Co.
102		4-6-0	F2	Baldwin	30436	1907	63-18¾x26-164,000	24,675	1932	Boiler at Biwabik Enginehouse
103		4-6-0	F2	Baldwin	30437	1907	63-18¾x26-164,000	24,675	1933	American Steel & Wire Co.
104		4-6-0	F3	Baldwin	34723	1907	63-20x26-164,000	28,100	1933	American Steel & Wire Co.
200	200	2-8-8-2	M	Baldwin	35165	1910	57-26x40x32-448,100	91,000	1953	Sold for Scrap
201	201	2-8-8-2	M	Baldwin	35166	1910	57-26x40x32-448,100	91,000	1953	Sold for Scrap
202	202	2-8-8-2	M	Baldwin	35167	1910	57-26x40x32-448,100	91,000	1953	Sold for Scrap
203	203	2-8-8-2	M	Baldwin	35168	1910	57-26x40x32-448,100	91,000	1950	Sold for Scrap
204	204	2-8-8-2	M	Baldwin	35169	1910	57-26x40x32-448,100	91,000	1950	Sold for Scrap
205	205	2-8-8-2	M	Baldwin	35170	1910	57-26x40x32-448,100	91,000	1950	Sold for Scrap
206	206	2-8-8-2	M	Baldwin	35171	1910	57-26x40x32-448,100	91,000	1950	Sold for Scrap
207	207	2-8-8-2	M	Baldwin	35172	1910	57-26x40x32-448,100	91,000		Rebuilt to Single-Expansion 1930
207*	207	2-8-8-2	MS	Baldwin	35172	1910	57-24x32 -494,500	110,000	1953	Sold for Scrap
208	208	2-8-8-2	M1	Baldwin	43530	1916	57-26x40x32-470,000	91,000		Rebuilt to Single-Expansion 1931
208*	208	2-8-8-2	M1S	Baldwin	43530	1916	57-24x32 -494,450	110,000	1954	Sold for Scrap
209	209	2-8-8-2	M1	Baldwin	43531	1916	57-26x40x32-470,000	91,000		Rebuilt to Single-Expansion 1937
209*	209	2-8-8-2	M1S	Baldwin	43531	1916	57-24x32 -494,450	110,000	1958	Sold for Scrap
210	210	2-8-8-2	M2	Baldwin	45769	1917	57-26x40x32-470,000	91,000		Rebuilt to Single-Expansion 1929
210*	210	2-8-8-2	M2S	Baldwin	45769	1917	57-24x32 -494,450	110,000	1957	Sold for Scrap
211	211	2-8-8-2	M2	Baldwin	45793	1917	57-26x40x32-470,000	91,000		Rebuilt to Single-Expansion 1931
211*	211	2-8-8-2	M2S	Baldwin	45793	1917	57-24x32 -494,450	110,000	1957	Sold for Scrap
300		2-8-0	C	Pittsburgh	1525	1894	50-22x28-160,000	36,800	1927	Duluth & Northwestern R.R. 22
301		2-8-0	C	Pittsburgh	1563	1895	50-22x28-160,000	36,800	1927	Duluth & Northwestern R.R. 23
302		2-8-0	C1	Pittsburgh	1966	1899	56-22x28-180,000	36,900	1933	American Steel & Wire Co.
303		2-8-0	C1	Pittsburgh	2099	1900	56-22x28-180,000	36,900	1934	American Steel & Wire Co.
304		2-8-0	C1	Dickson	26342	1902	56-22x28-180,000	36,900	1933	American Steel & Wire Co.
305		2-8-0	C1	Dickson	26343	1902	56-22x28-180,000	36,900	1933	American Steel & Wire Co.
306	306	2-8-0	C1	Dickson	26344	1902	56-22x28-180,000	36,900	1948	American Steel & Wire Co.
307	307	2-8-0	C1	Cooke	27063	1903	56-22x28-180,000	36,900	1948	American Steel & Wire Co.
308	308	2-8-0	C1	Cooke	27064	1903	56-22x28-180,000	36,900	1948	American Steel & Wire Co.
309		2-8-0	C1	Cooke	27065	1903	56-22x28-180,000	36,900	1933	American Steel & Wire Co.
310		2-8-0	C1	Cooke	27066	1903	56-22x28-180,000	36,900	1933	American Steel & Wire Co.
311		2-8-0	C1	Cooke	27067	1903	56-22x28-180,000	36,900	1933	American Steel & Wire Co.
312		2-8-0	C1	Cooke	27068	1903	56-22x28-180,000	36,900	1933	American Steel & Wire Co.
313		2-8-0	C2	Pittsburgh	28897	1904	56-22x28-180,000	37,026	1919	Oliver Iron Mining Co. 513+
314		2-8-0	C2	Pittsburgh	28898	1904	56-22x28-180,000	37,026	1919	Oliver Iron Mining Co. 514+
315		2-8-0	C2	Pittsburgh	28899	1904	56-22x28-180,000	37,026	1919	Oliver Iron Mining Co. 515+
316		2-8-0	C2	Pittsburgh	28900	1904	56-22x28-180,000	37,026	1919	Oliver Iron Mining Co. 516+
317		2-8-0	C2	Pittsburgh	28901	1904	56-22x28-180,000	37,026	1919	Oliver Iron Mining Co. 517+
318		2-8-0	C2	Pittsburgh	28902	1904	56-22x28-180,000	37,026	1919	Oliver Iron Mining Co. 518+
319	319	2-8-0	C3	Pittsburgh	30730	1905	56-22x28-185,500	39,080	1955	Sold for Scrap
320		2-8-0	C3	Pittsburgh	30731	1905	56-22x28-185,500	39,080	1919	Oliver Iron Mining Co. 520+

Orig. No.	DM&IR No.	Type & Class		Builder and Construction No.		Date Built	Dimensions Dr.—Cyls.—Wt.	Tractive Effort	Date Retired	Final Disposition and Remarks
321		2-8-0	C3	Pittsburgh	30732	1905	56-22x28-185,500	39,080	1928	Mpls. Northfield & So. Ry. 402
322		2-8-0	C3	Pittsburgh	30733	1905	56-22x28-185,500	39,080	1919	Oliver Iron Mining Co. 522+
323		2-8-0	C3	Pittsburgh	30734	1905	56-22x28-185,500	39,080	1919	Oliver Iron Mining Co. 523+
324	324	2-8-0	C3	Pittsburgh	30735	1905	56-22x28-185,500	39,080	1954	Sold for Scrap
325	325	2-8-0	C3	Pittsburgh	31232	1905	56-22x28-185,500	39,080	1948	Sold for Scrap
326		2-8-0	C3	Pittsburgh	31233	1905	56-22x28-185,500	39,080	1928	Mpls. Northfield & So. Ry. 403
327	327	2-8-0	C3	Pittsburgh	31334	1905	56-22x28-185,500	39,080	1955	Sold for Scrap
328		2-8-0	C3	Pittsburgh	31335	1905	56-22x28-185,500	39,080	1919	Oliver Iron Mining Co. 528+
329		2-8-0	C3	Pittsburgh	31236	1905	56-22x28-185,500	39,080	1928	Mpls. Northfield & So. Ry. 404
330	330	2-8-0	C3	Pittsburgh	31237	1905	56-22x28-185,500	39,080	1953	Sold for Scrap
331	331	2-8-0	C3	Pittsburgh	39586	1906	56-22x28-185,500	39,080	1955	Sold for Scrap
332	332	2-8-0	C3	Pittsburgh	39587	1906	56-22x28-185,500	39,080	1955	Duluth & Northeastern R.R. 28
333	333	2-8-0	C3	Pittsburgh	39588	1906	56-22x28-185,500	39,080	1950	Sold for Scrap
334	334	2-8-0	C3	Pittsburgh	39589	1906	56-22x28-185,500	39,080	1955	Sold for Scrap
335	335	2-8-0	C3	Pittsburgh	39590	1906	56-22x28-185,500	39,080	1955	Sold for Scrap
336	336	2-8-0	C3	Pittsburgh	39591	1906	56-22x28-185,500	39,080	1954	Sold for Scrap
337		2-8-0	C3	Pittsburgh	42275	1907	56-22x28-185,500	39,080	1929	Mpls. Northfield & So. Ry. 405
338	338	2-8-0	C3	Pittsburgh	42276	1907	56-22x28-185,500	39,080	1953	Sold for Scrap
339	339	2-8-0	C3	Pittsburgh	42277	1907	56-22x28-185,500	39,080	1955	Sold for Scrap
340	340	2-8-0	C3	Pittsburgh	42278	1907	56-22x28-185,500	39,080	1950	Sold for Scrap
341	341	2-8-0	C3	Pittsburgh	42279	1907	56-22x28-185,500	39,080	1953	Sold for Scrap
342	342	2-8-0	C3	Pittsburgh	42280	1907	56-22x28-185,500	39,080	1955	Sold for Scrap
343	343	2-8-0	C3	Pittsburgh	42281	1907	56-22x28-185,500	39,080	1950	Sold for Scrap
344		2-8-0	C3	Pittsburgh	42282	1907	56-22x28-185,500	39,080	1927	Mpls. Northfield & So. Ry. 400
345		2-8-0	C3	Pittsburgh	42283	1907	56-22x28-185,500	39,080	1927	Mpls. Northfield & So. Ry. 401
346	346	2-8-0	C3	Pittsburgh	42284	1907	56-22x28-185,500	39,080	1949	Sold for Scrap
347	347	2-8-0	C3	Pittsburgh	42285	1907	56-22x28-185,500	39,080	1953	Presented to Museum of Mining
348	348	2-8-0	C3	Pittsburgh	42286	1907	56-22x28-185,500	39,080	1955	Duluth & Northeastern R.R. 27
349	349	2-8-0	C3	Pittsburgh	42287	1907	56-22x28-185,500	39,080	1953	Sold for Scrap
350	350	2-8-0	C3	Pittsburgh	42288	1907	56-22x28-185,500	39,080	1955	Sold for Scrap
400	400	4-6-2	P	Baldwin	39877	1913	69-25x28-245,700	38,800	1959	Sold for Scrap
401	401	4-6-2	P	Baldwin	39878	1913	69-25x28-245,700	38,800	1955	Sold for Scrap
402	402	4-6-2	P	Baldwin	39879	1913	69-25x28-245,700	38,800	1958	Sold for Scrap
500	500	2-10-2	E	Baldwin	43409	1916	60-28x32-346,600	71,200	1962	Sold for Scrap
501	501	2-10-2	E	Baldwin	43410	1916	60-28x32-346,600	71,200	1959	Sold for Scrap
502	502	2-10-2	E	Baldwin	43411	1916	60-28x32-346,600	71,200	1962	Donated to Museum of Transportation
503	503	2-10-2	E	Baldwin	43412	1916	60-28x32-346,600	71,200	1962	Sold for Scrap
504	504	2-10-2	E	Baldwin	43501	1916	60-28x32-346,600	71,200	1962	Sold for Scrap
505	505	2-10-2	E	Baldwin	43502	1916	60-28x32-346,600	71,200	1962	Sold for Scrap
506	506	2-10-2	E1	Brooks	60075	1919	57-27x32-352,000	69,600	1962	Donated to National Ry. Museum
507	507	2-10-2	E1	Brooks	60076	1919	57-27x32-352,000	69,600	1962	Sold for Scrap
508	508	2-10-2	E1	Brooks	60077	1919	57-27x32-352,000	69,600	1959	Sold for Scrap
509	509	2-10-2	E1	Brooks	60078	1919	57-27x32-352,000	69,600	1962	Sold for Scrap
510	510	2-10-2	E1	Brooks	60079	1919	57-27x32-352,000	69,600	1963	Sold for Scrap
511	511	2-10-2	E1	Brooks	60080	1919	57-27x32-352,000	69,600	1959	Sold for Scrap
512	512	2-10-2	E1	Brooks	60081	1919	57-27x32-352,000	69,600	1962	Sold for Scrap
513	513	2-10-2	E1	Brooks	60082	1919	57-27x32-352,000	69,600	1962	Sold for Scrap
514	514	2-10-2	E1	Brooks	60083	1919	57-27x32-352,000	69,600	1962	Sold for Scrap
515	515	2-10-2	E1	Brooks	60084	1919	57-27x32-352,000	69,600	1959	Sold for Scrap

* — As Rebuilt

‡ — 92,100 lbs. Tractive Effort with Tender Booster

+ — Converted to 0-8-0 type by Oliver Iron Mining Co.

DULUTH, MISSABE & IRON RANGE RAILWAY

Orig. No.	Type & Class		Builder and Construction No.		Date Built	Date Acq.	Dimensions Dr.—Cyls.—Wt.	Tractive Effort	Date Retired	Final Disposition and Remarks
220	2-8-8-4	M3	Baldwin	62526	1941		63-26x32-695,040	140,000	1962	Sold for Scrap
221	2-8-8-4	M3	Baldwin	62527	1941		63-26x32-695,040	140,000	1963	Sold for Scrap
222	2-8-8-4	M3	Baldwin	62528	1941		63-26x32-695,040	140,000	1962	Sold for Scrap
223	2-8-8-4	M3	Baldwin	62529	1941		63-26x32-695,040	140,000	1962	Sold for Scrap
224	2-8-8-4	M3	Baldwin	62530	1941		63-26x32-695,040	140,000	1962	Sold for Scrap
225	2-8-8-4	M3	Baldwin	62531	1941		63-26x32-695,040	140,000	1963	Donated to Proctor Dev. Council
226	2-8-8-4	M3	Baldwin	62532	1941		63-26x32-695,040	140,000	1962	Sold for Scrap
227	2-8-8-4	M3	Baldwin	62533	1941		63-26x32-695,040	140,000		Stored at Proctor
228	2-8-8-4	M4	Baldwin	64707	1943		63-26x32-699,700	140,000	1962	Sold for Scrap
229	2-8-8-4	M4	Baldwin	64708	1943		63-26x32-699,700	140,000	1967	Lake County Hist. Society
230	2-8-8-4	M4	Baldwin	64709	1943		63-26x32-699,700	140,000	1962	Sold for Scrap
231	2-8-8-4	M4	Baldwin	64710	1943		63-26x32-699,700	140,000	1962	Sold for Scrap
232	2-8-8-4	M4	Baldwin	64711	1943		63-26x32-699,700	140,000	1962	Sold for Scrap
233	2-8-8-4	M4	Baldwin	64712	1943		63-26x32-699,700	140,000	1962	Sold for Scrap
234	2-8-8-4	M4	Baldwin	64713	1943		63-26x32-699,700	140,000	1962	Sold for Scrap
235	2-8-8-4	M4	Baldwin	64714	1943		63-26x32-699,700	140,000	1962	Sold for Scrap
236	2-8-8-4	M4	Baldwin	64715	1943		63-26x32-699,700	140,000	1962	Sold for Scrap
237	2-8-8-4	M4	Baldwin	64716	1943		63-26x32-699,700	140,000	1958	Sold for Scrap (Damaged in wreck)
601	0-10-2	S7	Baldwin	61907	1936	1949	61-28x32-422,000	90,900	1959	Ex Union R.R. 301 — Scrapped
602	0-10-2	S7	Baldwin	61908	1936	1949	61-28x32-422,000	90,900	1958	Ex Union R.R. 302 — Scrapped
603	0-10-2	S7	Baldwin	61909	1936	1949	61-28x32-422,000	90,900	1961	Ex Union R.R. 303 — Returned
604	0-10-2	S7	Baldwin	61910	1936	1949	61-28x32-422,000	90,900	1963	Ex Union R.R. 304 — Scrapped
605	0-10-2	S7	Baldwin	61911	1936	1949	61-28x32-422,000	90,900	1958	Ex Union R.R. 305 — Scrapped
606	0-10-2	S7	Baldwin	62059	1937	1949	61-28x32-422,000	90,900	1959	Ex Union R.R. 306 — Scrapped
607	0-10-2	S7	Baldwin	62060	1937	1949	61-28x32-422,000	90,900	1958	Ex Union R.R. 307 — Scrapped
608	0-10-2	S7	Baldwin	62061	1937	1949	61-28x32-422,000	90,900	1959	Ex Union R.R. 308 — Scrapped
609	0-10-2	S7	Baldwin	62062	1937	1949	61-28x32-422,000	90,900	1959	Ex Union R.R. 309 — Scrapped
700	2-10-4	E4	Alco	68891	1937	1951	64-31x32-520,000	96,700	1961	Ex B&LE 621 — Scrapped
701	2-10-4	E4	Alco	68892	1937	1951	64-31x32-520,000	96,700	1961	Ex B&LE 622 — Scrapped
702	2-10-4	E4	Alco	68893	1937	1951	64-31x32-520,000	96,700	1961	Ex B&LE 623 — Scrapped
703	2-10-4	E4	Alco	68894	1937	1951	64-31x32-520,000	96,700	1961	Ex B&LE 624 — Scrapped
704	2-10-4	E4	Alco	68895	1937	1951	64-31x32-520,000	96,700	1956	Ex B&LE 625 — Scrapped
705	2-10-4	E4	Alco	68896	1937	1951	64-31x32-520,000	96,700	1961	Ex B&LE 626 — Scrapped
706	2-10-4	E4	Alco	68897	1937	1951	64-31x32-520,000	96,700	1961	Ex B&LE 627 — Scrapped
707	2-10-4	E4	Alco	68898	1937	1951	64-31x32-520,000	96,700	1961	Ex B&LE 628 — Scrapped
708	2-10-4	E4	Alco	68899	1937	1951	64-31x32-520,000	96,700	1961	Ex B&LE 629 — Scrapped
709	2-10-4	E4	Alco	68900	1937	1951	64-31x32-520,000	96,700	1961	Ex B&LE 630 — Scrapped
710	2-10-4	E5	Baldwin	64150	1941	1951	64-31x32-519,740	96,700	1961	Ex B&LE 631 — Scrapped
711	2-10-4	E5	Baldwin	64154	1941	1951	64-31x32-519,740	96,700	1961	Ex B&LE 635 — Scrapped
712	2-10-4	E6	Baldwin	64578	1942	1951	64-31x32-524,382	96,700	1961	Ex B&LE 637 — Scrapped
713	2-10-4	E7	Baldwin	64718	1943	1951	64-31x32-523,600	96,700	1961	Ex B&LE 638 — Scrapped
714	2-10-4	E7	Baldwin	64721	1943	1951	64-31x32-523,600	96,700	1961	Ex B&LE 641 — Scrapped
715	2-10-4	E7	Baldwin	70059	1943	1951	64-31x32-523,600	96,700	1961	Ex B&LE 645 — Scrapped
716	2-10-4	E7	Baldwin	70060	1943	1951	64-31x32-523,600	96,700	1961	Ex B&LE 646 — Scrapped
717	2-10-4	E7	Baldwin	70061	1943	1951	64-31x32-523,600	96,700	1961	Ex B&LE 647 — Scrapped
1312	2-8-2	N4	Alco	64742	1923	1948	63-28x30-333,000	63,467	1958	Ex EJ&E 746 — Scrapped
1313	2-8-2	N4	Alco	64743	1923	1948	63-28x30-333,000	63,467	1961	Ex EJ&E 747 — Scrapped
1314	2-8-2	N4	Alco	64744	1923	1948	63-28x30-333,000	63,467	1961	Ex EJ&E 748 — Scrapped
1315	2-8-2	N4	Alco	64745	1923	1948	63-28x30-333,000	63,467	1958	Ex EJ&E 749 — Scrapped
1316	2-8-2	N4	Alco	64746	1923	1948	63-28x30-333,000	63,467	1959	Ex EJ&E 750 — Scrapped
1317	2-8-2	N4	Alco	64747	1923	1948	63-28x30-333,000	63,467	1959	Ex EJ&E 751 — Scrapped
1318	2-8-2	N4	Alco	64748	1932	1948	63-28x30-333,000	63,467	1959	Ex EJ&E 752 — Scrapped
1319	2-8-2	N4	Alco	64749	1923	1948	63-28x30-333,000	63,467	1959	Ex EJ&E 753 — Scrapped
1320	2-8-2	N4	Alco	64750	1923	1948	63-28x30-333,000	63,467	1958	Ex EJ&E 754 — Scrapped
1321	2-8-2	N4	Alco	64751	1923	1948	63-28x30-333,000	63,467	1959	Ex EJ&E 755 — Scrapped
1322	2-8-2	N5	Lima	6695	1923	1948	63-28x30-333,000	63,467	1958	Ex EJ&E 756 — Scrapped
1323	2-8-2	N5	Lima	6696	1923	1948	63-28x30-333,000	63,467	1961	Ex EJ&E 757 — Scrapped
1324	2-8-2	N5	Lima	6697	1923	1948	63-28x30-333,000	63,467	1959	Ex EJ&E 758 — Scrapped
1325	2-8-2	N5	Lima	6698	1923	1948	63-28x30-333,000	63,467	1958	Ex EJ&E 759 — Scrapped
1326	2-8-2	N6	Baldwin	61076	1929	1948	63-28x30-333,460	63,467	1958	Ex EJ&E 761 — Scrapped

Orig. No.	Type & Class		Builder and Construction No.		Date Built	Date Acq.	Dimensions Dr.–Cyls.–Wt.	Tractive Effort	Date Retired	Final Disposition and Remarks
1327	2-8-2	N6	Baldwin	61077	1929	1948	63-28x30-333,460	63,467	1961	Ex EJ&E 762 — Scrapped
1328	2-8-2	N6	Baldwin	61078	1929	1948	63-28x30-333,460	63,467	1958	Ex EJ&E 763 — Scrapped
1329	2-8-2	N6	Baldwin	61079	1929	1948	63-28x30-333,460	63,467	1958	Ex EJ&E 764 — Scrapped
1330	2-8-2	N6	Baldwin	61080	1929	1948	63-28x30-333,460	63,467	1962	Ex EJ&E 765 — At Gary, Indiana
1331	2-8-2	N6	Baldwin	61081	1929	1948	63-28x30-333,460	63,467	1959	Ex EJ&E 766 — Scrapped
1332	2-8-2	N6	Baldwin	61372	1930	1948	63-28x30-333,460	63,467	1958	Ex EJ&E 767 — Scrapped
1333	2-8-2	N6	Baldwin	61373	1930	1948	63-28x30-333,460	63,467	1959	Ex EJ&E 768 — Scrapped
1334	2-8-2	N6	Baldwin	61374	1930	1948	63-28x30-333,460	63,467	1958	Ex EJ&E 769 — Scrapped
1335	2-8-2	N6	Baldwin	61375	1930	1948	63-28x30-333,460	63,467	1958	Ex EJ&E 770 — Scrapped
1336	2-8-2	N6	Baldwin	61378	1930	1948	63-28x30-333,460	63,467	1959	Ex EJ&E 773 — Scrapped
1337	2-8-2	N6	Baldwin	61379	1930	1948	63-28x30-333,460	63,467	1958	Ex EJ&E 774 — Scrapped

DIESEL LOCOMOTIVES

DULUTH, MISSABE & IRON RANGE RAILWAY

Orig. No.	Type & Class		Builder, Type and Construction No.			Date Built	Dimensions Dr.–Wt.–H.P.	Tractive Effort	Date Retired	Final Disposition and Remarks
11	B-B	DS-1	Electro-Motive	SW-9	17870	1953	40-246,660-1,200	62,000	1958	Electro-Motive
12	B-B	DS-1	Electro-Motive	SW-9	17871	1953	40-246,660-1,200	62,000	1960	Electro-Motive
13	B-B	DS-1	Electro-Motive	SW-9	17872	1953	40-246,660-1,200	62,000	1963	Leased to Union R.R.
14	B-B	DS-1	Electro-Motive	SW-9	17873	1953	40-246,660-1,200	62,000	1958	Electro-Motive
15	B-B	DS-1	Electro-Motive	SW-9	17874	1953	40-246,660-1,200	62,000	1963	Leased to Union R.R.
16	B-B	DS-1	Electro-Motive	SW-9	17875	1953	40-246,660-1,200	62,000	1963	Leased to Union R.R.
17	B-B	DS-1	Electro-Motive	SW-9	17876	1953	40-246,660-1,200	62,000	1960	Electro-Motive
18	B-B	DS-1	Electro-Motive	SW-9	17877	1953	40-246,660-1,200	62,000	1960	Electro-Motive
19	B-B	DS-1	Electro-Motive	SW-9	17878	1953	40-246,660-1,200	62,000	1963	Leased to Union R.R.
20	B-B	DS-1	Electro-Motive	SW-9	17879	1953	40-246,660-1,200	62,000	1960	Electro-Motive
21	B-B	DS-1	Electro-Motive	SW-9	17880	1953	40-246,660-1,200	62,000	1960	Electro-Motive
22	B-B	DS-1	Electro-Motive	SW-9	17881	1953	40-246,660-1,200	62,000	1960	Electro-Motive
23	B-B	DS-1	Electro-Motive	SW-9	17882	1953	40-246,660-1,200	62,000	1963	Leased to Union R.R.
24	B-B	DS-1	Electro-Motive	SW-9	17883	1953	40-246,660-1,200	62,000	1962	Chicago Short Line
25	B-B	DS-1	Electro-Motive	SW-9	17884	1953	40-246,660-1,200	62,000	1962	Chicago Short Line
50	C-C	RS-5	Alco	DL-600-B	81756	1959	40-387,000-2,400	96,750	1964	Bessemer & Lake Erie 881
51	C-C	RS-5	Alco	DL-600-B	81757	1959	40-387,000-2,400	96,750	1964	Bessemer & Lake Erie 882
52	C-C	RS-5	Alco	DL-600-B	81758	1959	40-387,000-2,400	96,750	1964	Bessemer & Lake Erie 883
53	C-C	RS-5	Alco	DL-600-B	81759	1959	40-387,000-2,400	96,750	1964	Bessemer & Lake Erie 884
54	C-C	RS-5	Alco	DL-600-B	81760	1959	40-387,000-2,400	96,750	1964	Bessemer & Lake Erie 885
55	C-C	RS-5	Alco	DL-600-B	81761	1959	40-387,000-2,400	96,750	1964	Bessemer & Lake Erie 886
101	C-C	RS-1	Electro-Motive	SD-9-R	21727	1956	40-387,000-1,750	96,750	1965	Bessemer & Lake Erie 826
102	C-C	RS-1	Electro-Motive	SD-9-R	21728	1956	40-387,000-1,750	96,750	1965	Bessemer & Lake Erie 827
103	C-C	RS-1	Electro-Motive	SD-9-R	21729	1956	40-387,000-1,750	96,750	1965	Bessemer & Lake Erie 828
104	C-C	RS-1	Electro-Motive	SD-9-R	21730	1956	40-387,000-1,750	96,750	1965	Bessemer & Lake Erie 829
105	C-C	RS-1	Electro-Motive	SD-9-R	21731	1956	40-387,000-1,750	96,750	1968	Leased to Elgin, Joliet & Eastern
106	C-C	RS-1	Electro-Motive	SD-9-R	21732	1956	40-387,000-1,750	96,750	1967	Leased to Bessemer & Lake Erie 830
107	C-C	RS-1	Electro-Motive	SD-9-R	21733	1956	40-387,000-1,750	96,750	1968	Leased to Bessemer & Lake Erie
108	C-C	RS-1	Electro-Motive	SD-9-R	21734	1956	40-387,000-1,750	96,750	1968	Leased to Elgin, Joliet & Eastern
109	C-C	RS-1	Electro-Motive	SD-9-R	21735	1956	40-387,000-1,750	96,750	1968	Leased to Elgin, Joliet & Eastern
110	C-C	RS-1	Electro-Motive	SD-9-R	20655	1955	40-387,000-1,750	96,750	1967	Leased to Bessemer & Lake Erie 831
111	C-C	RS-2	Electro-Motive	SD-9-R	23099	1957	40-387,000-1,750	96,750		
112	C-C	RS-2	Electro-Motive	SD-9-R	23100	1957	40-387,000-1,750	96,750		
113	C-C	RS-2	Electro-Motive	SD-9-R	23101	1957	40-387,000-1,750	96,750	1968	Leased to Bessemer & Lake Erie 833
114	C-C	RS-2	Electro-Motive	SD-9-R	23102	1957	40-387,000-1,750	96,750	1968	Leased to Bessemer & Lake Erie 834
115	C-C	RS-2	Electro-Motive	SD-9-R	23103	1957	40-387,000-1,750	96,750		
116	C-C	RS-2	Electro-Motive	SD-9-R	23104	1957	40-387,000-1,750	96,750		
117	C-C	RS-2	Electro-Motive	SD-9-R	23105	1957	40-387,000-1,750	96,750		
118	C-C	RS-2	Electro-Motive	SD-9-R	23106	1957	40-387,000-1,750	96,750		
119	C-C	RS-2	Electro-Motive	SD-9-R	23107	1957	40-387,000-1,750	96,750		
120	C-C	RS-2	Electro-Motive	SD-9-R	23108	1957	40-387,000-1,750	96,750		
121	C-C	RS-2	Electro-Motive	SD-9-R	23109	1957	40-387,000-1,750	96,750		
122	C-C	RS-2	Electro-Motive	SD-9-R	23110	1957	40-387,000-1,750	96,750		
134	C-C	RS-2	Electro-Motive	SD-9-R	23119	1957	40-387,000-1,750	96,750		
124	C-C	RS-2	Elctro-Motive	SD-9-R	23112	1957	40-387,000-1,750	96,750		

Orig. No.	Type & Class		Builder, Type and Construction No.			Date Built	Dimensions Dr.—Wt.—H.P.	Tractive Effort	Date Retired	Final Disposition and Remarks
125	C-C	RS-2	Electro-Motive	SD-9-R	23113	1957	40-387,000-1,750	96,750		
126	C-C	RS-2	Electro-Motive	SD-9-R	23114	1957	40-387,000-1,750	96,750		
127	C-C	RS-2	Electro-Motive	SD-9-R	23115	1957	40-387,000-1,750	96,750	1968	Leased to Elgin, Joliet & Eastern
128	C-C	RS-2	Electro-Motive	SD-9-R	23116	1957	40-387,000-1,750	96,750		
129	C-C	RS-2	Electro-Motive	SD-9-R	23117	1957	40-387,000-1,750	96,750		
130	C-C	RS-2	Electro-Motive	SD-9-R	23118	1957	40-387,000-1,750	96,750		
131	C-C	RS-3	Electro-Motive	SD-9-R	23911	1958	40-387,000-1,750	96,750		
132	C-C	RS-3	Electro-Motive	SD-9-R	23912	1958	40-387,000-1,750	96,750		
133	C-C	RS-3	Electro-Motive	SD-9-R	23913	1958	40-387,000-1,750	96,750		
134	C-C	RS-3	Electro-Motive	SD-9-R	23914	1958	40-387,000-1,750	96,750		
135	C-C	RS-3	Electro-Motive	SD-9-R	23915	1958	40-387,000-1,750	96,750		
136	C-C	RS-3	Electro-Motive	SD-9-R	23916	1958	40-387,000-1,750	96,750	1964	Bessemer & Lake Erie 821
137	C-C	RS-3	Electro-Motive	SD-9-R	23917	1958	40-387,000-1,750	96,750		
138	C-C	RS-3	Electro-Motive	SD-9-R	23918	1958	40-387,000-1,750	96,750		
139	C-C	RS-3	Electro-Motive	SD-9-R	23919	1958	40-387,000-1,750	96,750		
140	C-C	RS-3	Electro-Motive	SD-9-R	23920	1958	40-387,000-1,750	96,750	1964	Bessemer & Lake Erie 822
141	C-C	RS-3	Electro-Motive	SD-9-R	23921	1958	40-387,000-1,750	96,750	1964	Bessemer & Lake Erie 823
142	C-C	RS-3	Electro-Motive	SD-9-R	23922	1958	40-387,000-1,750	96,750		
143	C-C	RS-3	Electro-Motive	SD-9-R	23923	1958	40-387,000-1,750	96,750		
144	C-C	RS-3	Electro-Motive	SD-9-R	23924	1958	40-387,000-1,750	96,750		
146	C-C	RS-3	Electro-Motive	SD-9-R	23926	1958	40-387,000-1,750	96,750	1964	Bessemer & Lake Erie 824
147	C-C	RS-3	Electro-Motive	SD-9-R	23927	1958	40-387,000-1,750	96,750		
148	C-C	RS-3	Electro-Motive	SD-9-R	23928	1958	40-387,000-1,750	96,750	1964	Bessemer & Lake Erie 825
149	C-C	RS-3	Electro-Motive	SD-9-R	23929	1958	40-387,000-1,750	96,750		
150	C-C	RS-3	Electro-Motive	SD-9-R	23930	1958	40-387,000-1,750	96,750		
151	C-C	RS-3	Electro-Motive	SD-9-R	23931	1958	40-387,000-1,750	96,750		
152	C-C	RS-3	Electro-Motive	SD-9-R	23932	1958	40-387,000-1,750	96,750		
153	C-C	RS-3	Electro-Motive	SD-9-R	23933	1958	40-387,000-1,750	96,750		
154	C-C	RS-3	Electro-Motive	SD-9-R	23934	1958	40-387,000-1,750	96,750		
155	C-C	RS-3	Electro-Motive	SD-9-R	23935	1958	40-387,000-1,750	96,750		
156	C-C	RS-3	Electro-Motive	SD-9-R	23936	1958	40-387,000-1,750	96,750		
157	C-C	RS-3	Electro-Motive	SD-9-R	23937	1958	40-387,000-1,750	96,750		
158	C-C	RS-3	Electro-Motive	SD-9-R	24487	1958	40-387,000-1,750	96,750		
159	C-C	RS-4	Electro-Motive	SD-9	25259	1959	40-387,000-1,750	96,750		
160	C-C	RS-4	Electro-Motive	SD-9	25260	1959	40-387,000-1,750	96,750		
161	C-C	RS-4	Electro-Motive	SD-9	25261	1959	40-387,000-1,750	96,750		
162	C-C	RS-4	Electro-Motive	SD-9	25262	1959	40-387,000-1,750	96,750		
163	C-C	RS-4	Electro-Motive	SD-9	25263	1959	40-387,000-1,750	96,750		
164	C-C	RS-4	Electro-Motive	SD-9	25264	1959	40-387,000-1,750	96,750		
165	C-C	RS-4	Electro-Motive	SD-9	25265	1959	40-387,000-1,750	96,750		
166	C-C	RS-4	Electro-Motive	SD-9	25266	1959	40-387,000-1,750	96,750		
167	C-C	RS-4	Electro-Motive	SD-9	25267	1959	40-387,000-1,750	96,750		
168	C-C	RS-4	Electro-Motive	SD-9	25268	1959	40-387,000-1,750	96,750		
169	C-C	RS-4	Electro-Motive	SD-9	25269	1959	40-387,000-1,750	96,750		
170	C-C	RS-4	Electro-Motive	SD-9	25270	1959	40-387,000-1,750	96,750		
171	C-C	RS-4	Electro-Motive	SD-9	25271	1959	40-387,000-1,750	96,750		
172	C-C	RS-4	Electro-Motive	SD-9	25272	1959	40-387,000-1,750	96,750		
173	C-C	RS-4	Electro-Motive	SD-9	25273	1959	40-387,000-1,750	96,750		
174	C-C	RS-4	Electro-Motive	SD-9	25274	1959	40-387,000-1,750	96,750		
175	C-C	RS-6	Electro-Motive	SD-18	25779	1960	40-387,000-1,800	96,750		
176	C-C	RS-6	Electro-Motive	SD-18	25780	1960	40-387,000-1,800	96,750		
177	C-C	RS-6	Electro-Motive	SD-18	25781	1960	40-387,000-1,800	96,750		
178	C-C	RS-6	Electro-Motive	SD-18	25782	1960	40-387,000-1,800	96,750		
179	C-C	RS-6	Electro-Motive	SD-18	25783	1960	40-387,000-1,800	96,750		
180	C-C	RS-6	Electro-Motive	SD-18	25784	1960	40-387,000-1,800	96,750		
181	C-C	RS-6	Electro-Motive	SD-18	25785	1960	40-387,000-1,800	96,750		
182	C-C	RS-6	Electro-Motive	SD-18	25786	1960	40-387,000-1,800	96,750		
183	C-C	RS-6	Electro-Motive	SD-18	25787	1960	40-387,000-1,800	96,750		
184	C-C	RS-6	Electro-Motive	SD-18	25788	1960	40-387,000-1,800	96,750		
185	C-C	RS-6	Electro-Motive	SD-18	25789	1960	40-387,000-1,800	96,750		
186	C-C	RS-6	Electro-Motive	SD-18	25790	1960	40-387,000-1,800	96,750		
187	C-C	RS-6	Electro-Motive	SD-18	35791	1960	40-387,000-1,800	96,750		
188	C-C	RS-6	Electro-Motive	SD-18	25792	1960	40-387,000-1,800	96,750		
189	C-C	RS-6	Electro-Motive	SD-18	25793	1960	40-387,000-1,800	96,750		
190	C-C	RS-6	Electro-Motive	SD-18	25794	1960	40-387,000-1,800	96,750		

Orig. No.	Type & Class		Builder, Type and Construction No.		Date Built	Dimensions Dr.—Wt.—H.P.	Tractive Effort	Date Retired	Final Disposition and Remarks
191	C-C	RS-6	Electro-Motive	SD-18 25795	1960	40-387,000-1,800	96,750		
192	C-C	RS-6	Electro-Motive	SD-18 25796	1960	40-387,000-1,800	96,750		
193	C-C	RS-6	Electro-Motive	SD-18 25797	1960	40-387,000-1,800	96,750		
201	C-C	RS-7	Electro-Motive	SD-38 37069	1971	40-387,000-2,000	96,750		
202	C-C	RS-7	Electro-Motive	SD-38 37070	1971	40-387,000-2,000	96,750		
203	C-C	RS-7	Electro-Motive	SD-38 37071	1971	40-387,000-2,000	96,750		
204	C-C	RS-7	Electro-Motive	SD-38 37072	1971	40-387,000-2,000	96,750		
205	C-C	RS-7	Electro-Motive	SD-38 37073	1971	40-387,000-2,000	96,750		
206	C-C	RS-7	Electro-Motive	SD-38 37074	1971	40-387,000-2,000	96,750		
207	C-C	RS-7	Electro-Motive	SD-38 37075	1971	40-387,000-2,000	96,750		
208	C-C	RS-7	Electro-Motive	SD-38 37076	1971	40-387,000-2,000	96,750		

SELF-PROPELLED RAIL CARS

No.	Railroad	Builder	Date Built	Remarks
MC-1	D&IR	Barney & Smith	1907	Remodeled from combine car No. 19 by D&IR in 1926. Equipped with two Red Seal Continental 104 hp, 6-cylinder gas engines. Seating capacity — 36 persons. Used on Western Mesaba Branch between Allen Junction and Virginia.
M-55	DM&N	Ohio Falls Car Co.	1901	Remodeled during 1927 from coach No. 55. Equipped with two Red Seal Continental 70 hp, 6-cylinder gas engines. Seating capacity — 64 persons. Used for Proctor roundhouse jitney service.
W-56	DM&IR	Twin City Rapid Transit Co.		Remodeled from Duluth Street Railway trolley car in 1939. Equipped with General Motors 160 hp diesel engine and generator by DM&IR. Seating capacity — 36 persons. Used for Proctor roundhouse jitney service. This motor car replaced M-55.
M-108	DM&N	American Car & Foundry	1908	Remodeled during 1928 from combine car No. 108. Equipped with two Red Seal Continental 104 hp, 6-cylinder gas engines. Seating capacity — 30 persons. Used on Alborn Branch.
RDC-1	DM&IR	Budd Co.	1953	Rail Diesel Car — type RDC-3. Equipped with two 275 hp model 61801 RA General Motors diesels. Builders No. 5701. Seating capacity — 48 persons. Sold to the Northern Pacific Railway (now Burlington Northern).

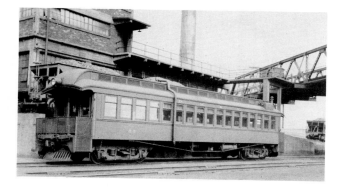

Motor car M-55 was remodeled from a coach in 1927 for use as a shop motor car at Proctor. —DM&IR COLLECTION

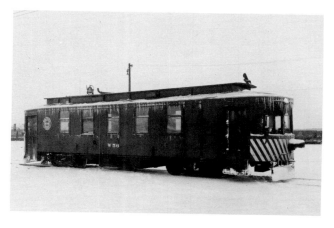

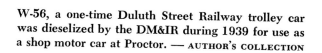

W-56, a one-time Duluth Street Railway trolley car was dieselized by the DM&IR during 1939 for use as a shop motor car at Proctor. — AUTHOR'S COLLECTION

MOTIVE POWER
THROUGH THE YEARS
-
A PICTORIAL REVIEW

SINCE 1884 the Missabe Road and its prede-cessor companies have owned and operated 352 steam locomotives and 122 diesel units. This motive power fleet has, through the years, moved over 1.7 billion tons of iron ore.

For its size, the road has had an exceptional number of notable steam locomotive types. The list begins with the D&IR's clean-lined 4-8-0's, one of which was exhibited at the 1893 World's Fair in Chicago by Schenectady as a prime motive power example of its day. Next were the DM&N's big 2-8-8-2 Mallets, among the world's largest lo-comotives when received from Baldwin during 1910. The husky 0-10-0 "Ore Sorters," built by Baldwin during 1928 for the DM&N, remained the heaviest of their type throughout the age of steam. The famous Yellowstones, received during 1941 and 1943, were acclaimed by many to have represented Baldwin's finest example of articulated power. The big 0-10-2's and 2-10-4's, received dur-ing the twilight of steam, each represented the most powerful examples of their respective types. Lastly, there were the faithful USRA Santa Fe's. These engines, though not unique to the Missabe,

were in keeping with other engines of USRA de-sign — all good performers.

The conversion from steam to diesel was for all practical purposes effected during 1960 with the last steam-powered ore extra being handled by Yellowstone No. 222 on July 5th of that year. The farewell trip for steam occurred on September 29, 1962, when a special train, carrying 325 pas-sengers, was sponsored to commemorate the build-ing of the DM&N Railway from Stony Brook to Mountain Iron, as well as the first shipment of ore from the Mesabi Range 70 years earlier. USRA Santa Fe type locomotive 514 did the honors.

The Missabe, which was noted for its well-main-tained steam locomotives, continues this practice with today's diesels, operating one of the finest locomotive repair facilities in the area. Standard-ization has been the Missabe's diesel motive power policy, the road now utilizing only one basic locomotive type for all its operations. This is in marked contrast to the latter days of steam operation when no less than ten different types (by wheel arrangement) of locomotives were em-ployed to perform the various services.

The *Three Spot*, the first locomotive to see service on the D&IR, is now on permanent exhibition at Two Harbors. She was built by Baldwin in 1883. (**LEFT**) The original bill of sale by the Baldwin Locomotive Works for D&IR No. 3 was located recently in the company files. Note the price of the engine in 1883 and the terms — cash. — **BOTH DM&IR COLLECTION**

Diamond-stacked No. 1, received from the Baldwin Locomotive Works in 1884, was the first passenger engine on the D&IR. — LAKE COUNTY HISTORICAL SOCIETY

D&IR No. 14 as it appeared in 1913, rebuilt for use as the Two Harbors shop switcher. — AUTHOR'S COLLECTION (BELOW) Switcher No. 27, built by Schenectady during 1889, was the only one of its class. She later became shop switcher No. 27, replacing No. 14. — LAKE COUNTY HISTORICAL SOCIETY

Locomotive No. 24 was one of the best looking 4-4-0's on the D&IR. With 63-inch drivers, she could roll the passenger trains over the line. — AUTHOR'S COLLECTION (BELOW) No. 4, along with four other identical four-wheel switchers, was the smallest locomotive owned by the D&IR. — LAKE COUNTY HISTORICAL SOCIETY

Consolidation No. 7 built by Baldwin in 1883, was identical to engine No. 8, which hauled the first train of iron ore over the D&IR in 1884. She was subsequently renumbered 37. — AUTHOR'S COLLECTION

210

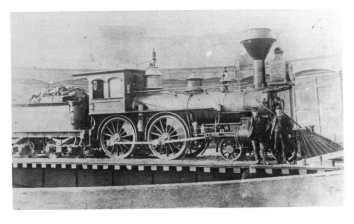

After nearly a decade of using 4-8-0's in main line ore service, the D&IR reverted to the Consolidation type. No. 92 was received from Baldwin in 1905. — AUTHOR'S COLLECTION (BELOW) Consolidation No. 208 was received during 1906. — H. L. BROAD-BELT COLLECTION

Chicago and Eastern Illinois No. 12 was built by Hinkley in 1871. She was acquired by the D&IR in 1887 for use in suburban service. — AUTHOR'S COL-LECTION

Schenectady-built No. 101 was one of six 10-Wheelers received during 1900 for passenger service. — AUTHOR'S COLLECTION

Trim-lined Schenectady-built No. 60 was one of ten 4-8-0's received during 1893. A sister engine was exhibited at the World's Fair in Chicago in the same year. —AUTHOR'S COLLECTION (BELOW) 12-Wheeler No. 83 was received from Baldwin during 1899. — AUTHOR'S COLLECTION

Pacific-type No. 110 was built by Baldwin in 1913. She, along with three others, was acquired to handle the heavier passenger trains, made up largely of all-steel equipment. — AUTHOR'S COLLECTION

No. 302 was one of four Mikados built by Baldwin for the D&IR in 1913. (BELOW) Mikados (Nos. 304 & 305), built by the Lima Locomotive Works during 1913, were nearly identical to those received from Baldwin. — BOTH AUTHOR'S COLLECTION

Mikados Nos. 309 to 311 were the last locomotives acquired by the D&IR (1923). They were the first on the road to be equipped with feedwater heaters and trailing truck boosters. (BELOW) Mikado No. 306 as equipped with a Coffin Feedwater Heater. — BOTH AUTHOR'S COLLECTION

Baldwin-built No. 307 (1916) featured a coal pusher on her Vanderbilt tender. — AUTHOR'S COLLECTION

The Two Harbors back shop was busy when this photograph was taken in 1914. All locomotives are 2-8-0's except for No. 68 which is a 4-8-0. Note the difference in size between Consolidation No. 38 built by Baldwin in 1883, and No. 44 erected in 1887, and No. 201 erected in 1906. — AUTHOR'S COLLECTION

10-Wheelers, such as Pittsburgh-built No. 7 (1893) formed the backbone of the DM&N's motive power fleet until the turn of the century, holding down main line ore, freight and passenger assignments. — AUTHOR'S COLLECTION

DM&N Nos. 1 and 2 were built by the Pittsburgh Locomotive Works in 1893. With 63-inch drivers, these locomotives were used in passenger service. — DM&IR COLLECTION

Pittsburgh-built Consolidation No. 300 was designed specifically for use on Proctor Hill. She, along with sister engine No. 301, was equipped with a slope-backed tender for improved visibility while backing down the Hill. — AUTHOR'S COLLECTION

Class C-1 Consolidation No. 306 was among three locomotives of this type received in 1902 for main line ore service. Within months after having this portrait taken, she was involved in a devastating boiler explosion. — AUTHOR'S COLLECTION

Trim-lined Consolidation No. 311 was received from the Cooke Works of the American Locomotive Company in 1903. — AUTHOR'S COLLECTION

Consolidation No. 315 (Class C-2) was one of six received during 1904. (BELOW) The Class C-3 Consolidations, represented by No. 327, were the first engines on the DM&N equipped with wide fire boxes. — BOTH AUTHOR'S COLLECTION

Baldwin-built 10-Wheeler No. 100, received in 1906, was the first DM&N locomotive designed specifically for passenger service. (BELOW) The three Class P Pacifics (Nos. 400-402), built by Baldwin during 1913, were the last passenger engines received by the DM&N. — BOTH AUTHOR'S COLLECTION

Mallet No. 207, when received from Baldwin in 1910, was among the world's largest locomotives. — AUTHOR'S COLLECTION (BELOW) No. 207, after her rebuilding to single expansion. — FRANK A. KING

No. 208 was one of two Mallets received from the Baldwin Locomotive Works during 1916. — AUTHOR'S COLLECTION

Santa Fe-type engines (Nos. 500-505), received from Baldwin during 1916, had double the tonnage rating of the Consolidations they displaced. (BELOW) The ten U.S.R.A. light Santa Fe locomotives received during 1919 were in many ways the most versatile steamers ever operated by the Missabe Road. — BOTH AUTHOR'S COLLECTION

DM&N No. 210 *Madame Queen*, was the first 2-8-8-2 type locomotive to be simplified. — FRANK A. KING

Pittsburgh-built 0-6-0 switchers, Nos. 56 & 57, were received in 1900. Both engines ended their days on the Minnesota, Dakota and Western Railway, a Minnesota short line. — AUTHOR'S COLLECTION

During 1928, the DM&N received the world's heaviest ten-coupled switchers, Nos. 90 to 93. They were built specifically for Proctor Yard ore sorting. — AUTHOR'S COLLECTION

Eight-coupled switcher No. 61 was received in 1907 for use on the Duluth ore docks. — AUTHOR'S COLLECTION

Schenectady-built No. 84, one of six 0-8-0's received during 1910, was considerably heavier than the earlier engines of this type. (BELOW) No. 86 was one of four Class S5 0-8-0's received from Baldwin during 1917. — BOTH AUTHOR'S COLLECTION

Busy 1920's scene at the Proctor back shop showing several locomotives under various stages of repair. Note the locomotive in the foreground is stripped down to its running gear, while two Santa Fe types are in for major repairs. — DM&IR COLLECTION

No. 222 was one of eight class M-3 Yellowstones received from the Baldwin Locomotive Works during 1941. (BELOW) Ten additional Yellowstones (Class M-4) were received in 1943. Total weight of engine and tender was 1,138,000 pounds. — BOTH AUTHOR'S COLLECTION

Nine 0-10-2 (Union-type) locomotives arrived during 1949 from the Union Railroad, replacing the old 1910 Mallets on Proctor Hill — FRANK A. KING

Eighteen 2-10-4 (Texas-type) locomotives were purchased during 1951 from the Bessemer and Lake Erie Railroad. No. 714 was photographed shortly after receiving a major overhaul at the Proctor back shop. — FRANK A. KING

Engine No. 1317 was one of 26 Mikados received during 1948 from the Elgin, Joliet and Eastern Railway. (RIGHT) DM&IR No. 1303, former D&IR locomotive No. 303, patiently waits on the turntable at Endion for a run. The date was May 1959, shortly before the locomotive was scrapped. — BOTH FRANK A. KING

The Missabe's first diesels consisted of 15 1,200 hp. EMD switching units. No. 18 is representative of the locomotives which were received during 1953. — DM&IR COLLECTION

No. 50 was one of six Alco-built diesels acquired primarily for use in Two Harbors yard ore service. Rated at 2,400 hp., they were the most powerful diesel units ever owned by the Missabe. — DM&IR COLLECTION

No. 111, which is representative of the Missabe's first road diesels, was received during 1957. The 1,750 hp. SD-9 units were built by Electro-Motive. — DM&IR COLLECTION (BELOW) SD-38 No. 208 was one of eight 2,000 hp. units received during 1971 from Electro-Motive. In this photo, the diesel leads a northbound Fairlane unit train near Payne. — HOWARD S. PATRICK

APPENDIX - D

EVOLUTION OF THE LAKE SUPERIOR REGION ORE CAR

The bottom-dump ore car used today by the majority of the Lake Superior ore railroads is a highly-specialized vehicle, measuring only 24 feet in length and having a capacity of 70 to 80 tons. The present standard length of 24 feet, which was established over 80 years ago, is compatible with the 12-foot pocket spacing of the gravity-type ore docks and the 12- or 24-foot hatch spacing of the Great Lakes ore-carrying vessels. These cars, when spotted on the dock for dumping, discharge into every other pocket.

The earliest ore cars used in the Lake Superior region (1855-1880) were small four-wheeled *jennies* of 7- to 10-ton capacity, very similar to those then in use on the eastern anthracite roads. By the early 1880's, the double-truck design was introduced and the capacity had risen to 20 tons.

The 50-ton capacity all-steel ore car was introduced around 1900. Throughout the years, many refinements were made to the 50-ton ore cars, the most important centering around the doors and door-operating mechanisms. The first 70-ton capacity cars were placed in service in the 1920's. All ore cars in use today are of this capacity or over. To enable capacity loading with taconite pellets, which have a lower weight per cubic foot than most natural ores, many roads have found it necessary to apply sideboard extensions to cars assigned to this service. Future cars, designed specifically for pellet service, will likely be of 90- to 100-ton capacity. In cases where it is not necessary to dump cars directly into gravity-type docks, a breakaway from the 24-foot standard length to a longer car may occur.

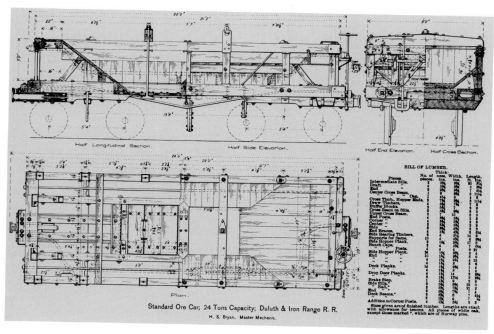

Standard Ore Car; 24 Tons Capacity; Duluth & Iron Range R. R.
H. S. Bryan, Master Mechanic.

This drawing shows construction and material details for the D&IR (1893) standard 24-ton, 24-foot ore car. The car was constructed primarily of oak. — AUTHOR'S COLLECTION

218

The D&IR's first ore cars were 28 feet in length and had a nominal capacity of 20 tons. Car No. 251, now on exhibition with the *Three Spot* at Two Harbors, was constructed during the 1930's from the original drawings. — HOWARD PATRICK

DM&N car No. 7013, which had a capacity of 35 tons, was one of 800 built by Pullman during 1900. They were the last ore cars of wooden construction received by either the DM&N or the D&IR. — AUTHOR'S COLLECTION

D&IR car No. 163 was typical of the first all-steel 50-ton capacity ore cars acquired shortly after the turn of the century. — DM&IR COLLECTION

The class U5 ore cars received by the DM&N during 1910 were the first equipped with two longitudinal bottom doors and patented dumping mechanism. All previous ore cars were equipped with four transverse doors, and had a restricted door opening. — DM&IR COLLECTION

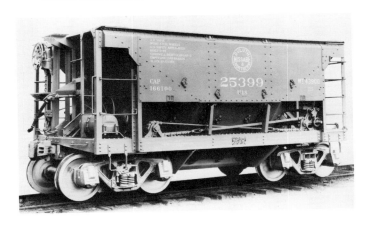

DM&N No. 25399 was one of 1,500 70-ton capacity ore cars received during 1937. This was the first major order by the Missabe for ore cars of this capacity. All subsequent 70-ton ore cars acquired were constructed to this design. — DM&IR COLLECTION (BELOW) DM&IR 70-ton ore car as equipped with 20-inch sideboard extensions for use in taconite pellet service. Such cars have a nominal capacity of 74 long tons of pellets. — NEIL HANSON

THE MISSABE ROAD'S NAVY
TUG BOATS AND FIRE BOATS
—
USED BY THE RAILROAD OVER THE YEARS

It is only natural that a road like the Missabe, with its waterfront operations, would have need for marine equipment. Over the years, the Missabe and its predecessors operated a total of four tugboats and fireboats. Two of them, the *Ella G. Stone* and the *Edna G*, were typical tugs in every sense. The other two, the *William A. McGonagle* and the *Torrent*, were somewhat unusual in that they were equipped for firefighting. In the early days of the present century, when the D&IR and the DM&N owned a total of nine highly-combustible wooden ore docks, the presence of a fire tug at both Duluth and Two Harbors was a matter of absolute necessity. Both tugs were disposed of following dismantling of the last wooden docks. Today, only one tug, the *Edna G*, remains. A veteran of 76 years, she is reputedly the last steam-powered tug operating in North America.

The tug *Ella G. Stone* was named after the wife of the D&IR's first president, George Stone. Until completion of the D&IR connection between Duluth and Two Harbors during 1886, she played a key role in moving new motive power and rolling stock to Two Harbors. She ended her days in towing service in the Chicago area. — DULUTH PUBLIC LIBRARY

Still going strong after 76 years, the Missabe Road's steam-powered tug *Edna G* is the last of her breed. Named after the daughter of D&IR president J. L. Greatsinger, she continues to assist giant ore carriers into and out of the port of Two Harbors (at Duluth, tug service is provided by an outside towing firm). During World War I, the *Edna G* left Two Harbors for active duty on the eastern seaboard. In spite of her years, she is in almost mint condition, looking every bit as young as her boilers, which were replaced in 1948. — A. C. ANDERSON

The DM&N's *William A. McGonagle*, shown above, was by far the largest of the four railway-owned tugs, having a weight of 416 gross tons. Equipped with powerful steam-driven pumps, she was capable of cascading 12,000 gallons of water per minute in fire-fighting service. The *McGonagle* was sold in 1935 to Canadian shipping interests, and continued in active service for another 30 years. — DM&IR COLLECTION (ABOVE RIGHT) The *William A. McGonagle* during fire-fighting practice at Duluth. (RIGHT) The fire tug *Torrent* was built in 1910 for the D&IR. She was stationed at Two Harbors until the retirement of the last wooden ore docks at that location, when she was sold to the city of Milwaukee for waterfront fire-fighting use. — BOTH AUTHOR'S COLLECTION

RAILWAY OWNED TUGS

Name	Type of Construction	Tonnage	Length	Beam	Depth	Year Built	Remarks
Ella G. Stone	Wood	42	69'	15'	--	1881	Built at Algonac, Michigan, for the D&IR Railroad. Sold in 1896 upon receipt of *Edna G.* Sold to Great Lakes Dredge & Dock Co., Chicago, Illinois (owners as of 1909).
Edna G.	Steel	154	110'	23'	15'6"	1896	Built at Cleveland, Ohio, for the D&IR Railroad. Replaced *Ella G. Stone.* Rated at 1,000 hp. In service — 1972. Reputed to be the last steam operated tug in United States Registry.
William A. McGonagle	Steel	416	125'	28'	15'6"	1908	Built at Lorain, Ohio, by the American Shipbuilding Company for the DM&N Railway. Equipped as a fire tug. Sold to Lakehead Transportation Co. Ltd. of Fort William, Ontario, Canada, in 1935, and renamed *Marguerite W.* Transferred to Great Lakes Lumber & Shipbuilding Co. Ltd., Fort William, Ontario, Canada, in 1943. Sold to Hindman Transportation Co., Ltd., Owen Sound, Ontario, Canada, in 1953, and renamed *Ruth Hindman.* Renamed *Lynda Hindman* in 1965. Sold to Siddal Fisheries, Goderich, Ontario, Canada, in 1966. Stripped to hull and used as pier at Goderich on Lake Huron.
Torrent	Steel	296	110'	28'	15'0"	1910	Built in 1910 for the D&IR Railroad. Equipped as a fire tug. Sold to the City of Milwaukee, Wisconsin.

BIBLIOGRAPHY

BOOKS

Beaver, Roy C., *The Bessemer and Lake Erie Railroad 1869-1969*. San Marino, Golden West Books, 1969.

Bennett, Russell H., *Quest for Ore*. Minneapolis, T. S. Denison & Co., 1963.

Bridges, Hal, *The Life of Charlemagne Tower*. Philadelphia, University of Pennsylvania Press, 1952.

Bruce, Alfred W., *The Steam Locomotive in America*. New York, W. W. Norton & Co., Inc., 1952.

Butler, Joseph G., Jr., *Fifty Years of Iron and Steel*. Cleveland, Penton Press, 1918.

Crowell & Murray, *The Iron Ores of Lake Superior*. Cleveland, Penton Press, 1917.

Davis, E. W., *Pioneering with Taconite*. St. Paul, Minnesota Historical Society, 1964.

De Kruif, Paul, *Seven Iron Men*. New York, Harcourt, Brace & Co., 1929.

Dorin, Patrick C., *The Lake Superior Iron Ore Railroads*. Seattle, Superior Publishing Co., 1969.

Evans, Henry O., *Iron Pioneer — Henry W. Oliver*. New York, E. P. Dutton & Co., 1942.

Fisher, Douglas A., *Steel Serves the Nation (1901-1951)*. Pittsburgh, United States Steel Corporation, 1951.

Hatcher, Harlan, *A Century of Iron and Men*. Indianapolis, Bobbs-Merrill Co., Inc., 1950.

Havighurst, Walter, *Vein of Iron*. Cleveland, The World Publishing Co., 1958.

Havighurst, Walter, *The Long Ships Passing*, New York, The Macmillan Co., 1942.

Hendrick, Burton J., *The Life of Andrew Carnegie*. New York, Doubleday, Doran & Co., 1932.

Hurd, Rukard, *Iron Ore Manual — Lake Superior District*. Minneapolis, Syndicate Printing Co., 1911.

McGannon, Harold E., (Edited by), *The Making, Shaping and Treating of Steel*. Pittsburgh, United States Steel Corporation, 1969.

Nevins, Allan D., and John D. Rockefeller, *The Heroic Age of American Enterprises*. Vol. II, New York, Charles Scribner's Sons, 1940.

Poor, Henry V., *Manual of Railroads of the United States*. Volumes 2-61 (1870-1930), New York, H.V. & H.W. Poor.

Pyle, Joseph G., *The Life of James J. Hill*. New York, Doubleday, Doran & Co., Inc., 1916.

Spurr, J. E., *The Mesabi Iron Bearing Rocks*. Minneapolis, Harrison & Smith — State Printers, 1894.

Spurr, J. E., *Lake Superior Iron Ores*. Cleveland, Lake Superior Iron Ore Association, 1938.

Tarbell, Ida M., *The Life of Elbert H. Gary — The Story of Steel*. New York, D. Appleton & Co., 1925.

Van Brunt, Walter, *Duluth and St. Louis County*. Volumes 1-3, Chicago, American Historical Society, 1921.

Wall, Joseph Frazier, *Andrew Carnegie*. New York, Oxford University Press, 1970.

Winchell, N. H., *The Iron Ores of Minnesota*. Minneapolis, Harrison & Smith — State Printers, 1891.

Wirth, Fremont P., *The Discovery and Exploitation of the Minnesota Iron Lands*. Cedar Rapids, Torch Press, 1937.

Woodbridge, Dwight E., *History of Duluth and St. Louis County*. Volumes 1-2, Chicago, C. F. Cooper & Co., 1910.

Woodbridge, Dwight, *My Many Years*, Duluth, —, 1942.

NEWSPAPERS

News-Tribune, Duluth, Minnesota, 1890-1971

MISCELLANEOUS RECORDS AND PUBLICATIONS

Geologic Sketch of Tower-Soudan State Park. Minneapolis, University of Minnesota, 1966.

John D. Rockefeller vs Alfred Merritt. Transcript of Record, U.S. District Court of Appeals — Eighth Circut. Filed September 2, 1895.

Leonidas Merritt vs. Duluth, Missabe & Northern Railway Company. State of Minnesota Supreme Court, April Term 1895.

Mining Directory Issue — Minnesota. University of Minnesota, School of Mines and Metallurgy, Minneapolis. 1920 to date.

State V. Duluth, Missabe and Iron Range Railway Company. St. Paul, Minnesota, Reports, Volume 246, 1956.

United States Steel Corporation, Annual Reports. 1901-1971.

COMPANY RECORDS

Annual reports to the officers and stockholders of the Duluth and Iron Range Rail Road Company; the Duluth, Missabe and Northern Railway Company; and the Duluth, Missabe and Iron Range Railway Company. Classification, Renumbering, and Assignments of Locomotives and Rolling Stock. Company periodicals: *DM&N-D&IR Employee Safety Magazine* 1919-1948, *Missabe Iron Ranger* 1948-1972. Records of the Traffic, Equipment and Transportation Departments.

INDEX